Practitioner Series

Springer
London
Berlin
Heidelberg
New York
Hong Kong
Milan
Paris
Tokyo

Other titles in this series:

Elizabeth Sparrow

Successful IT Outsourcing

**From Choosing a Provider to
Managing the Project**

 Springer

Elizabeth Sparrow, MSc, MBCS, CDipAF
Sparrow Associates, Surrey, UK

British Library Cataloguing in Publication Data
Sparrow, Elizabeth
    Successful IT outsourcing: from choosing a provider to
    managing the project. – (Practitioner series)
    1. Information technology – Management 2. Contracting out
    3. Electronic data processing departments – Contracting out
    I. Title
    658.4'038'011
    ISBN 1852336102

Library of Congress Cataloging-in-Publication Data
Sparrow, Elizabeth, 1952–
    Successful IT outsourcing: from choosing a provider to
    managing the project / Elizabeth Sparrow.
        p. cm. – (Practitioner series)
    Includes bibliographical references and index.
    ISBN 1-85233-610-2 (alk. paper)
    1. Computer service industry. 2. Information resources management.
    3. Information technology--Management. 4. Electronic data processing
    departments--Contracting out. I. Title. II. Series: Practitioner series
    (Springer-Verlag)
    HD9696.67 A2S66 2003
    004'.068'7--dc21
                                    2003042425

Practitioner series ISSN 1439-9245
ISBN 1-85233-610-2 Springer-Verlag London Berlin Heidelberg
A member of BertelsmannSpringer Science+Business Media GmbH
http://www.springer.co.uk

Typesetting: by Gray Publishing, Tunbridge Wells, Kent, UK
Printed and bound in the United States of America
34/3830-543210 Printed on acid-free paper SPIN 10875766

Series Editor's Foreword

IT outsourcing is in fashion (again). But how do you find out whether to outsource all or any of your IT, how to go about it, how to manage the outsourcing of your IT, and how to manage the outsourcing relationship? Elizabeth Sparrow's book provides answers to these and many other questions you might not have thought of asking, but need to. For example, how to manage the potential demotivation of in-house IT professionals, how to go about service level agreements, how to turn an outsourcing failure into a success in 10 steps, etc.? This book provides clear people-oriented comprehensive coverage of IT outsourcing, and if you are involved in any way in the latter, you should avoid some of its problems by reading this book.

One of my empirical observations about service departments I call *The Inverse Law of Service Departments* states that:

> The more people employed in a service department, the greater proportion of time each will spend on communications with other colleagues, and the less on customers. If the number continues to increase, there will come a time when there is no time left for customers. Any further increase in numbers will lead to the service department demanding time and effort from its customers, and the giving of nothing in return.

IT departments or computer services are classic followers of this law, and might provide some impetus for outsourcing. But service providers of outsourcing might easily succumb to the law as well. I mentioned above that outsourcing is in fashion – again! In the 1960s and 1970s time sharing was the equivalent approach to outsourcing, and it eventually became unpopular as the provider gained too much control, and the purchaser found that their business was being held back by an inability to persuade the provider to change the service provided quickly enough. This was exacerbated by the purchaser not having sufficient informed inside knowledge necessary to communicate the changes required from the provider.

If you are already outsourcing, or thinking of outsourcing, *Successful IT Outsourcing* will help you avoid the mistakes of history. It will also help providers give a more sustainable provision. And if you are none of these IT professionals, then you ought to read the book to find out if outsourcing should be investigated by you or not.

Ray Paul

Preface

A great deal has been written about IT outsourcing. Many have extolled its virtues – how it helps to improve company focus, to reduce and control operating costs and provides access to world-class technical capabilities. They have written about what might be achieved through IT outsourcing in a perfect world. Some have also written about the pitfalls and arguments against outsourcing.

Books on IT outsourcing aimed primarily at practitioners tend to focus on the concepts underpinning outsourcing, the historical development of the trend towards IT outsourcing and the current computer services market. Few venture far beyond signing the outsourcing contract and little practical advice has been published on the day-to-day challenges of working with outsourcing suppliers and what to do if the outsourcing relationship simply is not working.

The trend towards outsourcing some, or all, IT activities within an organization has had a profound impact on the careers of IT staff and managers. Decisions to outsource may be imposed on IT departments by senior executives but IT professionals have to deliver results. It is they who specify detailed requirements, set technical standards, specify technical interfaces, manage the outsourcing relationship day by day and pick up the pieces when things go wrong. This book is written for these IT professionals.

The IT outsourcing market continues to expand. Major new outsourcing deals are regularly announced in the press. Old outsourcing contracts come to an end and are re-tendered; contracts are awarded to new suppliers; and new requirements may lead to new outsourcing contracts. The growth of the Internet and expansion in broadband networks has opened up new ways of offering outsourced services and this has led to the creation of many new outsourcing suppliers. There are today many different ways of sourcing IT services. Most organizations outsource some IT activities and many have more than one outsourcing supplier. Any IT manager asked to undertake a major project or improve IT services needs to consider how best to source the activity. Many outsourcing decisions today are taken within the IT department.

IT professionals need to know about the whole outsourcing process and this book addresses this requirement. As well as considering the objectives behind outsourcing and the selection of service provider, it looks at managing performance after the contract is signed, measuring performance and tackling problems when outsourcing fails. Academic research has studied the outcome of outsourcing initiatives, examining successes and failures and offering some conclusions. I have drawn on this research and my own extensive experience managing outsourcing relationships in a number of different organizations to provide practical guidance and advice to IT professionals tackling the challenges of outsourcing.

The topics covered by this book are outlined below.

Chapter 1 defines IT outsourcing, gives a brief history and description of the current outsourcing market. Different types of sourcing such as selective sourcing, insourcing, strategic sourcing, business process outsourcing and joint ventures are described.

The arguments for and against outsourcing are covered in Chapter 2.

In Chapter 3 I examine the objectives that underpin outsourcing initiatives and how these will influence the outcome. The identification of which IT services can be outsourced profitably is considered and the use of benchmarking reviewed. This chapter also describes the definition of service requirements, preparation of the business case and the staff transfers that might be encompassed within an outsourcing exercise.

Chapter 4 considers the process of selecting a service provider through a competitive tendering exercise. Although specialists may lead some aspects of this process, such as the negotiation stage, IT professionals are inevitably called on to provide much of the input to the selection process. This chapter puts individual tasks into the broader perspective of the overall process.

Chapter 5 is the first to focus on the challenge of managing the outsourcing relationship once the contract is signed. It looks at building successful outsourcing relationships – what this means and how it can be achieved. Suggestions are given to help identify incentives for your supplier and ways in which added value can be derived from outsourcing contracts. The contract management function is described, including service management, contract administration and the role of users in outsourcing. The change control and issue management processes are discussed.

Measuring the performance of outsourcing suppliers is considered in Chapter 6. It looks at the principles of performance measurement systems, the use of benchmarking, measuring benefits and involving service users. Service level management and the role of service level agreements are described, and the chapter ends with a look at the challenges presented by managing multiple outsourcing suppliers.

Chapter 7 considers the outsourcing contract, looking at various elements within the agreement. Risk management is a key element of successful outsourcing and we look at the risks commonly associated with outsourcing and risk management techniques.

Outsourcing relationships sometimes run into serious problems and inevitably the task of trying to resolve differences and maintain adequate service levels falls to IT professionals. Chapter 8 looks at this important area of work, reviewing reasons for outsourcing failure and describing a ten-step programme to turn failure into success. If all attempts to resolve problems fail, the more formal action that can be taken, including arbitration and litigation, is outlined.

The book concludes in Chapter 9 with a review of the emerging hosted service provider market, a look at current outsourcing trends and the impact of outsourcing on today's IT department.

In preparing this book I have drawn from many years experience of working with IT teams and outsourcing suppliers in the delivery of IT services. I am indebted to all those – too numerous to mention – who have worked with me and from whom I have learnt so much. My thanks also go to Beverley Ford and Rebecca Mowat at Springer-Verlag for their help and encouragement in the preparation of this book; to the helpful staff at the Institution of Electrical Engineers Library; and finally to my husband Alan Gurney for his support and enthusiasm.

Contents

Introduction to IT Outsourcing 1

1.1 What Is IT Outsourcing?

Outsourcing is ubiquitous in the IT world. Pick up any IT newspaper and you will invariably find several reports about outsourcing initiatives. As complexity and change in IT increase perhaps it is only natural that organizations seek to contract out key IT services to those with specialist technical and professional skills.

People and organizations have always looked to others to assist in tasks that they are either too busy to do or lack the necessary skills to perform competently. I know a thing or two about gardening and so I choose to dig the soil, tend my plants and remove weeds myself. But I employ someone else to mend the central heating system since I do not possess the relevant skills nor do I have the time to learn.

We accept it as normal practice for an organization to "outsource" its postal service, provision of electricity and water and stationery supply. IT outsourcing, however, is seen as much more controversial. Perhaps this is in part because we have come so far in a relatively short period of time. Rapid technological change has been paralleled by many changes in the way in which IT is viewed and managed by organizations. To some, the trend towards outsourcing reflects maturity in the IT world.

Press reports about outsourcing in practice have highlighted bad news stories. Outsourcing is certainly not a quick fix to a badly managed process. There is no reason to suppose that someone else will be able to fix a problem overnight that an organization has failed to put right for months or even years. Outsourcing is best regarded as a long-term strategic management tool. It is not a simple option.

Outsourcing can take many forms but in this book it is defined as the practice of handing over the planning, management and operation of certain functions to an independent third party, under the terms of a formalized service level agreement. It is usually, but not always, characterized by the transfer of assets from the customer to the service provider.

Increasingly, organizations are both outsourcing customers and service providers. The major IT outsourcing companies focus on their core competencies too and find it profitable to outsource other functions such as staff recruitment or payroll processing.

IT outsourcing is a well-established, and growing, management practice. It is not easy to get right but we must learn to do so if we are to fully exploit the benefits and capabilities of IT.

1.2 History of IT Outsourcing

The concept of IT outsourcing is not a new phenomenon. When mainframe computers were first used to support business functions such as payroll processing they were expensive, bulky machines that required a special environment with strict controls on temperature, humidity and dust. Data and programs were input on punched cards or magnetic tape. Many organizations could not afford the investment in equipment or specialist operators needed to own and run their own computer. In the 1960s various computer bureaus were established, selling mainframe time to other organizations for data processing. This was effectively one of the earliest examples of IT outsourcing, used in this instance to gain the benefits of investment and specialist skills. As early as 1963, Perot's Electronic Data Systems (EDS) was handling data processing services for Frito-Lay and Blue Cross.

During the 1970s and 1980s first minicomputers and later microcomputers were introduced and these had a dramatic impact on the cost of computing power. Hardware costs fell to a level that was low enough to justify companies of all sizes owning and controlling their own IT assets. Standard software packages helped organizations set up their own systems with little programming effort (this was another form of outsourcing).

IT came to be seen as a source of competitive advantage. Companies invested large amounts of money in purchasing new hardware and application systems. Organizations often carried out a wide range of diverse and non-core activities in-house because at this stage:

- running all operations in-house was perceived to be beneficial;
- there was little competition in the IT services market;
- the wide span of activities came through acquisitions and mergers;
- vertical integration was pursued as it was seen to give greater control.

As the use of IT became widespread it was viewed as a necessity rather than a unique competitive advantage. Managers became more interested in the outcome of their investment in IT and its impact on the organization's efficiency and effectiveness. They were less concerned about the technical details of the IT infrastructure. The concept of outsourcing IT activities began to develop.

The first major outsourcing initiative to receive worldwide publicity came in 1989 when Eastman Kodak hired outsiders to buy, operate and maintain its information processing systems. IBM, Digital Equipment Corporation and Businessland were awarded outsourcing contracts worth in total approximately £500 million. In the early 1990s this and other high profile outsourcing exercises increased awareness of the outsourcing trend among business management, IT professionals and researchers.

Changing markets forced a reappraisal of the aggregation of activities and vertical integration seen in the 1980s. Whereas monopolies and multinationals had previously been regarded as strong, possessing economies of scale and able to support creative processes such as research and development, it became apparent that these large, highly formalized internal organizations could stifle and strangle good ideas. Companies recognized that survival required them to evolve from hierarchical, inflexible organizations to lean, flexible and nimble enterprises. A number of trends followed this evolution: downsizing, restructuring, re-engineering and just-in-time manufacturing.

Outsourcing was seen as a way of reshaping the organization to create more flexible companies, focused on core abilities and improving relationships with customers. Other factors supporting the trend towards outsourcing included:

- the global skills shortage;
- a more mobile workforce;
- increasing costs of in-house developed software;

- the need to move fast, adopting new technologies quickly and speeding up system development;

- the explosion of Internet technologies and services requiring a wide range of new skills and investments.

Initially, outsourcing was viewed as a move to transfer responsibility for the entire IT department to a third party. But in recent years, as experience and knowledge has deepened, outsourcing has become an option to be applied selectively or extensively to IT activities in line with an overall sourcing strategy.

The outsourcing market was given a further boost in the late 1980s/1990s by many national governments that sought to drive radical change by encouraging public sector bodies to adopt private sector efficiency techniques. In the UK, the government instigated a programme called "Market Testing" in which in-house services (including IT) were tested for value for money against what an external service provider could deliver. This resulted in the outsourcing of a substantial proportion of the government's IT services.

The UK government also laid down a timetable in which local authorities had to put their services out to competition from external providers in a process known as "compulsory competitive tendering".

Aside from these formal programmes, the trend towards outsourcing in the UK public sector was driven by:

- difficulties experienced by many central departments and local government organizations in recruiting and retaining staff;

- pressure on government departments and agencies to achieve greater value for money;

- the establishment of government agencies whose role was to encourage a more flexible, commercial outlook on delivering services;

- sales pressure from private sector companies wanting to take a more proactive part in helping government improve the delivery of services using IT;

- a growing interest in the opportunities that an outsourcing solution offers as a strategic alternative.

In the USA, public sector organizations have not made extensive use of outsourcing in the past but this is now changing as budgets tighten.

4

In the 1990s, as IT services came under greater scrutiny, several major service providers pushed to increase their share of the outsourcing market. These companies developed a wider and more comprehensive range of services. As organizations began to suffer from diseconomies of scale and experienced difficulties migrating from cumbersome legacy (existing) systems, these external service providers' offerings looked increasingly attractive and the market grew substantially. The major players such as Computer Sciences Corporation (CSC), EDS, IBM and ICL (now Fujitsu) took on increasingly large, multi-dimensional and complex deals.

During the dotcom boom, a large number of new, smaller service providers emerged, with outsourcing services operating at remote data centres (these are discussed in more detail in Chapter 9). These companies offered rapid implementation and simplified pricing, and were aimed primarily at small and medium-sized businesses.

In the 21st century we have a rich and mature IT outsourcing market, offering a wide variety of services to meet different needs.

1.3 Size and Scope of the IT Outsourcing Market

IT outsourcing has grown at a phenomenal rate over the past decade in the UK, North America and Australia. The trend towards outsourcing has also increased elsewhere in Western Europe, and in South America and parts of South-East Asia including Japan. Growth is particularly strongly linked to periods of economic downturn when IT outsourcing is seen as a way to contain costs. Companies try to lower IT spending and convert unpredictable costs into fixed costs.

An examination of the size of the outsourcing market is complicated because different research organizations combine different types of outsourcing in their surveys. Nevertheless, all agree that growth in the outsourcing market continues to outstrip other sectors of the IT industry and is currently running at around 10–15 per cent per annum.

Key Note has reported that the total UK outsourcing market grew from £3.5 billion in 1997 to £7.0 billion in 2001 and forecasts that it will grow to £13.8 billion in 2006 (Fenn 2002).

Gartner has estimated that in Western Europe expenditure on business process outsourcing and IT outsourcing will reach $115.6 billion (£82.6 billion) by 2005 and will account for more than half of the total IT services market (www.gartner.com). Merrill Lynch has estimated that the proportion of European IT budgets spent on external service providers will increase to 30 per cent by 2004. In a recent survey they found that two-thirds of the companies interviewed preferred to use a combination of best-of-breed suppliers rather than depend on one major outsourcing company for various IT functions (www.computing.co.uk).

Gartner predicts that the North American IT outsourcing market will grow from $101 billion in 2000 to $160 billion by 2005. According to IDC, the USA accounts for around half of global IT outsourcing expenditure (www.computerworld.com).

The leading suppliers of outsourced IT services include IBM, EDS, CSC, Fujitsu, Cap Gemini Ernst & Young, Accenture, SchlumbergerSema, Logica, Capita, Unisys and Xansa.

1.4 Different Sourcing Models

As experience has developed, a variety of sourcing models have evolved. Outsourcing can range from having all your organization's development, maintenance and operations performed by the service provider, through to simply contracting an external supplier to perform one single task such as to install a piece of software.

Many different terms have been adopted to describe various sourcing models.

1.4.1 Facilities Management

In this form of outsourcing, the customer owns the computer assets but hires an external service provider to run the computer operations either at the customer's premises or elsewhere. IT staff transfer to the supplier. All operational and systems programming tasks are usually included, but not the development of applications. Facilities management is sometimes not regarded as true outsourcing since it does not include the transfer of assets to the supplier and leaves little scope for the supplier to introduce service improvements through innovations.

> **Example**
>
> BT awarded a $40 million managed services deal to Unisys to run and maintain its growing consumer voicemail service. Under the 5-year deal, Unisys is responsible for 5.7 million BT customer voicemail boxes, including 4.1 million users of the free '1571' residential service. With experience of running 150 million voicemail mailboxes worldwide, Unisys is able to offer expertise and lower per-user costs. It provides 24-hour management and maintenance of the 12 voicemail platforms it has installed for BT around the UK, along with administration of new users and storage capacity management.

1.4.2 Selective Outsourcing

Although total outsourcing initiatives – in which at least 80 per cent of the functions of an IT department are transferred to an external provider – receive extensive press coverage, the most common approach is to selectively outsource IT functions. Academic research has found that selective outsourcing strategies are usually successful and more likely to succeed than total outsourcing. The IT services most commonly outsourced are infrastructure management and support.

Selective outsourcing is flexible and leaves sufficient IT capability within the customer organization to adapt to changes and new technological innovations and advances. It is also less risky than a total outsourcing approach. Each outsourcing project, however, requires evaluation, negotiation and management. Total costs, when several different initiatives are taken into account, can prove more expensive than a more comprehensive outsourcing model.

> **Example**
>
> The high street bank HSBC signed a multi-million pound outsourcing deal with systems integrator Dimension Data Logistics. The 3-year contract covers procurement and technical support for the bank's Cisco network in 78 countries. A UK-based team centrally manages the standardized network, with implementation

via regional teams in conjunction with HSBC's localized telecommunications hubs. Dimension Data Logistics designs, procures, implements and project manages the technology. There is a particular focus on new equipment such as content delivery networking, wide area network routers and local area network switches.

1.4.3 Tactical Outsourcing

This approach is also referred to as contracting out or out-tasking. Outsourcing is adopted as a rapid and often short-term solution to a particular need or problem. In recent years many companies have adopted tactical outsourcing solutions to contract out the development of Websites and services, using small innovative companies to gain rapid access to new technical skills.

Tactical outsourcing can also be applied to specific problems that, for whatever reason, are difficult to resolve using in-house resources without lengthy delays. For example, infrastructure upgrades may be achieved more quickly and effectively when outsourced if an organization does not have sufficient IT staff to carry out such a large-scale project in addition to other development and operations work.

Example

Archstone-Smith Trust, a real estate investment firm based in Colorado, outsourced a revenue management application, which analyzes peaks and troughs in demand so that the company can set appropriate prices for apartments and create a consistent, disciplined pricing methodology. The application was outsourced because it requires a Unix host with an Oracle database on the back end, while Archstone-Smith uses Windows NT and SQL Server for its other internal systems.

1.4.4 Strategic Sourcing

This model of sourcing puts decisions about what to outsource, how and when, into a wider business context. By working with one or more suppliers, the customer organization is aiming to achieve a significant improvement in business performance rather than a short-term cost saving alone. Managers will need to adopt a new perspective on control and are likely to be more successful if the focus is on outputs rather than inputs.

Within the strategic sourcing model the customer and supplier identify and work towards mutual interests: this approach is commonly referred to as a partnership. If this model is to be effective, the supplier needs to understand that its commercial success is intertwined with that of the customer. It is likely that, under the terms of the outsourcing agreement, the supplier will benefit financially from the customer organization's increased success. The supplier is encouraged to be innovative rather than to simply follow rigid service specifications. Both customer and supplier recognize the importance of managing the relationship, not just the outsourcing contract. They are more willing to share risk and reward and the customer is less likely to rely on penalizing poor performance.

Example

The UK mapping agency, Ordnance Survey, aims to conduct most of its business over the Internet in coming years, but its mix of best-of-breed software and internally developed applications was not up to handling a complex online strategy. One-third of the agency's revenues are generated from paper-based maps, sold either on the high street or through its Website. The remaining two-thirds is derived from the sale and distribution of digital geographical data to organizations such as energy and water utilities. The business objective is to offer information electronically as much as possible.

Ordnance Survey therefore decided to spend £9 million to replace its business software and implement new internal processes. Much of this investment will focus on staff training. A 5-year contract was awarded to Siemens Business Services to replace existing systems with enterprise resource planning and customer relationship management applications from SAP.

1.4.5 Transformational Outsourcing

This approach combines the outsourcing of an IT department with a comprehensive reorganization. Companies adopting this model hope to transform business processes and the technology infrastructure to reduce costs, improve services and empower employees.

Example

Industrial group Invensys signed a 10-year deal worth up to $100 million per year with IBM Global Services to provide application management, help desk services and support for 29,000 workstations in several countries. Around 600 Invensys IT staff transferred to IBM. The objective was to streamline business processes within the hundreds of businesses of various sizes that make up Invensys. Reducing costs was not a major factor. IBM provides an innovation team comprising research and development staff, consultants and business strategists to identify and address business needs through the use of IT.

1.4.6 Transitional Outsourcing

Companies use transitional outsourcing to introduce major change such as moving from one technological platform to another. Here there would be three phases: (1) management of the legacy systems; (2) transition to the new technology; and (3) operation and management of the new platform. Any or all of these phases may be outsourced. Since legacy systems are generally technically mature and stable, it is often possible to negotiate sound and economic contracts for managing the systems for a specified, short period. This frees up the in-house IT staff to focus on the new technology and to develop new skills.

Example

United Technologies underwent a complete IT infrastructure overhaul and consolidation that cost $4.5 billion but is expected to save the company $1 billion through efficiencies over the next

15 years. The project was outsourced to CSC and included a roll out of 45,000 PCs, standardizing on a single back-up and recovery platform and consolidating the business critical workloads from 20 major data centres down to three. Every critical system now has a disaster recovery plan.

After decades of growth, United Technologies data centres and server farms were dispersed throughout the USA. Its eight main-frames, 11 IBM AS/400 servers and 2,950 other servers were also dispersed among those data centres. Processing has now been consolidated onto two mainframes and two AS/400 systems, with the number of servers reduced to about 350. United Technologies also created two storage area networks and standardized its net-work on CSC's management tool. Fifteen help desks running nine applications have been consolidated into one centre running one system.

Moving from a position where every business unit was unique and had its own standards was a major challenge.

1.4.7 Business Process Outsourcing

As spending on outsourcing continues to increase, organizations are looking to bring in specialist service companies to manage entire busi-ness processes. These business process outsourcing (BPO) deals are not limited to IT but the services companies do spend a significant amount of time running and improving the computer systems that lie at the core of the process. The entire function, assets and staff are transferred to the external service provider; outsourcing is not limited to the IT activities. Commonly outsourced functions include hotlines, help desks, call cen-tres, document processing and storage, payroll and internal auditing.

Example

LloydsTSB signed a 7-year, multi-million pound deal with BT Ignite to provide a range of services spanning all areas of the busi-ness including Internet banking, key financial services and service delivery. The overall aim is to improve customer service. BT provides a fully managed customer contact centre that is integrated with the bank's customer database. This allows seamless and consistent levels of customer service covering all transactions and information requests. Higher bandwidth is provided to improve network capacity and performance.

Example

Under a 10-year, £100 million deal, Thomas Cook (the travel agency) transferred its UK IT and finance operations at its nerve centre at Peterborough to Accenture. The site houses IT operations and applications management as well as finance, accounting and payroll services. Accenture is responsible for reservations, tour operations and flight management systems with Thomas Cook retaining control over strategy, policy and investment. About 140 IT and 260 finance staff transferred from Thomas Cook to Accenture.

1.4.8 Joint Ventures

Rather than transfer IT services to an outsourcing supplier, some customers choose to set up a separate joint venture organization with an external service provider to gain access to technical skills and resources without transferring staff and losing control over the new IT organization.

Both customer organization and outsourcing supplier provide IT staff to work in the new joint venture, which has its own management team. The underlying commercial arrangement recognizes that both parties bear costs and take risks, and both are entitled to share profits or dividends. The joint venture may be given the freedom not only to reorganize IT functions and processes but also to investigate new sources of revenue.

Both organizations are responsible for the supply of resources to meet the objectives set for the joint venture. One of the risks of this approach is that there may be no redress if the objectives or targets are not met.

Example

Barclays Bank and LloydsTSB set up Intelligent Processing Solutions (IPSL) with Unisys to outsource the banks' cheque processing. The £80 million business was founded with the commercial freedom to investigate new sources of revenue such as electronic bill payment. IPSL has proved very successful and HSBC has joined as an equity partner.

1.4.9 Benefit-based Relationships

This type of outsourcing arrangement is based on both parties making an up-front investment in the relationship and sharing the benefits as they accrue. Both parties therefore take risks and share the rewards. If the benefits previously forecast and agreed do not materialize the supplier may not be guaranteed any recompense for their effort or input. This approach is relatively new and is still being developed. Since it is difficult to measure benefits in a way that can be agreed by both customer and supplier, it is not often adopted.

In the UK, the government's Private Finance Initiative applies some of the principles of the benefit-based outsourcing model. Private sector companies are invited to invest up-front in developing public sector services with payments based on outcomes or benefits derived from these services. Risks are identified and a negotiated agreement reached about which party is best placed to manage each risk. The private sector company must genuinely carry some risks.

Example

The UK government's Employment Service formed a Public Private Partnership with EDS to deliver IT services through a network of 1,000 job centres and 35,000 staff. The procurement was undertaken in 10 months, which proved challenging but highly cost effective to all parties. The deal links the use of IT to securing business benefits as well as a payment methodology that links EDS's reward to realizing those benefits. The evaluation process and model paid significant attention to future developments and the negotiations were undertaken in line with a framework that encouraged innovation.

1.4.10 Insourcing

Most companies retain some IT activities in-house. Even those who decide to pursue an outsourcing approach may invite their own IT department to submit proposals for quality and efficiency improvements. These may prove more attractive than any bids received from an external service provider. The organization may then decide to insource and the in-house IT department is formally adopted as the service provider. Service level agreements will be brought into operation and services improved and developed as indicated in the winning proposal. Spare capacity can be used to develop additional business, potentially outside the customer organization.

In this approach the customer organization retains its IT staff and assets and, hopefully, releases the potential for improvements and efficiency gains.

As a variant on insourcing, an organization may decide to hire an outsourcing company to manage IT activities while retaining IT staff and assets in an in-house IT department.

Example

Insurance group Axa rejected outsourcing and cut technology costs by 6 per cent by consolidating its IT operations using the in-house IT department. The economic downturn forced Axa to embark on a cost-cutting programme. The group decided to streamline its IT function and focus on innovation by re-using systems, instead of bringing in an external service provider to run its IT operations. The IT strategy was refocused, from creating business value to enhancing IT productivity. The first stage was to combine the corporate IT department with 500 staff and 60 separate business unit IT departments with another 2,800 people into one consolidated new department. The next step was to standardize the group's IT purchasing to allow the smaller business units to benefit from the same economies of scale as the larger parts of Axa. The number of contractors was cut by 43 per cent.

1.4.11 Offshore Outsourcing

Offshore programming and software development industries have emerged worldwide in countries such as India, China, Ireland, Israel, Malaysia, Hungary and the Philippines. Services offered include systems integration, legacy system maintenance and modernization, customized software development and package implementation. Major IT suppliers also use these offshore skills. IBM, AT&T, Novell, Microsoft, Oracle and Unisys all have development centres in India.

Remote sourcing has been growing rapidly and the market is now maturing. The value and viability of offshore outsourcing is becoming increasingly recognized despite political volatility in some offshore destinations. Intellect, the UK-based Information Technology, Telecommunications and Electronics Association (previously the Computing Services and Software Association) estimates that the annual global spending on offshore outsourcing is between $6 billion and $10 billion and is growing by 25–50 per cent each year (www.computing.co.uk).

India has about 60–80 per cent of the global market. With over 20 million English-speaking graduates, India is well placed to develop its IT services industry. Given the large numbers of technically skilled professionals, Indian companies can quickly mobilize teams to support outsourced projects. There has been an emphasis on creating strong processes and quality software in India where IT companies have given priority to quality standards and certification such as ISO 9001. This ensures that when applications are developed off-site, the service provider follows set processes to ensure consistent quality. Business process outsourcing to India is a specific growth area.

Communications could prove problematic given India's poor domestic telecommunications services but the outsourcing companies are based in numerous technology parks with modern infrastructure. They commonly have their own power plants making them independent of the local grid. Satellite links give direct connection to the Internet and foreign customers. The normal arrangement is for the Indian staff to use exactly the same IT equipment as the customer's IT department.

15

IT service companies based in other developing countries offer more competitive prices than India but are not always able to offer the same quality of service.

Lessons learnt from the experience of offshore outsourcing include:

- Overall savings may not be significant. Although development costs will be lower, specifications and documentation must be detailed and unambiguous to prevent misunderstandings when work is sent off-site. This means higher initial costs at the customer end.

- It is generally best to start with a simple, relatively small, non-critical project to resolve any difficulties in procedures and develop agreed ways of working.

- The customer normally gets to specify which country's law applies in any contractual agreement.

Example

In the UK, Channel 4 signed a multi-million pound outsourcing deal with an Indian offshore software developer to update its legacy systems. The £3.2 million deal with New Delhi-based NIIT is to transform the Airtime sales management system from Cobol to Java. It is envisaged that the project will take about 2 years to complete and will modify rather than rewrite the system, cutting both time and cost.

The system is central to Channel 4's business and will handle its multi-million pound revenue. No downtime can be tolerated so NIIT is working on a duplicate system with a dedicated team of 50 people at peak times. In its current form the costs of maintaining the system had been increasing. The transformation to Java is aimed at reducing problems and enhancing functionality.

The Case For and Against Outsourcing 2

2.1 Introduction

Talk of outsourcing generates heated debate among IT professionals. For some it represents an enlightened approach to the management of routine IT services and a mature development of partnerships with suppliers. Others see it as symptomatic of an organization that has failed to grasp the strategic importance of IT and is not prepared to invest in the professional development of its IT staff. Outsourcing – at least when it involves the transfer of staff from company to service provider – challenges our thinking about our ability to choose our own employer and our value as professionals.

In the first chapter we saw how outsourcing as a way of acquiring and managing IT services has developed since the Kodak landmark initiative. The term "outsourcing" is used to cover a range of activities from the transfer of an entire IT department to a third party to a joint venture supporting a new technological development. Whenever organizations consider the use of outsourcing, in whatever form, various arguments are put forward in favour of, and against, the use of outsourcing.

This chapter takes an impartial look at these arguments. It does not try to come to any firm recommendations – in any event the best way forward will vary from one instance to another. The purpose here is to consider the issues that will be addressed by any organization considering outsourcing.

2.2 Arguments in Favour of Outsourcing

This section examines the reasons that organizations give for adopting outsourcing and the benefits and advantages they anticipate.

2.2.1 Enabling the Organization to Focus on Its Core Business

Many organizations today see the use of outsourcing as an integral element of their overall business strategy. Any organization needs to address these questions if it is going to secure a successful future for itself:

- What do we do best?
- How can we do it better?
- What distinguishes us from our competitors?
- What value do our customers derive from our products and services?
- What competitive advantage could outsourcing provide?

Some IT operations consume a lot of resources and management attention but do not help distinguish a company from its competitors. By outsourcing these activities the organization can better focus on what it does best and what it needs to do tomorrow. IT professionals that remain in the organization can concentrate on strategic developments and supporting the business as it moves forward. This has the added advantage of raising the profile and status of the IT department.

Using outsourcing in this way also helps change the emphasis from operations and problem solving to thinking about how IT can be used most profitably. The focus is on interpreting information and exploiting IT systems rather than data processing and maintenance work.

Example

The USA National Security Agency (NSA) awarded a $2 billion outsourcing contract to a vendor team led by CSC to help revitalize the communications intelligence agency's Cold War era IT infrastructure. The 10-year contract, called Project Groundbreaker, is focused primarily on filling gaps in day-to-day support functions such as enterprise security and network management. The aim is to help the agency upgrade its IT infrastructure more quickly and allow it to focus more efficiently on its core business.

Example

IT service providers themselves make use of outsourcing to enable them to focus on their core business – IT services. CSC outsourced its UK hiring and running of contractors to a third party, Harvey Nash. The deal was worth £40 million over 2 years to handle around 200 contractors. Sema Group (now SchlumbergerSema) signed a 5-year deal to outsource recruitment of its permanent and freelance staff to Elan, up to 1,000 people a year.

Example

Scotiabank hired IBM Canada in an outsourcing deal worth $578.3 million over 7 years. IBM manages the bank's domestic computer operations including data centres, branches, automated teller machines (ATMs) and desktop PCs for 24,000 employees. Scotiabank decided to outsource key IT functions because it wanted to focus on its core business, which is delivering financial services.

2.2.2 New Business Development

Companies need to continually develop if they are to survive. Introducing technology in support of new business and implementing new technology can be difficult to run alongside daily operations that support current business activities. Outsourcing can help in two ways:

1. By freeing up resources, outsourcing helps organizations to focus on strategic new developments. New opportunities are opened up by being able to spend time looking for new business opportunities rather than solving operational problems.

2. Outsourcing can be used selectively to introduce new technology or applications. This approach has been especially evident during the introduction of e-commerce. Website design and set up, online order processing and integration of back office activities all require specialist skills which, initially at least, were in short supply in IT departments.

By outsourcing these activities to specialist companies, organizations were able to speedily introduce e-business and not lose ground to their competitors. Some of this work has now been taken back in-house as IT departments develop the appropriate skills base.

Outsourcing can also be used effectively for new applications which require specialized software support such as enterprise resource planning (ERP) systems. This may be the most economical way to implement and exploit the technology.

Example

ICL (now Fujitsu) was hired by Sainsbury to develop and implement a new point of sale system for their 400 out-of-town supermarkets and 100 local stores in high streets and petrol stations. Sainsbury's decision to outsource was based on ICL's expertise in retail systems. ICL made use of their GlobalStore software that handles around £100 billion of retail revenues worldwide.

Example

Eurotunnel outsourced the implementation of a content management system to hosting company 1eEurope. This is part of a 5-year initiative to transform Eurotunnel's Website from an online brochure to an interactive, revenue generating site. At least 30 per cent of all bookings for the Eurostar and freight trains made through Eurotunnel are carried out online.

2.2.3 Assisting Major Reorganizations

From time to time all companies, and IT departments, undergo major reorganizations, which inevitably take a great deal of time and effort. Outsourcing can be used to help make the transition smoother and quicker.

20

For IT service providers, their core business is IT. Over the years they have reorganized so that they can offer IT services most effectively and profitably. Companies can tap into this expertise by outsourcing their IT departments. The internal IT operations will be reorganized to maximize efficiency and integrate with the service provider's organization. This requires less management effort and time than reorganizing an internal IT department.

Outsourcing can also help with company mergers, acquisitions and divestments. Rather than tackle the complexity of integrating different IT departments, or splitting off part of a department, these challenges are left to the service provider. IT professionals can benefit too, as service providers can generally offer a wider range of alternative opportunities in such instances. This is particularly relevant when companies are looking for economies.

Major reorganizations in both public and private sectors can be difficult and take time to introduce. Internal politics, competing new initiatives and resistance to change can all slow down implementation. Outsourced services are less affected by these factors.

Example

Convenience food group Uniq signed a 7-year multi-million pound deal with Altos Origin to help support its growing business. The group, formerly known as Unigate, outsourced because its business had changed strategic direction towards a pan-European rather than just a UK focus. Acquisitions and structural changes made it necessary to outsource technology support. The in-house IT department could not provide the geographical coverage.

Example

Burger King outsourced its IT support, including data centre management, help desk support, enterprise systems management and global network management, to Perot Systems. The outsourcing deal was part of a series of moves to prepare Burger King for a

> separation from its parent company Diageo, an international food and beverage company. Perot moved Burger King's existing data centre operations to its technology centre in Texas. Burger King previously shared data centre facilities with other Diageo companies.

2.2.4 Quality and Service Improvements

Companies outsourcing do so in anticipation that their chosen service provider will offer a world-class service. An integral part of the outsourcing process will be to critically examine service level requirements. This helps both company and service provider to understand what is and what is not acceptable. Outsourcing suppliers can offer a track record of achievements in other organizations and can help improve the image of IT services by their general reputation.

Example

> BAA outsourced all voice communications at Heathrow, Gatwick and Stansted airports to BT in a £50 million, 5-year contract. The agreement covers all airport employees, including baggage handlers, check-in staff, customs and excise, emergency services and airport retailers. BT Ignite provides voice communications and paging services to BAA's 8,000 staff on 15,500 telephone extensions. BAA can manage all voice communications from a single point and has a dedicated help desk where orders can be placed and faults reported.
>
> The contract forms part of a long-term strategy to support and develop the telecommunications infrastructure at British airports. The aim of outsourcing the network through one provider is to allow greater focus on service delivery and development, ensuring high resilience and much shorter timescales for fault rectification. BT has also introduced a simplified billing process. BAA issues about 6,500 bills every year for its operations and BT invoices individual accounts on behalf of BAA.

> **Example**
>
> The Winterhur Group, part of the Credit Suisse banking and insurance conglomerate, is one of Europe's leading corporate insurers with 27,000 staff in 30 countries. The group initially outsourced IT systems, and later desktops, servers and telecommunications operations to IBM Global Services. The move was driven by a belief that it is better to rely on a company whose core competency is IT for these services. Winterhur anticipated some savings but this was not only a financial decision. Outsourcing was adopted in order to get more professional and higher quality work.

2.2.5 Access to Technical Expertise

This is a very important factor in outsourcing. IT outsourcing suppliers specialize in IT – it is their core business. They are able to offer extensive investment in technology, methodologies and people. The larger suppliers are able to offer worldwide coverage. Individual in-house IT departments are rarely able to match this level of technological expertise. IT service providers can provide access to new skills and capabilities and quicker implementation of technological changes. Outsourcing to a major supplier potentially offers the following advantages:

- Access to new technology, tools and techniques.
- Introduction of more structured methodologies, procedures and documentation.
- Access to more IT professionals with a wider span of technical knowledge and experience.
- Application of better tools and techniques for estimating costs of new solutions.
- IT service providers are well equipped to handle negotiations with multiple suppliers and can use volume purchasing agreements.
- Better IT career opportunities for those who transfer to the IT service provider.
- Can be used for implementation of leading edge technology to help minimize losses if the technology fails to take off.

- Enables an organization to use obsolete technology beyond its normal life span. The IT service provider may have several customers who use the old technology and may do its own maintenance rather than relying on the original supplier as an internal IT department might have to do.
- Avoids high costs of continually re-training in-house IT professionals in the latest technologies.

Example

Nationwide, the world's largest building society based in the UK, wanted to integrate telephone, online and branch customer data from its 681 branches and 5 administrative centres in the UK. The infrastructure at the time was not up to the job of supporting business growth. The company made the decision to upgrade its local and wide area networks but its in-house IT staff did not have the right skills set and time was short. Compaq Services were contracted to implement this major infrastructure change including skills transfer to in-house staff. Simplifying the network made it possible to introduce new voice, data, video and image services very quickly. Network maintenance costs were reduced by 25 per cent within one year of the project starting.

Example

South Northamptonshire District Council signed a £7.2 million deal with consultancy Capita to boost its skills base and help meet online targets. The 7-year contract covers the replacement of council tax, benefits, financial management and housing legacy systems. Support services and implementation of a customer relationship management system to make information available to the public are also included. Access to a wider skills base is seen as a major benefit in assisting the council to deliver the e-government agenda.

2.2.6 Financial Advantages

Cost reduction is the single most important tactical reason for outsourcing. Experience has shown, however, that if cost reduction is the sole or prime focus, outsourcing is less likely to succeed. The financial advantages of outsourcing fall into three categories:

1. Cost reduction: an outsourcing supplier can reduce costs by economy of scale, by specializing in IT services and by spreading research and training costs over a larger staff. It is also more economical for an organization to buy in technical expertise as and when required rather than investing in specialized technical training that is seldom used. Some outsourcing deals require the IT service provider to purchase IT assets and this provides a one-off cash sum to the outsourcing organization.

2. Predictable costs: an organization can achieve more predictable costs by negotiating and agreeing costs for specified service levels in an outsourcing deal. This also helps to achieve a clear understanding of business processes and to introduce improvements. More control can be exerted over future increases or decreases in costs.

3. Capital expenditure reduction: outsourcing can reduce the need to invest capital funds in IT functions. Instead of acquiring IT resources through capital expenditure, they are contracted for as an operational expense (variable cost). There is tremendous competition within most organizations for capital funds and outsourcing IT services can make more capital available for other core business functions.

Example

BAE Systems, formed by the merger of Marconi Electronic Systems IT operations and British Aerospace in 1999, rewrote its outsourcing contract with CSC to cut costs and help it better compare prices with other companies. The £1 billion contract was originally signed in 1994 as a traditional contract based on IT service commodities such as network and desktop services.

BAE now sets a price for IT services per head, and leaves it to CSC to work out how to deliver it. This makes it easier to work out cost and to compare value for money with other organizations. This is much simpler to administer and puts the focus on supporting users rather than the technology.

Example

American Express outsourced a major part of its IT operations to IBM in a deal that is likely to be worth more than $4 billion over 7 years. About one-third of the 6,000 technology staff have transferred to IBM. Under the agreement, American Express maintains oversight of its IT strategy, key supplier relationships, its voice and data network and development of applications and databases. IBM is responsible for the IT operations infrastructure, including major data centres in Phoenix and Minneapolis. About 1 billion transactions are processed daily.

IBM agreed to proactively reallocate IT resources and add new computing functions, as business needs change. IT support services are provided on an as needed, pay-as-you-go basis, giving a level of flexibility. American Express anticipates major savings in IT costs. Around 2,000 IT staff including IT operations workers, technical support staff and programmers have transferred to IBM.

2.2.7 Flexibility and Control

Buying in IT services as and when required gives greater flexibility and enables organizations to increase or decrease capacity for IT development and maintenance quickly and efficiently without the delays that are inevitable in recruiting more staff (or redundancies/redeployment).

Some organizations will also feel that poor performance can be confronted more immediately and effectively with an external outsourcing supplier. Action against an under-performing internal IT department may be seen to require more time and the problems may be difficult to resolve. The contractual obligations of an outsourcing arrangement mean that accountability is better defined whereas internal accountability may be seen as less definitive and therefore less effective.

Example

> IBM is working on a £35 million contract with Barclays Bank in which it has agreed to share the risks of a series of high profile IT ventures. The deal is part of a 2-year £700 million investment by Barclays to rebuild its IT infrastructure using Internet-based technologies. A joint IBM and Barclays team composed of senior executives from both organizations monitors the programmes. If the projects do not succeed, IBM shares the costs. At the outset Barclays indicated what products it expected to buy from IBM but is not contractually bound by this.

Example

> 7-Eleven extended its outsourcing contract with EDS in a $175 million, 7-year deal to provide systems and services integration, hosting and storage services. EDS continues to develop and expand the convenience store chain's ordering, distribution, financial and supplier systems. The deal has also enabled 7-Eleven to rapidly deploy Vcom, its new self-service application. Vcom, an ATM-like interactive device with a touch screen, was tested in 98 7-Eleven stores in Texas and Florida. 7-Eleven's customers can use Vcom to cash cheques, purchase money orders and obtain other financial services. The new agreement with EDS gives lower operating costs and greater flexibility to aggressively pursue e-business initiatives.

2.3 Arguments Against Outsourcing

We turn now to consider reasons given by companies deciding not to outsource and the pitfalls they foresee. Outsourcing is often seen as a cost saving opportunity, but IT departments may be able to achieve cost efficiencies without help from an external service provider. Savings depend largely on the adoption of efficient management practices and to a lesser extent on economies of scale. Implementing the efficiency measures requires IT departments to adopt policies that may not be accepted by other business units. Internal politics may drive what can and cannot be achieved. If senior management empowers the IT department it will have the necessary authority to implement the changes.

2.3.1 Negative Impact on Business Strategy

Outsourcing is unwise where an application or process gives an organization strategic or competitive advantage. An internal IT department is able to identify business needs and how to address them more readily than an external outsourcing company. In-house IT professionals should be in a better position to understand and implement strategic developments. Other reasons why outsourcing should not be used for projects or operations of strategic importance to the organization include:

- The business benefits of outsourcing are difficult to quantify analytically.

- Outsourcing is rarely appropriate for applications or processes that directly interact on a personal level with customers.

- The outsourcing supplier may not be able to keep pace with increasing market demand.

- The introduction of outsourcing may have drastic and unforeseen effects on the business.

Companies that do not want their competitors to know of any internal problems often keep the difficulties and complexities inherent in outsourcing secret.

Example

Citizen Connect develops personal training solutions for individuals excluded from social, economic and educational opportunities. The business is centred on Job-Connect, a Web-based application for career mentoring and retraining. This relies on solid infrastructure and its IP network has been outsourced to Redbus Interconnect. Benefits include access to business class connections without the hassles of installation and maintenance. It also eased the financial burden of Internet connectivity.

Expansion plans can, however, be affected by the outsourcing deal. A pan-Canadian roll-out was made easier because Redbus Interconnect was also planning expansion in that area. A launch in Asia could not be supported so readily because the supplier had no plans to move into that market.

2.3.2 Escalating Costs as Business Changes

Outsourcing agreements typically last 5–10 years. During this period any organization will face major business change whether driven by customer needs, technology developments, political or legislative change. No outsourcing contract can foresee what these changes will be and it is therefore not possible to negotiate and agree charges for all eventualities. New and changed requirements can easily lead to escalating costs.

2.3.3 Loss of Flexibility and Control

Services defined at the outset will be covered by the outsourcing contract but what about new services and changed requirements that develop over the life of the contract? Internal IT departments are under the direct control of the organization's senior management but an external third party provides outsourced services. Service changes have to be negotiated and agreed with the IT service provider. How can an organization guarantee that its needs and priorities will be recognized and adopted by the supplier?

If services fall below acceptable levels, the outsourcing provider may incur penalties but the business risk remains with the outsourcing customer organization. Outsourcing is a difficult decision to reverse. Setting up an in-house IT department from scratch or re-introducing an IT function is a lengthy and expensive process and one that would not be undertaken lightly.

Plans to outsource London's 999 emergency telephone service in a 15-year Private Finance Initiative were abandoned when it was decided that the risks were too great. The Metropolitan Police's Command Control Communications and Information (C3i) project would have been worth more than £1.5 billion. The project was high profile and the Metropolitan Police felt that it could have been too much for an external organization to manage. The Police wanted to integrate technology implementation with internal business process changes.

2.3.4 Service Provider Concerns

Organizations can become heavily dependent on their IT service provider and this presents various risks:

- The supplier may become financially unstable or even go bankrupt. Another company with a different and unwelcome approach to the outsourced service may acquire the service provider.

- There may be a lack of responsiveness, possibly as the supplier loses interest (or wins more lucrative outsourcing deals).

- Service levels may fall to unacceptable levels as a result of internal problems within the service provider.

The recruitment company Reed outsourced network provision and management in a £3 million deal to significantly increase bandwidth and enable new Web-based products to be introduced. Although it outsourced to Vanco, which buys and manages network facilities for its customers, Reed specified that BT infrastructure should be used to ensure continuity in the current economic climate. In selecting a network service provider, Reed paid particular attention to potential suppliers' financial viability. Many of the companies that submitted tenders were in financial difficulties. Reed sought stability, flexibility and the latest technology. Vanco uses BT infrastructure to provide links to Reed's wide area network.

2.3.5 Demotivated IT Professionals

A major concern for any organization considering outsourcing has to be the impact on staff in the IT department. A poorly planned outsourcing programme may lead to a loss of talent and expertise within the organization. Outsourcing can be seen as a threat and a vote of no confidence in the IT services. IT professionals may feel betrayed or unappreciated. Some will decide to leave and pursue their careers elsewhere and this can increase the pressure on those who stay. The situation is exacerbated by the period of uncertainty. Many months are likely to pass before the final selection of IT service provider is made and agreement reached on arrangements for any staff transfers that are to take place. Not knowing what the future holds can be the most demoralizing and demotivating factor.

Example

BT awarded a £150 million contract to Computacenter to provide IT support and services for 90,000 desktops. This outsourcing deal included the transfer of around 400 BT staff to Computacenter. Discussions between the trade union, the Communication Workers Union (CWU), BT and Computacenter initially broke down because of disagreement over pension rights. A ballot was held and a majority of affected staff voted to go on strike. Further negotiations led to an agreement on a package of measures aimed at job security and pensions.

31

Example

> The Winterhur Group, one of Europe's leading corporate insurers, outsourced to improve quality and service levels, but the move led to IT staff dissatisfaction. They perceived IBM Global Services to be a very process-oriented organization whereas the Winterhur IT department had been small and rather more flexible.

2.3.6 Loss of Technical Expertise

Once an organization has outsourced some of its IT functions, it no longer employs the specialists who once worked in those areas. How can it then be sure that the service provider is exploiting the technology effectively? How can the organization develop its IT strategy without access to the range of technical skills that it once possessed in-house? How will it know when the supplier is being economical with the truth? The loss of technical expertise through outsourcing can leave an organization vulnerable to poor service and inflated prices.

2.3.7 Security and Confidentiality Risks

The outsourcing relationship is a very intimate one in which the supplier has access to information and other assets that the organization would normally regard as confidential. There is little chance of privacy and few secrets from an outsourcing service provider. The potential risks include:

- The increased potential for misuse of confidential information: for example, internal email and accounting data may be processed by the service provider; strategic software that gives a competitive advantage may be operated and maintained by the supplier.

- Increased difficulties in protecting other people's confidentiality: for example, access to personnel files and customer data.

- Loss of control over physical and electronic security especially if the supplier transfers processing to a new site. How will this be monitored? Who will be allowed access? What are the procedures when there has been a breach of security? The service provider may use the site for processing systems belonging to several customers. How can you be sure that a competitor will not gain access to your data and systems?

2.4 If Your Department Is to Be Outsourced

You may be reading this chapter because you have heard that your organization is considering outsourcing your work. Perhaps you have read about the pitfalls of outsourcing and now feel ready to tackle your managers to enlighten them about the error of their ways.

By all means do take the opportunity to hear first-hand from your managers about outsourcing plans and expectations. And if you disagree that outsourcing is the best way forward take any opportunity given to put your point of view forward. But recognize that outsourcing is something you may have to live with. In the first chapter we saw how much outsourcing has grown over recent years. There will be few IT professionals with a career that has not at some stage been touched by outsourcing. Today many thousands of IT professionals pursue successful careers with outsourcing suppliers.

The arguments for and against outsourcing are often finely balanced. We have seen that some factors such as flexibility and control can be used both as arguments for and against outsourcing. Much will depend on the perception of senior management. Once the final decision in favour of outsourcing is made, the challenge becomes how to manage this relationship successfully. This is the focus in the following chapters.

If outsourcing is the way ahead for your organization, aim to start planning positively for the future. Here are some topics for further thought and research:

- What matters most to you in your career? Working directly in support of the objectives of your chosen organization or furthering your technical development and career in your chosen profession?

- Will you be given the chance of staying with your original organization or transferring to the IT service provider? Are there any associated guarantees of employment such as no redundancy agreements, or an agreement about terms and conditions and salary increases?

- What is the chosen IT service provider's performance as an employer? Try to talk to some of their employees if you can. Is it continuing to expand and prosper? Does it offer good training and development opportunities? Does it specialize in areas of technology that particularly interest you? Is it located in parts of the country where you want to work, now and in the future?

- Do you possess the IT and management skills that you will need for the future? If you want to stay with your original organization, brush up on your contract management skills. Look for training opportunities; attend relevant seminars, conferences and exhibitions. Review your IT skills. Identify any areas where you need updating and try to address these gaps before the outsourcing takes place.

- Review your CV. This makes sense for all IT professionals. Even if you do not plan to change jobs immediately it is well worthwhile revising and updating your CV each year. Are your skills and experience relevant to today's (and tomorrow's) technology and business developments? Undoubtedly some of your previous experience will be but you may need to bring out different facets or emphasize different elements in your CV. This process will also help identify gaps or areas that you might want to transfer to in future career moves.

- Remember that outsourcing presents challenging and worthwhile opportunities for IT professionals. You may stay with a smaller, higher profile IT team within your organization, focused on strategic new developments and working closely alongside other business units. Or you may transfer to a successful IT company specializing in technology and providing high quality services. Whichever path you follow, you can have an excellent future as an IT professional.

Objectives and Parameters for Outsourced Services

3

3.1 Introduction

The first critical step in any outsourcing initiative is to identify your key objectives. This will determine what you outsource, how you measure success or failure, and will also guide your choice of service provider. This chapter will cover the first tasks in any outsourcing programme:

- Set strategic objectives.
- Identify and take on board stakeholders' views.
- Select IT functions to be outsourced.
- Use benchmarking to assess current performance levels.
- Define service requirements.
- Prepare the business case.

Even if your IT department did not take the preliminary decision to outsource, as an IT professional you are very likely to be closely involved with these stages of the programme. This chapter will help you to identify the issues to be tackled and will put your work in the context of the overall programme.

At the end of this chapter we look at the question of staff transfers resulting from an outsourcing initiative and consider the regulations that apply (in certain countries) to these transfers.

Press reports on outsourcing tend to focus on very large deals providing comprehensive coverage of IT functions. But there are many more examples of organizations choosing to outsource specific services that go unreported. As you read through the following sections you might like to bear in mind the conclusions reached by academic research in this field:

- Selective outsourcing decisions and total insourcing decisions achieve success more often than total outsourcing decisions.

- If senior business executives and IT managers make decisions about outsourcing together, they are more likely to succeed than if one of these stakeholder groups acts alone.

- Organizations that invite both external service providers and the internal IT department to bid achieve success more often than organizations that simply compare a few external bids with the current IT performance.

- Short-term contracts achieve success more often than long-term deals.

- Detailed contracts, which are best suited to IT services that can be clearly defined, are more likely to be successful. Where technology is ill defined, immature or unstable it is not feasible to specify services in detail and outsourcing is less likely to be successful.

3.2 The Importance of Objectives

Not all organizations properly define the objectives of their outsourcing programme. At the start make sure you have defined what your organization wants to achieve and how it will know when it has met its aims.

These objectives will determine:

- How you structure and manage the outsourcing programme.

- How you identify which IT functions are to be outsourced.

- What type of service provider you will select.

- What type of contract (contents, format, specificity and so on) you will aim for.

- How you will manage the contract and the outsourced service provided.

- What type of relationship your organization will want with the service provider.

To illustrate the impact of different objectives we will look at three examples:

1. The organization that is focused solely on reducing IT costs.

2. An organization with multiple objectives – to reduce unit costs, gain access to modern technologies, achieve an early delivery of new technology benefits and maximize career development opportunities for IT professionals.

3. A company wishing to use outsourcing to tackle poor financial performance and problems in the IT department.

3.2.1 Single Aim: Reduce Costs

If the single objective is to reduce costs through outsourcing, then there must be a precise and detailed definition of service requirements to ensure that there are tight constraints on the supplier. The outsourcing programme will need to be closely monitored and controlled with fixed timescales for key activities. Suppliers will be encouraged to look for all possible economies and are likely to provide sufficient support to meet but not exceed minimum acceptable service levels. Profit margins are likely to be low and therefore the supplier's priority will be to maintain these margins and firmly control costs. Consequently there is likely to be little input by the supplier's managers to contract management.

This will probably result in minimum service flexibility and is likely to constrain business development. Changes to the services required may be difficult to negotiate because the supplier may see this as an opportunity to improve on the low margins.

The contract will leave little room for service variation or enhancement. Negotiations will be tough, there will be limited emphasis on developing a long-term, close working relationship and there may be maximum job losses. Once up and running, contract management will focus on the collection of quantitative performance measures.

3.2.2 Multiple Objectives: Value for Money and Technological Development

In this instance, the organization will be aiming for a reduction in unit costs, year on year, and will want to see continuing technological innovation. A career development programme will be an integral part of the agreement, ensuring that staff receive training to adapt to new roles and opportunities presented by the outsourcing deal.

The service provider will want to emphasize value for money. The deal offers greater commercial potential with the possibility of greater involvement in the management of the customer's operations and rewards for the delivery of business benefits through the use of new technology.

The outsourcing programme will be more complex and will need to remain flexible and ready to adapt as new business possibilities are identified through discussion and negotiation with potential suppliers. It may be difficult to strike an appropriate balance between the multiple objectives and regular liaison with all stakeholder groups will be necessary to ensure that the weight given to each objective continues to meet business priorities.

It will not be possible to include a precise definition of all services required in the contract. Formulae will need to be agreed to assess the value for money and business benefits delivered by the supplier. Negotiations may be lengthy because these formulae can be difficult to compile and to agree. Both parties will also see the negotiation stage as the first step in building a constructive working relationship.

A range of measures, some quantitative, others qualitative, will be collected to assess the performance of the outsourcing arrangement. The service provider is likely to be more flexible as service requirements change. Both customer organization and supplier will continue to invest in contract management.

IT professionals will increasingly take on new roles with some transferring to work with the supplier's other customers. There are likely to be minimum job losses.

3.2.3 Crisis Management: Escaping Financial Difficulties

In our third example, the organization is in severe financial difficulty and has identified a number of significant problems in the IT department. Improvements must be made fast if the organization is to survive. This sets the stage for a very different outsourcing programme.

Timescales will be short and will not allow sufficient time to draw up detailed service requirements. The programme will need to be structured to ensure rapid decision making by key executives. There will be little opportunity to seek out stakeholder views.

Through outsourcing the organization may, at least initially, be able to reduce ongoing IT operational costs and can additionally gain the advantages of IT investment without the need for up-front capital investment. This is, however, a high-risk strategy. Inadequate analysis and planning at the initial stage are likely to lead to many problems and escalating costs once the contract is signed.

Any organization facing this outsourcing model will need to recognize and address as far as possible the inherent dangers in this approach. Aim to avoid a long-term lock-in to a single supplier and seek to develop a relationship in which the supplier shares the risk and rewards of improving business fortunes.

3.3 Understanding Stakeholders' Objectives

Although your organization may have decided to pursue outsourcing, this does not mean that every department will share the same objectives and concerns at the outset. If your outsourcing programme is to be successful it needs to take account of these viewpoints. The first step, therefore, is to understand stakeholders' different perspectives.

There are many different stakeholders in an IT outsourcing programme, perhaps more than you might expect. Each might influence the programme, helpfully or not so constructively. Their interest may be direct or indirect. Identify those who have sufficient authority, influence or ability to make a significant contribution or cause a damaging delay if their views are not properly taken into account. These stakeholders can include:

- IT professionals concerned about their future careers.
- Trade unions who will not necessarily oppose outsourcing but will want to protect their members' employment and pension rights.
- Users who want to see improved IT performance.
- Business managers who may focus on business benefits.
- Purchasing specialists who will want to contribute to the outsourcing process and ensure that the organization gets value for money from its suppliers.

- The finance department concentrating on costs and capital expenditure.

- Auditors concerned to ensure that they continue to have sufficient access to systems and processes to enable them to do their job effectively.

- The legal department concerned about the major contractual commitment involved in outsourcing.

- Current IT suppliers who may either lose their business with your organization or may have to interface with a new outsourcing service provider.

- Top business executives concentrating on business strategy and shareholder value.

Aim to understand each stakeholder's perspective in your organization. This is best done through open discussion. Try to avoid broad generalizations that mask different viewpoints, especially at this stage in the programme. Plan the programme in such a way as to allow stakeholders to contribute, meeting their concerns. Thus the internal legal department will need to be closely involved in drawing up the outsourcing contract; the auditors will need to contribute to the specification of service requirements; and the trade unions will need an opportunity to meet with the short-listed potential new service providers. This will be an ongoing process throughout the outsourcing programme.

It is also important to ensure that senior management continue to support and encourage the outsourcing initiative. Identify key milestones such as finalizing the initial supplier short list, selecting the preferred supplier and agreeing contract terms. Schedule time for senior managers to get involved in these stages.

Once you have identified and understood the differing stakeholder viewpoints you can begin to create a shared agenda for IT outsourcing.

3.4 Analysing Objectives

In Chapter 2 we looked at the arguments in favour of outsourcing. The New York-based Outsourcing Institute categorizes the reasons why organizations outsource into tactical and strategic aims (www.outsourcing.com).

The top five tactical reasons are:

1. To reduce or control operating costs. This is the single most important objective and one of the most compelling short-term benefits.

Example

General Motors outsourced the development of a Web-based application for car owners to developers in Bangalore, India. The complex application was built in six months at a substantial cost-saving over using USA-based consultants. Owner Center is a Java-based Web application that allows registered General Motors vehicle owners to track warranty, recall and service information online.

Example

PacifiCare Health System outsourced its IT operations to IBM and consulting firm Keane in a 10-year, $1.2 billion deal that is expected to save PacifiCare around $380 million over the life of the contract. With 3.6 million members, California-based PacifiCare provides managed healthcare services for company health insurance plans and Medicare beneficiaries. The IT outsourcing agreement is part of a larger cost cutting programme that includes a reduction of about 15 per cent in the number of employees. Over 600 jobs have transferred from PacifiCare to IBM and Keane.

2. To increase the capital funds available for investment. If non-core functions are outsourced and paid for through operational expenditure, more capital funds can be invested in core, strategic activities.

Example

Amtrak, the American railway company, signed a $229 million IT outsourcing deal with IBM that will save the government-subsidized company $85 million over the course of a 7-year deal.

> The contract extends a previous agreement and because Amtrak still owes IBM $101 million from this earlier contract, the total value of the renegotiated deal is $330 million. IBM manages Amtrak's entire computing infrastructure from a data centre in Virginia. As a result of the new deal, IT services are being improved for Amtrak's 24,000 employees. Several projects can now be funded to take out costs and increase revenue.
>
> IBM provides Amtrak's desktop and help desk support for 7,500 workstations and manages voice and data networks, including the systems at Amtrak's reservation system, which processes up to 3,300 transactions per minute via the Internet, telephone and ticket counter channels. IBM and Amtrak are working together to increase the railway company's revenue by marketing the Arrow reservation system to other transport companies in Europe and the Asia-Pacific region.

3. To generate a one-off cash payment. Outsourcing can involve the transfer of assets from customer organization to service provider. Computer equipment and other facilities have a value and are, in effect, sold to the supplier as part of the outsourcing deal.

Example

> Texas-based Sabre Holdings and EDS agreed an outsourcing and IT asset sale in which EDS took over the management of Sabre's internal IT systems in a 10-year $2.2 billion contract and acquired Sabre's airline technology outsourcing business for $660 million. EDS also bought Sabre's IT infrastructure assets. About 4,200 Sabre employees transferred to EDS. Sabre now plans to focus primarily on its flagship travel reservations business and a companion software suite.

4. To give access to resources (including technical skills) that are not available within the organization.

Example

To compete in an increasingly technology-led sport, the Jaguar Racing team, which is based in Milton Keynes, needed to improve its testing and design process at an affordable cost. It therefore agreed an outsourcing deal that provides access to eight extra processors when it is really needed – during the Grand Prix season. The processors are made available over the Jaguar network and paid for only when they are required, making much better use of resources than purchasing these assets and leaving them idle for much of the year.

Outsourcer MSXI provides the extra systems over the Internet using Hewlett-Packard's Utility Data Centre software to allocate the resources and fit them into Jaguar's network. For Formula One designers, the more computing power available, the faster they can make the car. Jaguar uses the extra power for processor intensive aerodynamic modelling. The workload peaks according to the racing season, because from April to July staff work on both the current season's car and the specification for the following year. But when the initial design phase is over, the requirements reduce.

Example

Camden Borough Council decided to sign a multi-million pound contract for a strategic IT partner to help achieve its online government plans. The outsourcing arrangement will not replace the internal IT department, but will help provide technology and support in areas where there is no in-house expertise. Camden recognized that e-government was more about change than technology. The council wanted to make fundamental changes in how it was run and needed technological expertise from a partner to help achieve this. Cost was another important element. Camden wanted to invest significantly in IT, but did not have the capital funds, although it could meet the required operating or revenue costs.

5. To resolve difficult management problems. Managers should be aware, however, that they are still responsible for an outsourced function and cannot abdicate this role.

Example

Gillette consolidated all hosting and operations management of its global Websites using two outsourcing suppliers. From a central location in Virginia Exodus Communications hosts Gillette's Websites, while Redwood City provides systems monitoring, network services and enhanced site performance. The aim of the consolidation was to ensure more consistent service levels across Gillette's sites. For example, Web visitors accessing information about Braun products, which are developed in Germany, should receive the same level of service as those who access the Website for the USA-based Duracell unit. Content developers are located in various countries, but Gillette wanted to offer consistent Website services.

The top five strategic reasons for outsourcing identified by the Outsourcing Institute are:

1. To help companies focus on core, strategic issues leaving operational details to external experts.

Example

The car rental division of easyGroup, easyCar, has a 3-year £1 million Web hosting deal with Attenda. Under the agreement, Attenda acts as the outsourced operations department and the first point of call for any fault resolution. EasyCar remains in charge of all the main applications used to run the business, enabling the company to focus on enhancing the customer experience.

Baylor Health Care System outsourced billing and collection tasks to EDS to reduce administrative costs by 10–15 per cent and allow the company to focus more on its core business. The entire billing and collection business process is outsourced in a 10-year $200 million contract. The project's goal is to give Baylor Health Care an end-to-end digital system that improves the accuracy and speed of the billing and collection process by linking administrative and clinical data. Baylor is a private sector, non-profit healthcare company based in Dallas with a network including hospitals, primary care physician centres and rehabilitation clinics. It has about 14,000 employees and had $1.2 billion in total operating revenue in 2001.

EDS and Baylor are also working on a longer-term project to give healthcare workers wireless handheld devices to record and transmit data more quickly and accurately. Doctors and nurses will enter patient data into personal digital assistants instead of using clipboards. The data will then be transmitted wirelessly to the hospital's network and to the insurance companies' systems, which will reduce errors.

2. To provide access to world-class capabilities. Outsourcing suppliers can offer new technology, tools and techniques as well as better career opportunities to those who transfer to the supplier company. They can also bring structured methodologies, procedures and documentation.

Skills developed by EDS in running the UK Inland Revenue's computer systems are being used to improve the US Marine Corps' IT systems. The Intranet implementation programme, worth $6.9 billion, covers 300 bases in the USA and worldwide, as far afield as Iceland and Cuba. Relevant expertise from the UK Inland Revenue contract includes programme management, systems integration

> and large-scale desktop implementation projects. Change management and legacy system integration are some of the major challenges in the Marine Corps' programme.

3. To get the benefits of a reorganized function fast. Outsourcing service providers have considerable experience and expertise in their specialist areas and are organized to offer IT services most effectively and profitably. The customer's IT function can be reorganized quickly to deliver business benefits.

4. To share risks (and benefits) with the service provider. When non-core functions are outsourced, organizations can be more flexible, more dynamic and better able to respond to new business opportunities.

Example

The UK Highways Agency is planning to contract out the creation and management of a single telecommunications network covering the UK's motorways. The outsourcing service provider will be expected to connect 32 separate networks linking police control centres and roadside devices such as CCTV cameras and information signs. This initiative, known as the National Roads Telecommunications Services project (NRTS), will be a 10-year Public Private Partnership worth £400 million.

NRTS will create a high bandwidth digital network to serve the Highways Agency's future needs, offering the opportunity to plug new developments easily into the network. The outsourcing partner will be allowed to develop its own commercial opportunities using spare network capacity.

5. To free up resources for other tasks. Internal resources within an organization are always limited. By outsourcing non-core activities, more resources can be made available for strategic developments and serving customers.

Example

> Business jet maker Gulfstream Aerospace signed a 10-year, $510 million outsourcing contract with CSC. The Georgia-based aircraft company transferred all mainframe, mid-range and desktop computer operations, as well as the development and maintenance of all application software to CSC. About 220 Gulfstream IT workers move to CSC. The objective of the outsourcing deal was to help Gulfstream focus more effectively on its core business – building jets for corporate and other users – and to reduce competition for limited resources within the company.

To identify a set of objectives for your outsourcing programme you will need to ask:

- What are your high level corporate objectives and measures?

- Which areas provide real value to your organization?

- What are your organization's core competencies?

- Which IT functions differentiate your company from competitor organizations?

- What is the gap between your current IT services and your customers' needs?

- What are your customers' future needs?

- Where are the most serious problems of skills shortages, the greatest need for training and staff retention difficulties?

- To what extent is technological innovation important?

- What kind of supplier relationship best suits your organization's culture?

You will need clearly articulated and written objectives and measures for each IT function to be outsourced. Consider the potential and need for improving IT service performance. Look at what you might achieve internally without help from an external service provider and how much this would cost. Outsourcing only makes sense if a supplier can achieve greater service improvements and/or lower costs.

Once you have drawn up a set of objectives, review them:

- Does the outsourcing initiative fit with the overall business strategy of your organization?
- Do the objectives meet stakeholder requirements?
- Are the objectives clear?
- Have all the options been identified?

3.5 Selecting Outsourcing Candidates

Your organization will need to determine which IT services to outsource. An options analysis will help clarify the pros and cons of outsourcing or keeping the function in-house. A number of factors will need to be taken into account:

- The strategic importance of the IT services
- The availability of resources
- The importance of technological innovation
- The rate of change
- The gap between current services provided and user needs

1. *Strategic Importance.* IT services that provide a competitive edge or are key to an organization's future strategy are generally kept in-house. The company's focus will be on developing and improving these services. On the other hand, IT services which are common to many organizations and do not play a major role in business development may be profitably outsourced.

   Care needs to be taken in determining which IT services are strategically important. For many organizations with employees on standardized pay scales, payroll systems will not be regarded as strategic and may be seen as outsourcing candidates. There will be some companies, however, in which pay rates are specific to individuals and the ability to pay staff bonuses quickly and accurately is of critical importance in attracting and retaining staff to give the organization competitive advantage. In this instance payroll systems are likely to be kept in-house.

Strategic importance can also vary with time. ATMs offered competitive advantage when some banks first introduced them, but this is no longer the case. All banks offer ATMs today. They are commodity services and do not differentiate one bank from another and hence have become candidates for outsourcing.

2. *Resource Availability.* We have seen how outsourcing provides an opportunity to bring fresh resources and new technical skills into an organization. Small and medium-sized IT departments in particular may not find it possible to provide the breadth and depth of technical expertise needed today. As technological developments continue to demand ever-greater specialist knowledge it makes sense to consider outsourcing as a way of providing needed technical expertise.

Organizations developing new systems will also want to consider whether they have sufficient in-house resources to support the development and maintenance of new IT services. Outsourcing system development may be a sensible way to deliver the new service fast.

3. *Technical Innovation.* Does the IT service depend on leading edge technology? Is it critical to your organization's business strategy that you are among the first to adopt new technology? Your organization may be at the forefront of technological innovation in this area with a well-established team of specialists. In this instance outsourcing is unlikely to be advantageous, particularly if the IT service is of strategic importance. There will be circumstances, however, when a new service is to be developed where an alliance or joint venture with an outsourcing supplier with expertise in the appropriate areas will be an effective way forward.

4. *Rate of Change.* IT services that change very frequently can be difficult to outsource satisfactorily. Specifying, costing, agreeing and implementing changes through a third party can be a laborious process. It is important, however, to review the need for regular, small changes. Is the cost justified? What are the business benefits?

A service that has well-founded business needs for frequent change may be unsuitable for outsourcing. Services that are relatively mature and stable make good outsourcing candidates.

5 *Gap Between Current Services and User Needs.* If the difference between current service levels and user needs (these requirements must have a sound business justification) is significant you will need to ask what needs to be done to close the gap. Are there actions that can be taken within current resource levels to narrow the gap quickly

or is this simply not possible? If there are significant business benefits to be gained by improving the current IT services to meet user needs, but this requires additional resources and/or technical skills, then outsourcing is a potential option.

The options analysis will need to cover:

- Arguments for and against outsourcing.
- Information relating to the outsourcing and in-house options:
  - impact of proceeding with each option;
  - risks inherent in each option;
  - likelihood of the risks occurring;
  - costs of each option;
  - timescales for each option.

The choice of which IT services to outsource is sometimes referred to as best sourcing or right sourcing:

- What is best for my company?
- Who will bring about the most effective change?
- Who will make changes fast?
- What skills need to be retained in-house to ensure my company stays in control?

One method of identifying functions that are best outsourced is known as value chain analysis. Each segment of the internal value chain within a company must add maximum value in the delivery of services to the end customer. Activities are analyzed by their strategic relevance to understand the behaviour of internal costs and to identify existing and potential sources of differentiation between the company and its competitors. The value chain analysis helps identify business activities that may be eligible candidates for outsourcing. The analysis identifies which functions are strategic or a source of competitive advantage (to be kept in-house) and which functions need to be performed at maximum efficiency or lowest cost (candidates for outsourcing).

3.6 Benchmarking

Comparing IT services against industry standards and best practice in other organizations helps to identify where performance improvements can be made and which services might be beneficially outsourced. Benchmarking is a management process used by organizations to investigate, study, measure, enhance and apply best practice. Strengths and weaknesses of IT activities are identified. Benchmarking can also provide performance measures against which outsourced services can be assessed.

Several benchmarking methods exist. The exercise will depend on the resources and time available and the difficulty of identifying similar IT functions in other comparable organizations. The process generally consists of four key steps:

1. Determine the scope of the study, in other words the IT service or function to be assessed and the information requirements. You will need to determine the data to be collected and the external sources of information to be used. For example, you might look for information on customer satisfaction, staff numbers, salary levels, equipment used, response times and financial performance. The project will need to be planned and managed. It will be important to balance quantitative measures with more qualitative assessments and to avoid getting overloaded with numbers.

2. Collect data from customers, analysts' reports, published industry data and organizations that specialize in benchmarking. It may be helpful to approach other organizations that are known to operate excellent IT services with a view to exchanging performance data and best practice. Look particularly for organizations that have achieved standards such as ISO 9001, the international standard for quality management systems.

3. Analyze and verify the data. Validation is usually carried out through a seminar in which participants from different areas in your organization review the data to spot any inaccuracies or inconsistencies. Data normalization is an attempt to ensure fair comparisons between organizations. If you use an external benchmarking service they will have their own formulae based on, for example, the cost of IT staff in each geographic region.

4. The final step is to repeat the benchmarking process on an ongoing basis. For maximum benefit, benchmarking should become an integral part of IT operations and can be used to demonstrate improvements in performance over time.

The results from the benchmarking exercise can be used in a number of ways:

● They may show some improvements that can be made in-house regardless of whether the IT service is outsourced.

● Benchmark results may provide baseline data to be used in the specification of the outsourced service requirements.

● They may be used as a yardstick against which to measure proposals from prospective outsourcing suppliers.

A word of warning – if your IT department is organizing the benchmarking process it is especially important to be able to demonstrate that the data you gather is reliable and that assessments are objective. Perception is important and without care it may appear that results have been skewed to put the IT department's operations in a favourable light. Choose performance criteria that are important to business managers. If you use an external benchmarking service, get senior business managers involved in the selection of the service. When comparing with other organizations make sure that these are highly respected by your senior managers. Benchmarking services that monitor peak capacity may provide a better measure of service levels and resource requirements than monitoring operations that average out peaks and troughs suggesting that there is spare capacity.

3.7 In-house Improvements

It is a mistake to assume that supplier bids should be compared against current IT service performance. Take the opportunity to consider what might be done in-house to improve service levels and value for money. Question assumptions that limit the IT department's ability to make changes. Ask the staff running the service what they would do to

52

improve it, given a free hand. Experience in outsourcing has shown that the best approach is to review and rationalize internal IT operations before launching outsourcing initiatives. By ensuring that IT objectives are aligned to business strategy and that there are governance structures in place to monitor progress, organizations create a better foundation for assessing outsourcing proposals.

Some organizations decide to invite the internal IT department to submit a bid for formal evaluation against the external suppliers' proposals. You may be pleasantly surprised at how many constructive ideas for change this process can generate. With outsourcing on the agenda, organizations begin to look afresh at how they operate and why they need certain IT functions. Changes that previously were unacceptable to users may be seriously considered if they can be shown to improve value for money. Many medium or large IT departments can achieve economies of scale promised by external service providers. Internal IT departments can also introduce efficient management practices developed by suppliers.

When an external bid is superior to proposals from the internal IT department it is useful to question where and how the improvements will be made:

- Some savings may be more realistic than others.
- Take care to compare like with like: are total in-house IT costs being compared against a supplier's selective bid?
- Outsourcing can carry hidden costs such as the (internal) cost of contract management and excess fees for service changes.
- The economics of the different sourcing options can change over the life of the contract.
- The supplier's bid might suggest new ways of improving performance within the internal IT department.

If you are closely involved in the preparation of an internal bid do remember that an external provider might still submit the winning proposal. In the excitement of putting together ideas for change it is easy to forget that the outcome might be an outsourced IT service. Try to remain flexible and ready to adapt to whatever career development opportunities arise.

3.8 Defining Service Requirements

Outsourcing service requirements need to be clear, complete, measurable and based on the outsourcing objectives. They will form the basis for all the subsequent decisions in the selection of a suitable service provider and the construction of the contract. You should first decide on the outcomes you require from the IT function to be outsourced and then determine what services you need to achieve these results.

Your organization may have decided to outsource several IT functions or activities. It will be important to decide whether to package them together or to break them down into components and invite suppliers to bid for separate elements. There is no easy solution to this question. Commercially the greater the volume of services provided and the longer the timeframe the lower the unit costs should be and vice versa. On the other hand, some organizations prefer to appoint multiple suppliers to avoid becoming over reliant on one service provider and potentially losing a degree of control.

The specification of service requirements needs a clear definition of service boundaries and interfaces. Service requirements may include:

● business services with supporting IT, such as a call centre;

● IT services for the organization's internal use, such as intranet-enabled information services delivered to the user's desktop;

● support for major change programmes;

● advice on strategy or programme management;

● application development;

● adoption of new technology;

● operational services, such as help desk support or application maintenance;

● infrastructure, such as extending and updating telecommunications networks and facilities.

You can collect input to the statement of service requirements from various sources:

- Structured working sessions with users, business managers and technical staff, facilitated by an external expert or outsourcing programme team member. These discussions can provide valuable input and a means of verifying other data.

- Customer surveys.

- In-house manuals and guides.

- Benchmarking data.

- Quality, financial, environmental and other standards.

- Reference site visits to other organizations that have outsourced IT functions. Learn from their successes and failures. Include users, finance and legal representatives in these visits.

Using a variety of sources will help you prepare a balanced and reasonable set of requirements. The best people to specify the detail of the service requirements may be those whose careers will be significantly affected by the outcome of the outsourcing initiative. This can make it difficult to be impartial.

If a key business objective is to reduce costs then there is no justification for specifying enhanced services with little business benefit. Managers will need to be more specific than asking for lower costs and a better quality of service. Cost and quality need to be linked. What about future years? Is it practical to keep reducing costs year by year? It is all too easy to over-specify service requirements, so assess the impact of different service levels on your organization.

The statement of service requirements should cover the following topics:

- a general description of service requirements;

- target service levels;

- projected service volumes over the life of the contract;

- design constraints such as standards and interfaces to other systems and services;

- user support requirements;

- training and education requirements;

- performance measurement information and report requirements;

- service monitoring;

- security requirements;

- change control and a description of the types of change envisaged;

- a definition of the supplier's functional responsibilities;

- a definition of the customer's responsibilities;

- proposed charging structures and objectives;

- liaison requirements between customer and supplier;

- transition arrangements;

- timetables and target dates for outsourcing.

The statement of service requirements is also known by several other names: statement of requirements, operational requirement, output-based specification and specification of business requirements. Aim to set down what is required rather than how it should be delivered. Avoid specifying technical solutions and give the service providers scope to propose innovative ways of meeting the business needs. The requirements specification must be realistic, clear and unambiguous.

3.9 Business Case Analysis

The business case sets out the reasons, advantages and justifications for continuing with the outsourcing initiative. It should demonstrate that outsourcing is achievable, affordable and represents good value for money, both now and in the future. It is useful not only for focusing attention on the genuine need for outsourcing but also as a way to demonstrate to senior executives why outsourcing should proceed. It is also a valuable planning tool that will support informed decisions.

As the outsourcing progresses, the information you possess about services to be delivered, costs and timescales will become more accurate and precise. At the start the business case may only be developed in outline but by the time your organization is ready to select a preferred service provider there should be a full business case with validated assumptions.

The business case should cover the financial and non-financial issues. The financial arguments for proceeding with outsourcing need to be especially compelling. Existing problems should be identified with a list of the actions that could be taken to resolve the difficulties. Each option should be costed over the life of a potential outsourcing contract. There needs to be a cost analysis of current IT services against which everything else is measured.

The precise content and format of business cases will depend on the financial policies and practices in your organization and on whether you work in the private or public sector. What follows provides a general indication of the components of a business case.

3.9.1 Executive Summary

This section should provide a simple, clear and logical synopsis on why outsourcing is needed and what benefits it will bring. The arguments should be persuasive and the financial case unambiguous. The summary should be capable of standing on its own and should include references to other sections in the business case that provide more detail.

3.9.2 Strategic Case

This sets the scene and gives background information. It describes the strategic context – how the outsourcing initiative will fit with your organization's business strategy and related projects. It explains the need and drivers for change and explains the key stakeholders' viewpoints. Importantly it covers the objectives of the initiative, the service boundaries and the desired outcomes.

3.9.3 Current Services

Here the current IT services are described and costed. This section will be time consuming to prepare; rarely will an organization have access to the detailed costings and business benefits that are required here. It is important to analyze the business contribution made by the IT services. An accurate measure of staff costs will be needed. Busy people in your organization may be reluctant to spend time on this work especially if they are uncertain about, or unsupportive of, outsourcing.

3.9.4 Options Analysis

Each option for change should be identified, and assessed in detail. There will generally be three principal options:

1. maintain the current service provision, in other words do nothing;

2. improve service levels using in-house resources only;

3. outsource, that is identify and select a supplier capable of delivering the service that is needed.

3.9.5 Benefits Analysis

You will need to set parameters for appraising the options in terms of service quality benefits. Define the criteria to be applied to each option; for example, you may want to assess reliability, responsiveness to customer needs, service improvements and management effort. Estimate the potential financial impact of these benefits. Rank the benefit criteria on a scale of relative importance and apply a weighting system to produce a score for each option. Note that each option has an impact on a number of indirect costs such as costs associated with management time and cost differences that arise through changes in business responsiveness.

3.9.6 Cost Analysis

This section will invariably attract the most interest and is pivotal to the decision to proceed with outsourcing. No management board is likely to sign off a business case unless the financial director has given his or her sign of approval. It is important, but not always easy, to get the board to look beyond the short term and to focus on the long-term benefits. The up-front additional costs in outsourcing (or any major service improvement initiative) will not be welcomed especially since budgets for the current and following one or two years will already have been agreed and set.

Each option is costed over the life of the contract. Some cost elements will need to be estimated using market data. There are four key financial decision making methods. Your organization's financial policies will determine which you use.

1. *Net present value (NPV) method.* This is generally considered the best method. It begins by calculating the net cash flow generated by the option. The NPV measures the benefit that accrues to the organization and is calculated by taking the sum of the present value of all future cash flows minus the initial cost. A positive NPV means that the option yields a rate of return greater than the cost of the invest-

ment. A negative NPV means that the option earns less than the organization could obtain by keeping the money in the bank.

2. *Internal rate of return (IRR) method.* The IRR is the rate at which the NPV is exactly zero. The aim is to achieve an IRR that exceeds the cost of the investment. It is a percentage rather than an amount and so a higher IRR on a small investment might be worth less than a somewhat lower IRR on a large investment. The option with the highest IRR is therefore not necessarily the best choice.

3. *Payback period.* This method measures the length of time it takes to recover the initial investment. The option will be recommended only if the payback period is less than a set amount, say 3 years. In comparing options, the one with the shortest payback period is selected. This technique is not as effective as the NPV method as it takes no account of cash flows beyond the payback period, even though these are relevant and should be considered.

4. *Accounting rate of return or return on investment.* This measures the average annual after tax accounting profit generated by the investment in the option divided by the initial expense. It is inferior to the NPV method as it does not evaluate cash flows or take into account the cost of money.

All cost data should be displayed in spreadsheets together with a detailed breakdown of assumptions used. It is essential that each option put forward and each variant described is costed. All too often boards have a habit of choosing a solution that is a variation on the final recommendation in the business case.

3.9.7 Sensitivity Analysis

The cost and benefit analysis of the various options will depend on a number of estimates and assumptions. The sensitivity analysis will consider the impact on the business case of variations in these assumptions. For example, "what if" the supplier's costs are higher than anticipated for the specified service levels, "what if" in-house improvements lead to fewer cost reductions than forecast and so on. This process is applied to all relevant financial variables to give a clearer picture of the best case and worst case scenarios. The aim is to demonstrate that, even under the most extreme of circumstances, the recommended option continues to be the most financially advantageous solution.

3.9.8 Affordability Analysis

This section of the business case analyzes the budget needed to run the outsourcing programme and assesses the ability and willingness of the organization's budget holders to meet these resource implications. A statement of support from the key stakeholders is a useful addition.

3.9.9 Commercial Case

This explains any further work required to sound out the IT services market to establish whether there are sufficient companies able to supply the services required by your organization. Ideally you will want to receive a number of bids to be able to negotiate a competitive deal.

3.9.10 Risk Management

Potential risks and their possible causes should be listed. Each risk should be assigned to an owner and an indication given of contingency measures and risk management. There will be two types of risk: first, risks affecting the programme as a whole and, secondly, risks that impact the business case. Both types of risk need to be identified but the focus should be on the risks affecting the business case. Each risk should be scored against the likelihood of its occurrence and the severity of its impact. There is more on risk management in Chapter 7.

3.10 Staff Transfers

Where an in-house IT service is outsourced, the support and morale of the staff who maintain and operate the service are critical to success. If you are working on an outsourcing initiative remember the people issues:

- Think about the background to the decision to outsource. Did the idea come from within the IT department or was it imposed by senior executives?

- Be aware that people may fear the unknown and be very concerned about their future. They may be nostalgic for the old days. They may feel out of control, having little or no say in the choice of their future employer.

- People will want to hear what is happening from their own senior management. Make sure that there is no communication vacuum. Give clear information on timescales and make sure that those who might be transferring to a new service provider understand how their employment rights and conditions will be affected.

The personnel department will need to be closely involved with this aspect of the outsourcing programme. Current personnel policies will need to be reviewed within the context of outsourcing. Some may set constraints on the programme. Relevant personnel policies will need to be included in the statement of service requirements. Some policies may need to be modified and some new policies may need to be prepared. Internal agreements or legislation may require a certain level of consultation with trade unions. Failure to consult at an appropriate time could, at worst, lead to damaging disputes and a major disruption to the outsourcing initiative.

Employment law varies from country to country. In the USA staff have a contract with their employers and, as long as they comply with the contractual notice periods and benefits, or the benefits are bought off, employers are considered to have observed employees' rights.

Many countries have employment protection legislation that applies to any staff transferred to a new employer as a result of outsourcing. In Europe the Acquired Rights Directive 1977 is designed to safeguard employees' rights when a business is transferred. The original intention was to protect employees from redundancy when a company was restructured, merged within another company or was acquired by another business. The application of the Directive has been extended to other situations such as outsourcing.

In the UK, the Acquired Rights Directive has been implemented through the Transfer of Undertakings (Protection of Employment) Regulations 1981 or TUPE (as amended by the Trades Union and Employee Rights Act 1993). What follows is a description of the implications of TUPE but it carries a health warning! This is a very complex legal area fraught with difficulty, and employment law changes frequently. It is vital that any outsourcing programme that involves the transfer of in-house services has access to specialist legal advice on this area.

TUPE applies when an "undertaking" or "stable economic entity" is transferred. This does not have to be a self-contained business, nor does it have to be carried out for profit. It applies when only part of a business is transferred as long as the part is separately identifiable. For TUPE to apply there also has to be a direct transfer of significant assets or the new owner must take over a major part of the previous employer's workforce.

The regulations set out to preserve employees' rights and benefits, though TUPE may not cover everything. If staff are to transfer, information will need to be given in the statement of service requirements sent to potential service providers.

The TUPE regulations provide that:

● On the "transfer of an undertaking" the contracts of employment belonging to the employees engaged in the undertaking immediately prior to the transfer are not terminated. Instead they automatically transfer on the same terms and conditions to the new employer.

● Any dismissal connected with the transfer is automatically unfair unless there is an "economic, technical or organizational reason entailing changes in the workforce". In other words, an employee has the right not to be dismissed in connection with the transfer.

● Collective rights also automatically transfer to the new employer and there are obligations to consult with employees' representatives such as trade unions about the transfer. This consultation must be meaningful and take place "with a view to seeking" amongst other things "agreement". Thus employees have the right to be informed and consulted about the way in which the transfer will affect them.

When the transfer takes place, staff immediately become employees of the outsourcing service provider with accrued rights of continuous service such as holiday entitlements and redundancy rights. Modification of terms and conditions of employment constitutes grounds for a claim of constructive unfair dismissal (and will also be void).

Each employee has the fundamental legal right not to be compelled to work for an employer not of his or her choice. TUPE is designed to ensure continuity of employment. If an employee chooses not to transfer to the outsourcing supplier and the customer organization is not willing or not able to offer an alternative job, then this constitutes resignation not dismissal under UK legislation.

TUPE does not provide a legal framework for the transfer of occupational pensions. The customer organization may choose to require the outsourcing supplier to provide benefits equivalent to the employees' pension transfer values.

In such a complex area it is hardly surprising that problems can occur. Two examples illustrate the difficulties:

1. If some staff who work on the "undertaking" were to be given the choice not to transfer, opponents could argue that a coherent undertaking has not been transferred and hence TUPE does not apply. All staff who are being transferred could then argue that they have been made redundant and could claim redundancy payments. If the customer organization decided to make the staff redundant, the outsourcing supplier would not be legally obliged to offer them jobs, but if jobs were provided the employees would in effect be new starters and would lose previously accrued employment benefits.

2. If either the customer organization or outsourcing supplier dismisses anyone who worked on the "undertaking" just before the transfer or shortly afterwards, then the supplier can be brought before an Industrial Tribunal for unfair dismissal of that employee. Note that any claim for unfair dismissal is brought against the outsourcing supplier, not the customer organization. Any costs of unfair dismissal compensation therefore fall on the supplier.

The outsourcing supplier must take specialist advice prior to signing the contract and needs to price the contract to take account of any hidden employment risks. A risk evaluation and assessment will need to be carried out and the supplier will need access to staff files for those who are transferring with the service. The outsourcing supplier will want to check the standard of personnel record-keeping in order to assess the risks of acquiring the new staff. The supplier should also make enquiries about any changes in the workforce prior to the transfer in case any employees who might otherwise have transferred have been dismissed and would be eligible to make a claim.

The list of employees to whom TUPE might apply needs to be agreed by the customer organization and the outsourcing supplier for inclusion in the outsourcing contract. The information in the contract schedule will include:

- the number of staff who will be transferred if TUPE applies;

- the age and gender of staff so that pension entitlements, details of salary and pay settlements can be calculated;
- information about existing terms and conditions or references to where this information can be found.

3.11 Outsourcing Programme Management

By any account, an outsourcing initiative is a complex change process and will greatly benefit from a structured programme or project management approach. The business case should drive the programme management process and the focus should be on what the programme is to deliver, why, when and for whom. Responsibility for each key task needs to be formally assigned and the risks carefully managed.

The programme should have:

- a controlled and organized start, middle and end;
- regular reviews of progress against the plan and against the business case;
- flexible decision points;
- effective management control of any deviation from the plan;
- the involvement of management and stakeholders at the right time and place throughout the programme;
- good communication channels with senior business executives, users, the IT department and the potential service providers.

There should be a detailed outsourcing plan to set out what needs to be done, when and by whom and with what resources. The main activities to be covered by the plan include:

- clarify and document the objectives;
- carry out an options analysis;
- define the boundaries of the services to be outsourced;
- prepare and validate the service requirements;

- identify potential suppliers and establish a dialogue with them to determine their level of interest in the deal;

- prepare the business case;

- involve senior management and key stakeholders as appropriate throughout the process;

- communicate with staff who may transfer to the service provider, other members of the IT department and others in your organization;

- short-list suppliers and provide information and service requirements to them;

- evaluate suppliers' proposals and continue the dialogue with them;

- identify and train the contract management team;

- negotiate the contract and agree the service level agreement;

- manage the transition;

- manage the contract.

Throughout the outsourcing process remember these key points:

- Never lose sight of the business driven objectives of the programme. Outsourcing is a means to an end, not an end in itself. Review the programme regularly to ensure that the outcome continues to contribute effectively to your organization's goals.

- Understand the strategic, managerial and technical implications of the scope of the outsourcing programme. Look for the wider context. Do not treat the programme as if it were a back room technical project. Effective communications and setting realistic expectations are important.

- Clearly define the scope and interfaces of what is being outsourced. Unambiguous roles and responsibilities will help reduce confusion and hence cost and risk.

Choosing a Service Provider **4**

4.1 Introduction

Outsourcing has been described as a marriage between two organizations. It is a serious commitment, with long-term consequences. It is also a formal relationship underpinned by a contractual agreement. Critically, it depends on the relationship that is developed between the parties.

The choice of outsourcing service provider is clearly vital. In Chapter 3 we looked at the need to establish objectives and service boundaries for the outsourcing initiative, how to benchmark service levels and prepare a business case. This chapter describes techniques for choosing an outsourcing supplier. To select the best service provider for your organization you will need to define clearly and unambiguously what you want the supplier to do; devise the criteria used to evaluate the bids you receive; and be clear how you are going to manage your organization's relationships with the suppliers that compete for the business. You will need to be sure that short-listed suppliers are both motivated and capable of providing the required services and that your organization will want to develop a strategic relationship with them.

The selection process described below is best suited to a medium to large organization seeking to outsource an IT service that is currently provided in-house. It can be adapted as necessary for different circumstances. For example, some organizations use preferred suppliers and will not go through a competitive tendering exercise.

Some organizations have specialist purchasing units that take the lead on elements of this selection process. The whole process is described here so that you can see where tasks undertaken by the IT department fit into the bigger picture.

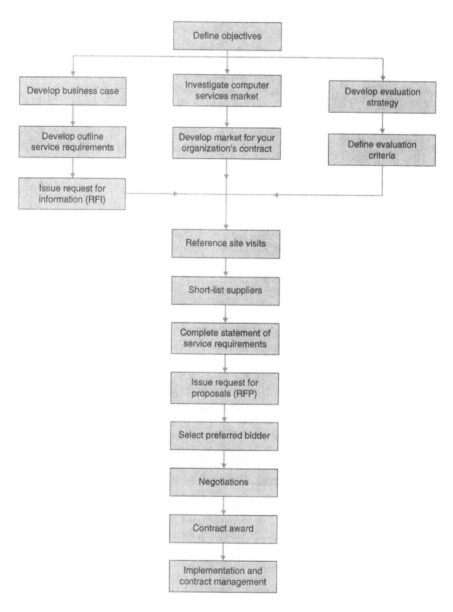

Figure 4.1 Selection process outline.

The steps in the selection process are illustrated in Figure 4.1. Especially during the early stages of the process, a number of parallel activities will be taking place as you work to define service requirements and the evaluation strategy within your organization, while investigating the computer services market to determine which companies might be interested in bidding. Throughout the process you will be laying the foundation for the future relationship between your organization and the chosen service provider.

4.2 Managing the Selection Process

This is a complex undertaking and the quality of the programme management of the process is critical to the successful selection of the best supplier. The key project roles at this stage in the outsourcing programme are senior executives, business managers and users, the purchasing team led by the project manager and a number of expert advisors.

4.2.1 Senior Executives

As with any major change programme, outsourcing needs the visible support of senior management if it is to succeed. A senior executive should be appointed as the programme owner, responsible for the overall success of the outsourcing process. He or she will present the business case and final recommendations to your organization's management board who are ultimately responsible for business strategy and achieving best value for money from IT investment.

4.2.2 Business Managers

Business managers are responsible for ensuring that the user requirements are accurately specified and that business benefits are correctly stated in the business case. They will help define the evaluation criteria to be used in the selection process and will play a part in developing the relationship between your organization and the chosen service provider. The business managers will also specify the required business outcomes that determine the service levels defined for the outsourced functions.

69

4.2.3 Purchasing Team

A team will need to be appointed to manage and support the selection process. Their normal day-to-day responsibilities will need to be reassigned to allow them to focus on this project. To ensure that the process is objective it is important that none of those on the team are at risk of losing their jobs as a result of the outsourcing initiative.

Between them, the purchasing team will need to offer a range of skills and expertise:

- scoping possible deals;
- knowledge of the computer services market;
- business and financial modelling skills for developing the business case;
- analysis of service requirements;
- co-ordinating business and user input to the requirements analysis and specification;
- specialist purchasing expertise including knowledge of your organization's purchasing strategy and policies;
- negotiating skills;
- managing the transition to new systems, services and providers;
- setting up contract management arrangements.

The programme manager's role will be to lead the purchasing team and manage the purchasing process. He or she will need to plan the process and manage any deviations from plan. Contributions from business managers and consultation with senior executives, users and others need to be scheduled and managed throughout. The programme manager will also need to ensure that access to experts outside the team is available as and when required.

4.2.4 Expert Advisors

It is unlikely that the purchasing team can provide all the specialist skills required during the selection process. Any gaps need to be identified at an early stage and advisors appointed as necessary. Other departments in your organization may provide some expertise. Do ensure that the finance, personnel, purchasing and legal departments have been consulted. They may wish to be represented on the purchasing team and might also be able to offer expertise in specific areas such as contract warranties and liabilities and employment law. These specialist skills can be brought into the project when required in the selection process.

Once you have consulted internally, you may find that some expertise has to be purchased and external consultants have to be appointed. Expert advisors are an expensive resource. To make the most of them, ensure that:

- their credentials are checked and their knowledge and depth of expertise are tested;
- their role is clearly documented and explained to everyone working on the programme – advisors cannot make decisions for your organization;
- the external advisors are properly managed and remain focused only on their assigned roles.

Do watch out for potential difficulties:

- Always make sure that you have sought out expertise available within your own organization. Avoid making a false assumption about in-house skills in other departments (and remember how frustrating this can be when others make similarly misguided assumptions about skills in the IT department). At worst, buying in external skills when it is not necessary can lead to a backlash from another department that can delay or even jeopardize the outsourcing initiative.
- Watch out for scope creep in the tasks assigned to external advisors. Some consultancies working in this field will be only too happy to expand their responsibilities (and fees of course!) to play a significant programme management role when the intention was only to use them to fill gaps in the skills base required.

4.3 Investigating the Computer Services Market

Before your procurement begins in earnest there is a lot to be gained from talking to a number of computer services companies. Make the most of this opportunity before you enter the more formal selection process.

There are three main reasons for talking to suppliers at this stage:

1. To find out more about the types of service being offered to other companies and to learn from their experiences. Suppliers will be developing services for other customers and these may suggest alternative options for your own organization. Aim to find out how successful different approaches have been and what developments the suppliers envisage over future years. Use the intelligence gleaned to refine your statement of service requirements and to ensure that the scope and objectives of your outsourcing initiative are sound.

2. To promote your outsourcing initiative to the market. At this stage you will be aiming to convince the best suppliers that it is worth bidding for your organization's outsourcing deal. The outsourcing market remains buoyant and has always been so through periods of economic downturn or uncertainty. The most competent computer services companies can afford to be more selective in the opportunities they pursue. Submitting bids and negotiating deals can be an expensive and risky business. So experienced suppliers will not bid if they do not think that the outsourcing initiative is being well managed or they may withdraw from the selection process if they come to believe that a potential customer is unreliable or insufficiently skilled to deliver on their side of the contractual agreement.

3. If your outsourcing initiative is innovative or novel it will be helpful to sound out the market. Explain your organization's objectives and plans and answer questions the suppliers raise. Listen to any concerns the service providers might have and aim to resolve them, amending the scope of your outsourcing programme if necessary. This gives suppliers an opportunity to hear about and explore what your organization has in mind. The aim is to ensure that the market place is well informed about your outsourcing programme and to avoid misunderstandings when your formal selection process is launched. This should help maximize the competition for your organization's outsourcing deal. In effect you are creating a market for your outsourcing programme.

There are several ways in which you can promote your outsourcing programme to the computer services market:

- Arrange a conference to which many prospective suppliers are invited. Use this occasion to explain the background, objectives and scope of the outsourcing initiative. Ask a senior executive to contribute to demonstrate to suppliers your organization's commitment to the programme. Include a question and answer session so that suppliers can clarify their understanding of the initiative.

- Issue an information pack to the main suppliers and others on request.

- Schedule a series of meetings with main suppliers. You will need to make it clear that this is not simply a sales opportunity for the supplier. The primary purpose is to promote a clear understanding of the outsourcing initiative and to give service providers an opportunity to influence your organization's thinking and approach. Three meetings with each supplier may be required; the first to hand over and discuss an information pack; the second to take questions from the supplier and provide answers; and the third to discuss refinements to the outsourcing programme that are being introduced as a result of the meetings with various suppliers.

- Issue a press release about the proposed outsourcing programme. Computer newspapers such as *Computing* and *Computer World* often include this material in their publications.

Organizations in the pubic sector in particular will need to take care that they treat all prospective suppliers equally. In the European Community (EC), public sector organizations can place a Prior Information Notice (PIN) in the *Official Journal of the European Community* (*OJEC*) at the beginning of the financial year. PINs give an outline of the organization's likely procurement needs for the coming year. This gives service providers time to consider their responses and to make contact to discuss opportunities in general terms. PINs do not specify requirements in detail. They should be broad enough to allow for opportunities to extend the boundaries of services to be provided under any subsequent contract and precise enough to avoid sending misleading messages to the market.

4.4 Evaluation

Service providers should be evaluated objectively throughout the selection process. This is a very different decision-making process to traditional

IT equipment purchases, when it is possible to define a fixed requirement and invite tenders at arm's length from suppliers.

The development of the evaluation framework and criteria should proceed in parallel with the preparation of the business case and statement of service requirements. The criteria driving the evaluation should be reflected in the information pack and requirements documents sent to potential suppliers. The evaluation process should be well organized and based on the business objectives agreed for the outsourcing programme. A typical evaluation strategy might cover the following factors:

- an assessment of the potential relationship with the service provider;
- the quality of the proposed service solution;
- commercial issues (risk management and payment mechanisms);
- costs (direct and indirect);
- business benefits;
- people issues.

Evaluation scores should be weighted to reflect business priorities. The evaluation method and criteria should be defined and agreed before you contact potential suppliers to help ensure an objective assessment. A formal evaluation panel may be set up, including representatives from business areas, the finance department and other key stakeholders. Your organization will need to agree about management levels involved in the evaluation, how the decision-making process is going to work and whether the evaluation panel is going to report to the management board. You will also need to determine how the process is going to be described to potential suppliers and whether they are going to be given feedback about the outcome of the evaluation.

4.4.1 Evaluating Relationships

Successful outsourcing depends critically on establishing and maintaining a productive relationship with the service provider. Your organization will need to meet with potential suppliers to establish whether or not there is a cultural and philosophical match between your two organizations. The evaluation process needs to create a forum and opportunities for open discussion about service expectations and ideas. The selection process should be interactive. The evaluation should also draw attention to any potential risks in the outsourcing solutions proposed by service providers and should identify ways in which these risks can be managed.

How exactly do you evaluate the future working relationship between your organization and a service provider? The first year of any outsourcing relationship can be a difficult one and may not give a true indication of the success (or failure) of the longer-term relationship. Initially there may be misunderstandings and disagreements about the interpretation of contract clauses. Your organization will need to be assured that the selected service provider has previously demonstrated a high level of integrity and shown that ultimately it can be trusted.

To evaluate the service provider's relationships with its customers look at five factors:

1. *Values.* Has the service provider demonstrated to its customers that it is trustworthy? Is it open and transparent in its dealings with customers? Is it flexible and accommodating as service requirements change? Does it show commitment to the relationship? Are high standards of service maintained? What are the ethical standards of behaviour in the company? Are there current codes of practice? Do the service provider's representatives show pride in their organization? Are they concerned to maintain the reputation of the company?

2. *Corporate emphasis.* How does the service provider balance the need to meet customers' requirements against staff management concerns? Are the interests of both customers and staff served well? How does it balance the needs of current service delivery against the need to innovate and introduce service improvements? How are shareholders' interests protected? Is quality management in evidence and an integral part of the way in which the service provider does business?

3. *Responsiveness.* How quickly does the supplier respond to service requests? How willing is it to adapt proposals to meet customer concerns? Does the supplier understand, and respond to, its customers' business priorities?

4. *Reliability.* To what extent does the service need to be supervised? Does it deliver against agreed timescales? Does it deliver within agreed costs? Does it regularly meet quality standards?

5. *Consistency.* Are the service provider's values, corporate emphasis, responsiveness and reliability stable over time and across relationships with different customers? How frequently are key contract and

support staff changed? Are the level and quality of staff working on the contract maintained? How consistent is service performance?

For this facet of the evaluation your organization will need to investigate each potential supplier's track record and the experience of other customers. Ask for a full customer list and select three to five so that you have a better chance of getting a balanced assessment. Reference site visits should use standardized questionnaires that encompass the values, corporate emphasis, responsiveness, reliability and consistency questions designed to evaluate the suppliers' relationships.

The evaluation criteria will need to allow for all forms of contact with potential suppliers throughout the selection process. Introduce procedures to ensure that the findings and outcome of each contact are recorded in a standardized format.

Don't forget that the potential service providers will also be evaluating your organization as a potential customer. They too will have questions about your company's culture, integrity and openness. They will want to determine whether your organization wants a more formal relationship with an emphasis on penalties where services do not meet set performance levels or whether a more collaborative approach is envisaged with risks and rewards shared.

4.4.2 Evaluating Service Solutions

You will need to assess whether the service provider has the capability and technical ability to deliver the services you require, to adapt to change and to offer innovations. Other areas to evaluate include:

- evidence of re-engineering capability, with examples that demonstrate that results have been delivered;
- technical span of resources;
- integration experience and achievements working with other suppliers, including development of interfaces to other systems;
- scale of resources available;
- management of large-scale operational environments;
- service provision methodology;
- specific industry experience.

4.4.3 Commercial Evaluation

The evaluation will need to assess the severity and impact of risks inherent in the service provider's proposals. This will include an assessment of:

- the service provider's objectives for the relationship;

- outsourcing experience;

- implementation and transition plans;

- evidence of the service provider managing change in their own company and in organizations that it has acquired or absorbed;

- the extent to which the service provider has demonstrated the ability to support multi-vendor environments (where this is applicable to your IT department);

- the financial stability and future prospects of potential suppliers;

- the nature of any consortia bidding and relationships between the parties;

- the primary supplier's sub-contracting arrangements (if any) and the potential risks to service stability.

Payment mechanisms also need to be evaluated. It is not easy to devise charging methods that are suitable for long-term relationships within which service requirements will change in unpredictable ways. Experienced suppliers should have little difficulty adopting unusual approaches or implementing open book accounting. The charging formulae should be straightforward to administer and monitor, leaving the service provider in day-to-day control of resources with the customer organization in strategic control. The formulae should give the supplier strong incentive to reduce operating costs and to help the customer improve its business performance.

4.4.4 Evaluating Costs and Benefits

The financial appraisal should establish whether the service provider's proposals are financially sound and will deliver value for money, balancing costs and quality throughout the contract period.

Proposals should be compared on a like-for-like basis. This approach, however, may lead to over-prescribed service requirements that leave little scope for potential service providers to innovate and devise alternative solutions that produce even greater business benefits. Your organization may decide to accept two proposals from a potential supplier, the first being a "standard" bid that meets the specified requirements fully and the second a "non-standard" proposal. The "standard" bid is used to get an accurate comparison with other suppliers' bids. The evaluation of the "non-standard" proposal needs to consider the extent to which your organization's existing processes and policies would need to be changed to get the enhanced benefits. The statement of requirements should make it clear that your organization is not compelled to accept "non-standard" bids. Both "standard" and "non-standard" proposals should be evaluated against the same criteria.

4.4.5 Evaluating People Issues

The evaluation criteria should include:

- general approach to staff transfers;
- staff training and development;
- pension arrangements;
- the management of growth or reduction in staff numbers over recent years.

4.4.6 Evaluation Process

There are three main stages in the evaluation process:

1. The evaluation strategy and criteria are devised at the outset of the selection process, before any significant discussions with potential service providers. The evaluation criteria are reflected in the information given to prospective bidders.

2. Proposals received in response to an initial request for information are evaluated in order to select a short list of potential service providers.

3. Detailed, fully costed proposals received from the short-listed suppliers are evaluated to identify a preferred bidder.

4.5 Short-listing Potential Suppliers

Once the evaluation strategy and criteria have been agreed, the next step in the selection process is to produce a short list of service providers. The selection of outsourcing supplier can be a lengthy, complex exercise that is expensive for both the customer organization and potential suppliers. Aim therefore for a short list of around three service providers (never less than two and ideally not more than four).

The short list selection is made by requesting information from a number of potential suppliers and evaluating their responses. This process is sometimes referred to as "Request for Information" (RFI) or inviting "expressions of interest" from suppliers. The objective is to identify service providers who would all be capable of meeting your service requirements, offering value for money and developing effective customer relationships. The companies must also be financially sound. It follows that your organization should be prepared – indeed should be more than willing – to award the outsourcing contract to any of the short-listed suppliers with the final selection dependent on a more detailed evaluation at a later stage.

At this stage in the process an outline statement of service requirements should be available. This should be an output-based specification that gives suppliers an opportunity to introduce new, more efficient processes. List the desired outcomes first or what must happen and then the outputs or what must be produced to make it happen. Take care not to make the outcomes more grandiose than an external service provider can realistically deliver. Make sure that within the service boundaries set for the outsourcing programme, the service provider will have the equipment and other assets needed to deliver the outputs. This will help determine the assets to be transferred as part of the outsourcing deal. Set a timeframe for the services – not all will be required from day one of the outsourcing arrangement.

A short list questionnaire should be sent to potential service providers together with the outline statement of service requirements. Information should be provided on your organization's current business strategy and the objectives of the outsourcing programme. The questionnaire should ask potential suppliers for specific information, such as:

● What is their background in this market?

- A brief synopsis of work undertaken for current customers.
- What competitive advantages can the supplier provide?
- How much will the supplier's services cost? (It will only be possible to provide an indicative cost or estimate at this stage.)
- Will the supplier base computer operations at your organization's offices or off-site?
- What application software will be used?
- What are their back-up and disaster recovery plans?
- How will your organization's staff be affected?
- What support and training will the supplier provide?
- How will they incorporate flexibility into the outsourcing programme?
- How will they take into account the need for growth in service use (or reduction, whichever is indicated in your service specifications)?
- Information about the company's structure – is it publicly quoted or private or a partnership?
- The last three years' audited accounts.
- Annual turnover figures in total and those relating to outsourced IT services.
- Number of staff employed on outsourced IT services and annual staff turnover.
- Company policy statements relating to health and safety, quality management, equal opportunities, industrial relations, environmental standards and so on.
- Professional liability insurance information.
- Information on any outsourcing contracts terminated at the customer's request. When did this happen and why?
- A list of current outsourcing customers (from which your organization can select its reference sites).

The request for information should be sent to about 12 potential service providers to give a sufficiently wide field from which to select a short list.

Public sector organizations follow specified procedures to ensure that their business is open to all possible suppliers. In the European Community, public authorities must place a notice in the *Official Journal of the European Community (OJEC)* for all deals over a set threshold advertising the service requirement.

The number of responses received from suppliers will depend not only on the quality of the information that you have sent them but also on how effectively you have promoted your outsourcing initiative to the market, the reputation of your organization and the number of other interesting business opportunities that the suppliers are pursuing at the time. It helps if you can avoid launching the selection process at the same time as other organizations similar to your own.

Given that you are unlikely to receive a large number of responses to your requests for information if these have been properly targeted, it will be practical to follow up with visits to each of the suppliers. Involve your senior managers in these meetings. Use the opportunity to confirm the suppliers' core competencies, track record, system and process capabilities. See how their strengths could match your organization's weaknesses. Learn more about their aspirations and aims. Can you see how your organization fits with their future plans? Will your organization be one of their larger or smaller clients? How will this affect their commitment to your contract? Get a better understanding of the company's culture and assess how well this would fit with your own organization.

If practical, schedule reference site visits at this stage in the evaluation. Select sites from the customer lists provided by the suppliers. Choose sites that will be informative both as companies offering services comparable to your own organization and as organizations with substantial outsourcing experience with the supplier. Observations made by the supplier about your choice of site will be informative: are they genuinely concerned to inform your choice or primarily guiding you away from dissatisfied customers?

Gathering the information sent to you by suppliers together with data from meetings with suppliers and site visits, your organization can now begin to evaluate the responses in order to select a short list. The evaluation strategy and criteria will have been decided before the selection process is launched. The aim of the evaluation at this point is to determine:

- Is there sufficient evidence to show that the services your organization requires are part of the suppliers' core business? Do they invest in these services and expect to continue to develop them?

- Has the supplier provided tangible evidence of professionalism and a methodical approach? A quality endorsement such as ISO 9001 provides such an assurance. Does the supplier use recognized metrics and proven methodologies such as PRINCE2? Does it adhere to industry codes of practice and is it committed to best practice?

- Does the supplier possess wide ranging managerial and technical competence and expertise?

- Can you foresee any difficulties in delivering the services your organization requires? If your organization would be a pioneer with the supplier, note the risks and make an allowance for additional time and cost. Otherwise look for a demonstrable track record and references.

- Has the supplier demonstrated an understanding of your organization's business and the current and likely future IT service requirements?

- Will the supplier be a good partner, with values and a culture that fits well with your own organization?

Here is a criteria checklist for the evaluation of initial supplier responses:

- Customer base, numbers and industry sectors
- Track record, company status and management capability
- Insurance provision
- Company culture
- Geographical coverage
- Relationships with customers and staff
- Resources available to meet your organization's requirements
- Indicative costs
- Risks and risk management plans
- Competitive advantage (supplier's unique selling points)
- Employment, health and safety, and environmental policies
- Support services such as help desks and maintenance systems.

In the European Community (EC) public sector, this stage in the selection process is sometimes referred to as Pre-Qualification. The purpose is to promote strong competition by producing a short list of suppliers who are likely to meet the requirements. The EC Procurement Rules set out detailed criteria and describe the nature of the information that can be taken into account in circumstances where the Rules apply. The Pre-Qualification questionnaire is designed to provide sufficient evidence so that potential bidders' suitability, including commercial, financial and technical track records, can be assessed.

As we have seen, the short list is commonly selected on the basis of the capability to develop and deliver the outsourced services rather than on the basis of specific proposed solutions, and without specific technical details or costs. The outsourcing programme team will usually be responsible for co-ordinating the evaluation data and presenting the findings to the evaluation panel who will make recommendations for a short list of potential service providers to your management board.

While this evaluation is underway and before the final short list is announced it will be important to ensure that discussions remain com-mercial-in-confidence and that your organization respects the rights of potential suppliers to a fair appraisal and prompt notification of the results. Plan your communications carefully so that information does not leak out and staff are informed about the short list from their man-agers while, at the same time, suppliers receive feedback from the out-sourcing programme team and do not hear the outcome "on the grapevine". How your organization handles this assessment and the communications says much about its performance as a customer and the way in which it will seek to develop its relationship with the future outsourcing service provider.

4.6 Selecting the Preferred Bidder

From the short list of suppliers, which have all demonstrated that they are capable of meeting the service requirements and forming an effec-tive relationship with your organization, a preferred bidder is selected in the next stage of the evaluation process. From this point on the discus-sions will be at a more detailed level as your organization tests precisely what service levels will be delivered at what cost, and the service providers in turn check the details of the requirements to make sure that they are fully informed about the service commitment and any risks involved from their perspective.

This step in the evaluation process is launched by the issue of a "Request for Proposals" (RFP); an "Invitation to Tender" (ITT); or an "Invitation to Negotiate" (ITN) by your organization to the short-listed suppliers.

4.6.1 Tender Documents

The tender documents are likely to be lengthy and will cover the following topics:

- Background information and context
- Confidentiality issues
- Outsourcing programme and evaluation process
- Service requirements
- Staff information
- Assets
- Costs and charging mechanisms
- Security and contingency requirements
- Draft contract
- Implementation and contract management
- Appendices.

A covering letter should explain how, to whom and by what date tenders should be returned. It should also say if an in-house bid is being invited.

Background Information

The tender documents should describe your organization, its core businesses, overall business strategy and plans, size and resources. It should outline the IT function to be outsourced and the current in-house department and explain any corporate policies or initiatives that led to the outsourcing decision. The documents should also describe the user community, its size and other main characteristics.

Confidentiality Issues

These documents will contain sensitive information both about your organization's business and financial status and about the staff who will be directly affected by outsourcing. It is important therefore to secure a commitment from the short-listed suppliers that they, and any external advisors that they appoint, will treat the tender material with care to preserve its confidentiality. For this reason you may request the return of any tender documents at the end of the evaluation process. Being a good customer, your organization will similarly wish to reassure service providers that any sensitive information, including pricing data, that they supply will be handled in confidence.

Outsourcing Programme Information

Describe the overall objectives for the outsourcing programme, the selection process and overall timetable. Let bidders know what you are going to evaluate and the reasons why. Provide guidance on the formalities such as the handling of pre-tender enquiries, the format and submission of tenders and the treatment of standard and non-standard bids.

You will need to decide how to handle the many queries and points for clarification that suppliers are likely to raise during the preparation of their tenders. Remember that it is in your organization's long-term interest to ensure that potential suppliers are as fully informed as possible about service requirements. If there are any uncertainties you can be sure that suppliers will leave room for manoeuvre in their responses to increase prices for any unforeseen costs. The better they understand your organization's requirements before they submit their tenders, the more likely it is that negotiations and the agreed contract will meet requirements and a productive relationship with the supplier will develop.

Do make sure that all short-listed suppliers receive the same information as far as possible. Composite answer packs can be prepared in response to queries raised by different suppliers. Each supplier will be trying to find out more about the other suppliers' proposals, keeping track of who looks most likely to win the deal. Intelligence can be gleaned from the particular queries raised by other suppliers so try not to indicate who has raised a specific question.

Consider inviting the short-listed suppliers into your organization for a few weeks. Provide an office and other facilities for each supplier on one of your main sites close to the IT operations and users if possible. Make sure that business managers are well informed about this process and that key stakeholders make themselves available to answer queries from each short-listed supplier. The service providers should have access to systems and IT staff so that they can clarify service requirements and operational issues. This approach can be particularly effective when there is an incumbent service provider. The challenge in this instance is to persuade other potential suppliers that they have an equal chance of winning the deal so that there is a real competition for your organization's business.

Service Requirements

The statement of service requirements must be completed by this stage. This specification will include details about current operations and applications, hardware and telecommunications configurations, data storage requirements, processing cycles, reports required, staffing levels, schedules, assets used, volumes, service performance and quality issues and costs. Of course it is not always feasible to specify future service requirements that may evolve during the course of the contract. The evaluation criteria must give due weight to an assessment of the ease with which future service requirements will be met by the service provider. The relationship between your organization and the service provider will be a significant element.

Staff Information

For potential outsourcing suppliers to fully cost their proposals and meet the staff transfer requirements, they will need to review your organization's personnel policies to identify any issues of concern or difficulties in matching these terms and conditions of employment after the staff have transferred. The tender documents need to give full details of personnel policies covering, for example, maternity leave, holiday entitlements, early retirement provision, flexible working schemes, official travel rules, trade union representation, long service awards and training.

Don't forget to include details of any consultants or contractors working on the service. The service providers may be able to use their own staff in these roles, which may be more efficient.

You will also need to include specific information about the staff who would transfer with the outsourced service including:

- staff numbers, job titles and descriptions;
- salary details;

- pension benefits earned;

- overtime allowances;

- travel and expenses arrangements;

- other benefits and entitlements.

Assets

Details of assets to be included in the outsourcing deal, such as computer hardware, telecommunications equipment and application software, are also given in the tender documents. In effect the service provider will be making a one-off payment for these assets, with ownership passing to the supplier. The cash can provide a useful injection of funds into the customer's core business. The supplier now owns additional assets that can be put to multiple uses. For example, it may be possible to use spare capacity to support IT services provided to other customers. The transfer of software, in particular, carries a number of possible risks that are explored further in Chapter 7.

Costs and Charging Mechanisms

Where large and potentially complex IT services are to be outsourced, detailed cost information and internal performance data can sharpen the competition by ensuring that all suppliers are aware of the bid threshold below which it would be uneconomic for your organization to accept a tender. The cost base is an important input to either the due diligence exercise pre-contract signature or post-contract verification exercises.

The charging formulae to be incorporated into the outsourcing contract can be based on inputs, outputs or sharing risks and rewards or a mixture of these elements. Which types of formulae are used can have a strong impact on both the customer's and supplier's behaviour and attitude towards the relationship. It can therefore influence service performance levels and perceptions of success or failure of the outsourced arrangement.

Suppliers should be asked to present their costs in a specified format to help in the evaluation of bids and comparisons between the different service providers. Preferred charging formulae should also be indicated where appropriate.

1. *Input charging.* The charges made for various IT services are based on the inputs used by the service provider. In order to have a degree of

certainty about prices and maintain service flexibility, the input charges may consist of:

- a standard component or routine base requirement;
- a variable component based on known service requirements with irregular frequency and volume;
- an additional services component covering unpredictable or novel service requirements that are within the range of outsourced service offerings;
- a transitional component that covers the costs of launching a new service.

2. *Output charging.* Output charges are based upon an agreed price per identified unit of output. This charging formula only works if it is possible to identify and count units of service output. You will need to test the price per unit to make sure that it is set at a reasonable level – perhaps by taking account of the supplier's direct costs, overhead costs and profit margin. Sensitivity analyses will be needed to test the potential charges against the range of likely levels of service use.

3. *Risk/Reward Charging.* This approach to charging establishes a link between the supplier's performance level and the business value derived from the outsourced services by the customer. Risk/reward charging formulae are based on a number of principles:

- Influencing the supplier's behaviour: the aim is to stimulate the supplier to work towards reducing service costs, helping the customer improve profit margins or efficiency savings.
- Impact on the customer's behaviour: the customer needs to recognize and accept that there will be pressure and support from the supplier to make changes in business processes. Where open book accounting is adopted so that the customer sees the supplier's costs and profit margins in detail, some form of reciprocal arrangement may be needed to assure the supplier that the customer is accurately reporting business benefits from improved service levels.
- General principles for new capital investments: either party may identify opportunities for such investments. The supplier will always provide the capital funding. Each proposal will have a business case that determines the percentage return anticipated. When

this return cannot be agreed, the customer organization's external auditors may arbitrate. A target percentage return on investment is agreed prior to the start of the contract. The new capital investment project proceeds if the relevant business case shows a return above the target and the customer wants the project to continue. If the return is above target but the customer does not want to proceed, the supplier can still continue if the project is purely related to the supplier's infrastructure. Note that if the return is above target and the customer wants the investment to continue, the supplier is compelled to proceed.

4. *Indexation.* The contract should make provision for inflation and a cost of living adjustment. Without such a mechanism the supplier is forced to increase initial prices to cover the risk of inflation during a long-term contract. With no provision for inflation and with open book accounting in which prices are set at a percentage above the costs incurred by the supplier, costs could increase as a result of pay awards and other cost changes well above inflation. Indexation therefore offers both parties some protection. This does not mean that the supplier should feel entitled to full price indexation, but there should be a mechanism to put a ceiling on any potential price increase.

Security and Contingency Requirements

Sensitive security requirements may be included in separate documents to be dealt with by a small team of staff from your organization and the short-listed suppliers. The tender documents should also specify service contingency or disaster recovery arrangements.

Draft Contract

You will need to consider who produces the first draft contract for discussion. If your organization as the customer produces the draft, this helps you to stay in control of the negotiations and ultimate agreement. It also alerts the potential suppliers to your requirements. Raising contractual issues at a later stage once the business deal is agreed can be difficult to manage. The earlier any possible contractual difficulties are raised, the easier they are to resolve. A draft contract produced by your organization also ensures that all short-listed suppliers are on a level footing and makes comparisons of the bids easier. The downside is that the draft may alert suppliers to your overall negotiation strategy. To some extent the draft will lock you into specific terms and conditions and reduce your flexibility in negotiations.

Experienced suppliers might put forward their own draft contracts. It is not a good idea to accept these. Starting from the supplier's own draft, your organization will be forced to argue for changes giving the supplier the negotiating advantage. The supplier's draft may specify that the supplier has to maintain the service levels delivered by the internal IT department during a baseline period. But this is not the same as setting performance standards and does not include penalty clauses if the supplier fails to meet the requirements.

Where large-scale outsourcing deals are envisaged, separate contracts for staff transfers, charging mechanisms and so on may be advisable so that parallel negotiations on different facets of the deal can be scheduled. The narrow focus on specific areas makes better use of specialist skills and gives greater clarity. This approach does, however, require very careful co-ordination. Further information on outsourcing contracts is included in Chapter 7.

Implementation and Contract Management

Consider what structures your organization should put in place to ensure that there is a smooth transition to the outsourced services and the contract is well managed. The tender documents should describe the contract management team that is to be set up; arrangements for liaison with users; the strategic and operational performance reporting requirements; the contract management meeting arrangements; and change control requirements.

Suppliers should be asked to provide information on how they will manage and successfully implement the new outsourced services. They should indicate the names and management levels of the staff involved; describe the customer's role during the transition; provide project plans and indicate how they will manage the staff transfers. The service providers should also state what due diligence or post-contract verification reviews they would need to carry out.

Appendices

For ease of use, the tender documents should incorporate appendices for technical data, booklets, internal manuals, policy statements and so on.

4.6.2 Evaluating the Responses

The responses received from the short-listed suppliers may be lengthy, often exceeding 100 pages. The final stage of the evaluation process requires, therefore, a considerable amount of effort. The evaluation framework and criteria agreed before the selection process began now defines how your organization should approach the selection of a preferred bidder. It would be a mistake to be over-reliant on a paper evaluation alone. Equally significant is your organization's confidence in the supplier's proposals and the perceived likelihood of establishing a good relationship with the supplier. Data will be drawn not only from the written tenders but also from the formal records of discussions with the suppliers and feedback from any time they have spent working alongside your business managers and other users.

There needs to be a formal evaluation process that produces a report summarizing each evaluation stage. The evaluation should be systematic, objective and well documented and seen to be so. The tender documents explained the evaluation criteria – make sure you follow through on what you have said. Within the bounds of commercial confidentiality, be open about your objectives and processes.

A tender evaluation panel can be set up to evaluate the bids. It is important that the panel has the necessary expertise for this complex task. There should be a chairman and at least two other members, depending on the size and nature of the outsourcing contract. The views of business managers/users should be represented. Independent observers may be appointed to witness the evaluation and provide an independent assurance that the evaluation has been carried out fairly.

The aim of the final evaluation stage is to select the service provider that is most likely to deliver excellent services and best value for money; to be capable of meeting future service requirements; and to be reliable, open and trustworthy. Here is a checklist for the key criteria assessed at this stage:

● Business requirements met by services offered

● Service costs over the life of the contract

● Service quality

● Support services such as help desks and user training

- Service flexibility

- Risk assessment

- Contingency and security proposals

- Charging mechanisms including influence on supplier performance

- Affordability: ensuring service costs are within your organization's budget levels

- Potential for service improvements and innovation

- Staff transfer plans

- Training and development for transferred staff

- Implementation and transition plans

- Contract management organization and personnel

- Future relationship with the supplier.

The evaluation panel should make a reasoned judgement, supported by the scores awarded to each supplier's proposal using weighted evaluation criteria. Some clarifications may be required from the bidders but this does not mean that they should be amending their proposals at this stage.

A detailed record of the evaluation panel's conclusions should be prepared. A "commercial-in-confidence" note should be sent to your management board for approval. At this point the aim is to select a preferred bidder and, possibly, a reserve. Once the choice of preferred bidder is confirmed, an announcement should be made to all bidders, business managers and staff. As with the short list decision, it is important to recognize and honour the commercial confidentiality of the suppliers' proposals and to plan the communications about the outcome of the evaluation so that the key stakeholders hear the results directly and not informally via a third party.

Try to ensure that bidders who were not selected have an opportunity to meet with outsourcing programme team representatives to discuss why they were unsuccessful and what they might do to improve their chances in future competitions. Cover performance across the range of selection criteria and contract prices. It is in your organization's interests to maintain good relations with all major suppliers if possible. There will be a range of IT service requirements in the future and a supplier who fails to be selected for one contract may be ideally suited to another.

Keep your options open and demonstrate your organization's competence as a potential customer by providing helpful debriefing information.

The purchase of services by EC public authorities is governed by the EC Procurement Rules, which are implemented in the UK by the Public Services Contract Regulations. These rules lay down procedures including the advertising of contracts in the *Official Journal of the European Community (OJEC)*, the use of technical specifications, the selection of tenderers and the award of the contract. They are designed to ensure that all service providers established in the EC Member States are treated on equal terms. There are three formal options:

1. *Open procedure.* This option requires that all service providers who respond to the contract notice published in the *OJEC* must be invited to tender. The services acquired using this option are typically very straightforward, low risk and well understood by both customer and providers.

2. *Restricted procedure.* This is appropriate when the service requirement can be specified in sufficient detail for proposals to be developed by service providers and evaluated by the customer without significant negotiation.

3. *Negotiated procedure.* Applies where the customer organization seeks an innovative approach from the computer services industry and/or where it is not appropriate (or possible) to specify a detailed requirement in advance. The negotiated procedure may only be used in certain circumstances as set out in the EC Rules. Outsourcing projects in the public sector generally adopt the negotiated procedure.

4.7 Negotiations

By this stage you will have a draft contract, a preferred set of proposals from a service provider and, most likely, a number of issues or difficulties that need to be resolved before your organization can confidently conclude the deal.

The aim of the negotiations in an outsourcing initiative is to deal with all outstanding issues in a way that leaves each party content that they have struck a fair deal and that the relationship between them will enhance the business performance of both organizations. This is not the place for tactics that seek to drive through the lowest (or highest) contract prices possible. If your organization believes that it has been persuaded to pay over the odds for the outsourced services, resentment towards the supplier will fester and grow. The contract is unlikely to deliver the anticipated business benefits. Equally if the supplier perceives that their profit margins have been squeezed to an unrealistic level, their commitment to the outsourcing relationship will tail off and they will constantly look for ways of reducing their costs.

Recognize that negotiating is a skilled activity. Computer services companies have lots of experience in negotiating outsourcing contracts. You will need to ensure that your organization is not disadvantaged by a lack of skills. Arrange training for those involved in the negotiations. Although your organization should set the objectives and tone of the negotiations it can be very helpful to recruit a negotiating expert to advise and assist. The negotiating style should reflect the ultimate relationship your organization hopes to have with the supplier:

- Use logical persuasion and explain your interests in a businesslike manner.
- Aim to decide issues on their merits rather than seek to impose your view.
- Focus on interests, not positions; be definite but flexible.
- Look for mutual gains wherever possible.
- Be creative; look for alternative solutions when your organization and the supplier cannot agree.
- Use joint brainstorming when first starting out to tackle tricky issues.
- Acknowledge the supplier's legitimate interests and the wider context from their point of view.
- Use silence wisely; don't be pushed into speaking before you are ready.
- Be aware of body language and make sure as far as you can that, on your negotiating team, no one's body language contradicts the position stated in words. In particular, avoid nodding before points have been agreed.
- Always do your own calculations (don't simply hand over control of the numbers to the supplier).
- Use every negotiation session with the supplier as an opportunity to find out more about their position and objectives.

It is important that at the outset of the negotiations the customer organization and supplier start from a position of equal strength. Getting the contract right is critical because once the deal is agreed the contract is the key mechanism that maintains a reasonable balance of power in the outsourcing relationship. Your organization can take a number of steps to ensure that it is not in a weak position as it enters the negotiations:

- Start from a contract drafted by your organization.

- Even when there is one preferred bidder, make it clear that you have a reserve bidder. There is little pressure on a supplier who believes that your organization has no alternative choice of service provider.

- Consider negotiating in parallel with two potential suppliers. This will maintain a strong competition for as long as possible. Obviously this approach is resource intensive and may be impractical in some circumstances.

- Retain responsibility for drafting the legal documents throughout the negotiations.

- Make sure your organization has access to negotiating, commercial, legal and technical experts. Suppliers regularly negotiate outsourcing deals and will have this expertise on board to protect their interests.

The negotiating team should possess a blend of relevant skills and should be capable of sustaining a clear negotiating focus and strong continuity. They need to keep in view both the overall shape of the deal and the way in which individual components interrelate. The team will need to be highly disciplined and prepared for working long hours during the negotiations.

The key team roles are:

1. *Negotiation leader.* The leader (often a senior manager) is responsible for the conduct of the negotiations as a whole, directing the team activities, reporting progress and clearing issues. Other team members will only contribute to the negotiations by invitation from the leader so as to avoid interruptions or contradictions. The team leader must know what other team members are going to say. The leader will be empowered to conclude the negotiations.

2. *Negotiation manager.* The manager is in charge of administration – scheduling, accommodation, agendas and minutes. He/she does not

have a speaking role but tracks the position throughout discussions and watches for potential problems.

3. *Commercial and technical experts.* It is important that experts are fully briefed and informed about the role they are to play in the negotiating tactics.

4. *Legal advisors.* It is sometimes helpful to negotiate tricky IT service and technical issues without lawyers present and agree that any points settled are subject to legal advice. If one party has a legal advisor present, however, the other is also obliged to do so.

5. *Administration/secretariat.* There is a substantial amount of administration behind any negotiations. An audit trail needs to be created and this involves someone attending the meetings, writing up notes of the meeting, circulating papers and maintaining a document library.

Negotiations require careful and comprehensive planning. Several hours planning will be needed for each hour spent in negotiation. Topics to be covered include preparing the agenda and the opening statement, checking documents, identifying the supplier's key players, reviewing draft and updated contract clauses, identifying contentious areas, preparing the line to take on main issues, identifying different options to resolve problem areas and points that cannot be conceded. If the contract is a complex one, negotiations on specific schedules can be delegated to teams of specialists from both parties.

A typical negotiating timetable will follow a cycle, for example:

Day 1   Internal planning meeting

Day 2   Negotiation meeting with the supplier

Day 3   Internal review meeting to discuss previous day's negotiation and task lawyer to draft or amend contract

Day 4   Update the draft contract

Day 5   Release updated draft to supplier

The customer organization should host the negotiation sessions. Choose meeting rooms that reflect the chosen negotiation style. Provide a room with office facilities and refreshments nearby for the supplier to use for private discussions.

Throughout the negotiation process keep a look out for potential problems:

- Do not allow the supplier's negotiators or senior executives to bypass the negotiations. This might be an attempt to get top management in your organization to make concessions without being fully aware of the implications.

- Resist the temptation to agree to a very loose contract on the basis of vague promises about the partnership between your organization and the supplier. Of course your organization will want an effective relationship with the supplier, but the contract is an invaluable insurance policy, a risk countermeasure to ensure your organization does not end up with poor IT services.

- Similarly, do not sign up to an incomplete contract in the interests of speeding up implementation. It is very difficult to resolve tricky issues satisfactorily once the deal is agreed.

- Do not agree to pay a bonus when service exceeds agreed performance levels without considering the implementations very carefully. Why pay for a service that is better than your organization needs?

- Be wary if the supplier glosses over technical issues. Are there hidden problems or is an alternative technical approach more suitable and more cost effective?

Occasionally negotiations break down and a decision will be needed on whether to start negotiations with the reserve preferred bidder. Sometimes the supplier treats the prospective customer badly enough during negotiations that they are replaced as preferred bidder.

4.8 Contract Award

Reaching agreement on the outsourcing contract is a major achievement and significant milestone in the outsourcing programme. It is, however, only the beginning. But take the opportunity to savour the moment and plan a small celebration with all key players who have worked so hard on the selection and evaluation process. Joint events with your selected service provider are of course most appropriate and in keeping with the spirit of the outsourcing relationship envisaged.

The press offices from both organizations should jointly agree press releases. Public authorities in the EC must submit a contract award notice to the OJEC.

4.9 The Importance of the Relationship Between Customer and Supplier

Previous sections have highlighted the importance of an effective relationship between customer and outsourcing supplier, but it is worth emphasizing here the significance of this factor in selecting the best service provider for your organization.

Cultural fit between the two organizations is a vital element. Look for similar values, similar ways of tackling problems and similar ways of managing business. Select a service provider on their total capabilities not just on price or one other facet of the outsourced service, and negotiate reasonable prices and performance measures. This has to be an ongoing relationship that will be successful for both organizations. Aim for a tough but fair agreement with the service provider.

It is important to recognize that every contact with suppliers during the selection process can influence the outcome. Keep formal records of impressions made on all who meet with potential service providers and use the suppliers' reactions to the selection process to inform your organization what type of relationship each supplier is seeking.

Suppliers should be keen to meet with your organization throughout the selection process. How your organization manages this process will influence how the suppliers evaluate the future potential of the outsourcing relationship. Begin, even in the selection process, to build an open constructive relationship. Provide information and meet with suppliers. Facilitate meetings with your senior executives. This degree of openness does not mean that communications are uncontrolled. Ask suppliers to channel all contacts with your organization and requests for information through key individuals in the outsourcing programme team. Object if they do not respect this arrangement – their attitude does not augur well for the future outsourcing relationship.

Your organization and the chosen supplier should share responsibility for, and be jointly committed to, achieving shared goals. Outsourcing needs trust, confidence, clear objectives and regular performance monitoring.

Managing Performance **5**

5.1 Introduction

Now comes the challenge of making outsourcing deliver value to your organization – can you make a success of it? After the excitement of choosing a service provider and celebrating the award of the contract, how do you ensure that outsourcing produces the benefits that were promised? At first you may have a sense of anticlimax – or calm before the storm – depending on your perspective! The consultants and other expert advisors that helped guide your organization through the selection of the supplier and the negotiation of the contract have probably packed their bags and left.

The supplier that worked so hard to win your business, anxious to meet the service requirements, keen to meet with your organization, enthusiastic about what could be achieved and the improvements that could be made, now has the contract to provide the outsourced services. What difference will this make to the supplier's attitude? How will it approach the task? If your organization has followed the guidelines in Chapters 2 and 3, the risk of serious problems will have been minimized but it is not possible to guarantee success.

Much has been written about the decision to outsource, and many management consultancies offer expert advice on sourcing decisions and the evaluation of suppliers' proposals. Considerable analysis is available on the rational and contractual aspects of reaching an outsourcing agreement. Relatively little attention, however, has been given to the task of actually making outsourcing work once the contract is signed, which is a vital component of the work of many IT professionals. In the following chapters we will be looking at the challenges and opportunities presented by IT outsourcing in practice, how to manage the inherent risks and ways of tackling failure in the outsourcing relationship. This chapter covers the management of the outsourced services and the maintenance of the outsourcing contract.

If an outsourcing initiative is to be successful it needs to be managed with care, attention to detail, vision about what might be achieved, close monitoring of financial issues and sensitivity to the needs of different stakeholders such as your senior executive and the service users. Both your organization and the service provider need to invest time in gaining deeper understanding of each other's working culture, establishing lines of communication between your two organizations and making sure that all those working on the outsourcing initiative are well informed, confident and motivated.

It is important that senior management continues to be involved in the management of information services. Few information systems operate in isolation. IT is integral to many business processes and cannot be divorced from business targets or outcomes. Try to devise systems that allow senior managers to participate in the co-ordination, monitoring and management of the outsourcing relationship, bearing in mind the other demands on their time. After all, we know that technology is ineffective unless it is aligned with business objectives.

As we first saw in Chapter 3, clear objectives should underpin the entire outsourcing initiative. Without agreed objectives, you will not know what you are trying to achieve through outsourcing and you will not be able to monitor your success.

5.2 Building Outsourcing Relationships

The key to successful outsourcing is building a relationship with your service provider that works in the longer term, not a quick fix economy drive. Put time and energy into deciding in advance how you are going to manage this relationship. An organization (whether customer or supplier) that is satisfied with its outsourcing relationship is likely to see it as successful and to take steps to reinforce and develop the relationship. From experience and research in this field we can draw lessons that will help your organization develop an effective outsourcing relationship:

1. *Build trust.* Work towards an open and honest relationship that is built on mutual trust. Trust needs to be earned. Where trust exists,

each party believes that the other organization will behave in a way that is mutually beneficial and will not act opportunistically. Express the wish to develop trust during negotiations and give the supplier opportunities to earn it. Acknowledge good performance and be open about concerns.

Your organization will have made a number of contractual commitments – payment procedures, the standard of assets transferred, assistance to be given during implementation and so on. Monitor these activities and alert the supplier to any difficulties. Deliver on time and demonstrate that your organization can be trusted.

The supplier needs to develop a track record for delivering services that meet contractual standards. Once this is established, your organization may invite the supplier to take part in strategy and planning discussions. The relationship can then evolve into a more strategic and closer alliance.

2. *Look for win-win solutions.* Recognize that both parties must benefit financially from the contract. Trying to create a "win–lose" position leads to resentment and a loss of commitment. It may also lead to a confrontational rather than collaborative style of relationship. Within some organizations there is a culture that encourages adversarial relationships with suppliers. There is an emphasis on "beating the supplier down" to the lowest price, fighting to win on every detail of contract interpretation. Those who are seen as "soft" on suppliers are criticized and probably feel that they have damaged their promotion prospects. Such an approach is unlikely to be successful in the longer term in IT outsourcing deals. It is a question of balance – there is no point conceding so much that your organization tips over into a "lose–win" position.

Both organizations should be able to understand and respect each other's goals and requirements. Work together to show the business community the benefits that can be delivered by IT services.

3. *Aim for co-operation not domination.* Outsourcing should not be based on a relationship of domination and dependence but on a spirit of co-operation and collaboration driven by shared benefits. During the negotiation stage, your organization and the supplier may have felt like adversaries, both sides defending the interests of their own organization. The relationship shifts when the contract is signed to become one in which co-operation is increasingly important if the IT services are to be successfully delivered. There will, of course,

continue to be discussions about contract changes that will require tough negotiation. But in the operation of services and in liaison with users, the style of relationship needs to become more co-operative and this change takes conscious effort.

4. *Good communications.* Effective relationships depend on good communication. Consider various ways in which your organization can communicate with the service provider at all levels within your two organizations. Map out a communications programme. You will be alerting your supplier to service failures, but remember too to congratulate them for good work. Share with the supplier as much as you can about your organization's processes and IT costs. The aim is to create a long-term relationship and one of the first steps towards this is to create an environment in which information is readily shared between your two organizations.

   A programme of liaison visits or secondments between your two organizations also encourages good working relationships.

5. *Aim for mutual understanding.* Take time to talk to your supplier about your organization – its plans, targets, organizational structure and core business. Don't limit discussions to the outsourced services or contractual issues, and don't let any personal prejudices get in the way. Try to give your service provider a better understanding of what makes your organization tick and what it hopes for in the future.

   Similarly, take an active interest in your supplier's affairs. Learn more about the organization, its culture and the services it offers. Celebrate with them when they succeed in winning new business; commiserate when they lose a potentially lucrative contract. Read their annual report and keep a look out for any relevant articles in the press.

   We are all inclined to make assumptions about organizations from the few individuals we meet: aim for a deeper understanding and you will be able to get more out of the outsourcing relationship.

6. *Criticize if you must, openly.* There is no room in an open and honest relationship for either organization to criticize the other behind their back. Problems or concerns should be tackled straightaway, before they fester and grow. Recognize that there may be a different perspective or point of view that is not apparent to your organization. Find out what this might be before you jump to any conclusions or take precipitous action.

This applies to service providers too. Work hard to co-operate with other suppliers and do not run down your customers in front of other organizations.

7. *Learn when to compromise.* Establish an open relationship and be prepared to compromise. Encourage a shared determination to make the contract work. Accept that your organization and your supplier will have different perspectives on the outsourcing arrangement. Expect value for money but accept the supplier's need to make a profit. Outsourcing contracts last for a long period and success depends on both parties being able to achieve business benefits from the deal.

8. *Resolve personality conflicts.* It can happen, unfortunately, that there is a personality clash between individuals appointed by your organization and the supplier to work on the outsourcing contract. These things happen and need to be resolved. Personality conflicts can be very damaging to the relationship between organizations. Try to avoid confrontations developing and avoid a blame culture. Be alert to the potential for problems developing and ensure that none of your own dealings with the supplier's representatives are soured.

9. *Foster realistic expectations.* Some users may expect miracles from your outsourcing supplier: minimal costs, improved quality and new services introduced immediately with no effort on their part. The reality of outsourcing throws into sharp relief facts about IT services and costs that relate to in-house provision too but may have been less visible in the past. Examples include:

- IT services cost money and appropriate budget allocations must be made to cover costs.

- New services take time to implement and users need to be closely involved not only in specifying but also in testing the services prior to formal acceptance.

- Customized services with minor modifications to meet each section's preferences are more expensive than standardized services and difficult to justify.

  Everyone in your organization who is concerned with the outsourced services needs to have an accurate understanding of the contract and a realistic expectation of the services to be delivered by the supplier. Otherwise the relationship between your organization and the service provider will be dominated by disappointment and dissatisfaction.

103

5.3 Understanding Stakeholder Perspectives

In Chapter 3 we looked at different perspectives within your organization on the outsourcing initiative. Once the contract is signed and implementation is underway, different viewpoints begin to emerge. Stakeholders in the outsourcing initiative include not only members of your organization but also staff in the supplier's company. They can behave co-operatively, enthusiastically, antagonistically, collaboratively or destructively depending on the issue at hand. Rather than look for a superficial harmony or agreement, it helps to face up to the realities of shared, complementary or conflicting goals. By understanding that stakeholders' goals sometimes conflict, we can recognize other positions while still protecting our own interests.

Table 5.1 illustrates some typical perspectives on outsourced services.

Table 5.1 Perspectives on outsourcing.

Stakeholder	Viewpoint
Customer's senior managers	Concerned that outsourcing should deliver business benefits. Looking for added value.
Customer's senior IT managers	Anxious that supplier meets contractual commitments. Will want to curtail excessive demands for service improvements so that expenditure on outsourced services stays within budget.
Customer's IT staff	Want to ensure that outsourcing is well managed and that the outsourcing service provider works well with other suppliers. Will watch for any negative impact on other in-house IT activities and will be concerned about possible extensions to the outsourcing contract to incorporate additional IT services and staff transfers.
Service users	Expect service excellence, however may have little knowledge of the costs incurred.
Supplier's senior management	Proud of winning outsourcing deal. Subject to keeping the customer satisfied will look to maximize profits.
Supplier's contract manager	Will carefully balance customer service and profitability to meet set targets. Concerned to ensure that problems are not escalated and referred to senior management.
Supplier's IT staff	The technical experts who will take professional pride in providing a good service but will also be aware of the budget and time constraints.

5.4 Outsourcing "Partnerships"

In all that has been written about outsourcing, the word "partnership" is the most commonly used description of the relationship between customer organization and supplier.

The dictionary describes a partner as "one who shares or takes part with another or others, especially in business firm with shared risks and profits; companion in dancing; player on same side in game; husband or wife" (*Pocket Oxford Dictionary*, 1984). Unless a joint venture company has been set up, the outsourcing customer and supplier are not true business partners. Although payments for outsourced services may be based on shared risks and rewards, the customer and supplier remain independent organizations, each ultimately concerned with protecting their own interests. The two companies might "play on the same side" in the "game" of promoting the possibilities of exploiting technology to deliver business benefit, but they will not be entirely on the same side when costs and timescales are discussed. The supplier is responsible for ensuring an adequate profit margin that maintains the viability of its business and meets shareholders' requirements. The customer needs to acquire IT services as economically as possible, compatible with the quality standard required.

Suppliers especially like to talk about their outsourcing partners and the term certainly does convey a warm feeling of collaboration and mutually beneficial activities.

This book promotes co-operation, collaboration, open, supportive and honest relationships between customer organization and supplier. But the word "partnership" does not frequently appear because it has been over-used and it is not entirely accurate.

Here are two extremes of the outsourcing relationship:

1. An arm's length relationship in which the customer organization fosters competition between multiple suppliers and awards contracts for each new piece of work on the basis of quality, time to delivery and price.

2. A very close, long-term strategic relationship in which the outsourcing parties do repeated business with each other and endeavour to share risks and rewards. This style of relationship takes time to evolve.

Your organization will need to determine the style of outsourcing relationship best suited to its needs and approach to business. Whichever style is chosen, outsourcing remains a commercial transaction in which the supplier has to keep earning business every day.

5.5 Communicate, Communicate, Communicate

Outsourcing introduces a whole new set of roles and responsibilities into your organization. This can produce uncertainty, doubt and fear. It can also lead to confusion and disorganization. Communication, not only between yourself and the supplier, but also with senior executives, business managers and users, will be a key element in delivering outsourced services successfully.

Communication takes place at various levels between your organization and the service provider:

- Senior managers, who review the overall outsourcing relationship, consider whether strategic objectives are being met and identify future direction, will discuss strategic matters.

- At the contract management level, discussions will focus on whether both parties are meeting their contractual obligations; they will agree contract charges, monitor performance, respond to contract change requests and provide an escalation route for service problems.

- With business managers and users, the supplier will discuss developing or changing service requirements.

- At the day-to-day operational level, discussions between your organization and the supplier will monitor performance against agreed service levels and review project progress.

You will need to devise a new organization structure to manage these communications effectively and this will be discussed in later sections.

It is important that regular communication is maintained at these various levels even when things are going well. Liaison should not simply be about problem resolution but should also include planning, identifying opportunities and celebrating success. Communicate early and often and allow time for the outsourcing relationship to mature: don't expect liaison to work well from day one.

Remember to continue communicating with business managers and users in your organization. Their awareness, understanding and commitment are important factors in the overall success of outsourcing. Initially their expectations may be unreasonable and they may find it hard to come to terms with the more structured and formal approach that may be necessary now that some IT services are purchased from an external provider. This happens in part because the concept of outsourcing will have been sold enthusiastically before the contract is signed. People throughout your organization need to be aware of the reasons behind the decision to outsource and the objectives, and they need to understand the impact on their work. Consider preparing newsletters, posters, leaflets and presentations jointly with your supplier to communicate these key messages to others in your organization.

Communications with staff who are transferring to the supplier are particularly significant. As their new employer, the supplier should take the lead but it is helpful if senior management from both your organization and the supplier are involved. It is only natural that this group of staff will be wary of what the future holds. They may fear a loss of control, increased workloads without compensation and working in a new culture. Communications will be needed at group and individual level, briefings, road shows, Intranet sites, personalized letters and enquiry points.

5.6 Transition

The implementation of the outsourcing contract, or transition from in-house to outsourced IT services, should be well managed just as any other IT project. The overall transition plan is initially put together by the supplier and submitted as part of the response to the statement of service requirements. The plan is refined during negotiations and put into effect once the contract is signed.

Transition commonly takes place in phases and may take up to a year to complete. Any longer and there is a danger that the state of transition becomes the norm and the incentive to complete the task is lost.

The first few weeks are significant in that they create an initial perception of outsourcing that, like all first impressions, can be difficult to change at a later date. The supplier will want to make a good start and you will want to demonstrate that you have chosen the best supplier. So it helps to choose some activities that can be completed readily and do not carry too many risks. Effective communications with service users will be important because there may be an unrealistic expectation that services will improve from day one and the supplier will be fully responsible for all aspects of service performance immediately the contract is signed.

The transition phases can best be managed as a series of projects, with the completion of each project a checkpoint in the transition to outsourced services. There should be a timetable for these checkpoints and this can form a useful measure of the supplier's performance during transition. Although the supplier will lead the overall transition programme and will be responsible for many of the activities, your organization will also have a number of responsibilities, particularly tasks that involve internal communications.

The transition plan should cover:

- transfer of responsibility for IT services;
- all activities relating to the transfer of staff to the supplier;
- transfer of assets, reassignment of software licences and so on (this is discussed further in Chapter 7);
- set up and introduction of contract management structures;
- implementation of contract management processes including invoicing and payment procedures;
- post-contract verification of service costs, performance levels and assets if this was agreed during negotiations;
- compilation and distribution of guides to the contract and to the outsourced services to users;
- communications programme;

- introduction of change request processes (there will probably be a backlog of requests if system changes were frozen during the selection of supplier and negotiations);

- implementation of problem management and escalation procedures.

5.7 Incentives and Disincentives

Think through carefully what incentives you are able to give to encourage your new supplier to innovate or propose service improvements and what discourages poor performance.

Contracts often include penalty clauses for serious breaches. These are necessary to protect the interests of your organization but represent a significant failure. Fines are not generally imposed lightly on suppliers and must be backed up by detailed, accurate service performance records. Although some allowance may be made for isolated reductions in service levels, any failure to meet contractual standards should be resolved quickly before it becomes accepted as normal practice. If hefty fines are imposed, the supplier's account managers will spend a lot of time verifying data in order to protect their organization's interests. As a consequence, there is a risk that insufficient attention will be paid to correcting service faults and raising standards, which is of course the objective of imposing the fines in the first place.

Day-to-day management of minor service lapses are therefore probably best dealt with by a system of service credits, which can be paid as fixed sums or treated as a rebate to charges. Alternatively, a sliding scale of charges can be used, so that lower charges (or no charges at all) are paid if service levels fall.

Although compensation, penalties or service credits are frequently incorporated into outsourcing contracts to discourage poor performance, they do little actively to encourage service excellence. It is not easy to formulate incentives that encourage innovation and service improvements but here are a few suggestions to consider:

- Encourage suppliers to propose service improvements based on their expertise, perhaps by setting up quarterly meetings dedicated to considering proposals put forward by your service provider.

- Set aside a modest research fund to be used in whichever way the supplier chooses in the development of innovative proposals. This fund can be topped up at your discretion if and when these proposals are accepted by your organization.

- Devise formulae that allow you to share the benefits of service improvements with your supplier.

- Act as a prime reference site for your service provider.

- Publish articles about the success of the outsourced services provided by your supplier.

- Award bonus payments to the supplier's team related to the findings of independent user satisfaction surveys in your organization.

- Pay a proportion of the operational savings made through technology upgrades to your service provider.

Think through the consequences of any incentives planned; they can sometimes produce unanticipated results. For example, if payments are linked to system availability, your organization will pay more for 98 per cent availability than 95 per cent even though the lower performance level may be quite sufficient for your organization and you gain no benefit from the higher availability level. If your service provider is under contract to make IT purchases on behalf of your organization and is paid commission on each acquisition, more equipment may be purchased than you need because this increases your supplier's income.

In all cases your organization should stay in control and have the final say on the adoption of innovative proposals for service development. But you can take steps to encourage your service provider to come forward with ideas and guide them on the type of proposal that would be welcomed by your organization.

5.8 Adding Value

It is one thing to get your supplier to provide the outsourced IT services to contractual levels; it is quite another to derive added value from the outsourcing relationship.

What do we mean by "added value"?

- More services for the same cost?

- Access to new technological skills?

- Ready access to additional IT skills?

- Innovation and fresh thinking?

- Reduced operating costs?

Different stakeholders have different perspectives. Users will probably expect more services without increased charges. Business managers may think about exploiting technology more effectively. Suppliers may consider the delivery of operational savings, as specified in the contract, to be "added value".

Initially when the outsourcing contract is signed, the focus needs to be on critical transition tasks. Get the basics right first and ensure that outsourcing processes are functioning correctly. Once this has been accomplished, work with your supplier to consider ways in which the outsourcing relationship can add value to your organization. Draw on ideas from both organizations and put together a package of initiatives to take forward. Here are a few ideas to get you going:

- Aim for a culture of continuous improvement in the management of the contract. Set targets each year for service enhancements (those that deliver business benefit) and cost reduction.

- Empower staff in the supplier's organization to make service improvements subject only to reasonable constraints.

- Maintain a record of the technical skills available from the supplier and make sure that all new project managers within your organization are aware of this potential resource.

- With the service provider, carry out annual reviews of key performance indicators. Remove those that no longer serve a useful purpose and divert the supplier's resources away from priority areas. Introduce new measures that reflect current business needs.

- Set up an Added Value Forum that meets to discuss ways in which technology can be exploited to deliver greater business benefits within your organization.

- Explore potential commercial possibilities through, for example, joint ventures with your service provider.

An environment in which innovation is welcomed and service excellence valued is challenging and motivating for everyone.

5.9 Contract Management

The contract management process ensures that both customer and supplier fully meet their respective obligations as efficiently as possible to meet the overall business objectives of the outsourcing initiative. The customer organization will want to buy IT services economically and the supplier must make a profit to stay in business and there is a natural tension between these objectives. The contract managers from both customer and supplier will aim to get the best possible deal for their respective organizations while maintaining a good working relationship. Effective contract management is based on:

- a shared understanding of outsourced service boundaries and costs;
- an unambiguous and comprehensive contract with supporting schedules including service level agreements;
- mechanisms for proposing, negotiating and incorporating contract changes;
- clear contract management structures and reporting procedures;
- effective channels of communication;
- regular and frequent meetings.

Contract management plans need to be developed at an early stage in the outsourcing programme so that you can hit the ground running when the contract is signed. It is not helpful to discover shortly after the deal is agreed that all suitably skilled staff have either transferred to the supplier or have been assigned to new projects within your organization! Initially, the emphasis in contract management will be on disseminating information about the contracted services and discussing interpretation of the contract in detail with the supplier's representatives. It is vital that your organization has people with the right blend of skills and knowledge to tackle these tasks.

The responsibilities of the contract management function include:

- disseminating information about the outsourcing contract and clarifying details;

- agreeing contract interpretations with the supplier;
- monitoring compliance with the contract, ensuring an appropriate balance between the cost of monitoring and the risk of problems occurring;
- managing the contract change process;
- managing disputes;
- regular liaison with the supplier's contract manager;
- negotiating financial arrangements for new services;
- monitoring the total value of the outsourcing deal, business benefits delivered and expenditure;
- reviewing delivery against overall outsourcing objectives.

Contract management is a distinct role within the IT function and it would be a mistake to assume that any IT manager could readily succeed as a contract manager. Here are some of the qualities, skills and expertise needed by the customer's contract manager:

- Credibility and authority within both customer and supplier organizations
- Determination and self motivation
- Excellent communication and negotiation skills
- Good understanding of business requirements
- Broad technical understanding and awareness of technology developments
- Knowledge of financial matters
- Political skill to retain the support and confidence of business managers and service users
- Sound understanding of the contract
- A firm but fair approach when dealing with the supplier
- Courage to stand up to tough negotiation by the supplier and to resist unreasonable demands from service users
- Ability to manage conflicts
- Awareness of computer services industry issues.

Having an appropriate person to manage the outsourcing contract is key to its success. The right blend of knowledge, attitudes and skills earns the confidence and trust of business managers and service users. The supplier will regard such a contract manager highly, as someone who enjoys wide support within your organization and a high degree of credibility.

The contract manager treads a fine line between your organization and the supplier. It is important that your organization feels that the contract manager is close to hand and not unduly influenced by the service provider's point of view. It therefore makes sense for the contract manager to be based in an office where he/she is readily accessible to the service users. If the supplier's contract manager is offered an office nearby, this can enhance communication between the two managers and to help them resolve disputes. If your organization's contract manager is offered accommodation at the supplier's site, he/she should use this only occasionally.

5.10 Service Management

In outsourcing relationships the focus of service management shifts to service performance monitoring and review. The service management function covers:

- monitoring services to assess whether performance targets are met;
- carrying out periodic reviews of service level agreements, performance measures and service requirements;
- maintaining service quality and technology interface standards, which help create a predictable and measurable environment – these standards make it easier to integrate services from different suppliers and will facilitate the transfer to a new service provider when the current outsourcing contract comes to an end;
- discussing business plans that could affect the outsourced services as early as possible with your supplier;
- involving your service provider in your organization's planning process – they may be able to offer valuable input to the review of the viability, costs and timescales of different options.

114

Measure services at the point of delivery. Your service provider should have the option of changing the method of service delivery over time, as long as performance standards are met. Monitor features such as capacity, availability, business continuity, security services, desktop facilities, problem management and user satisfaction.

To carry out this function you will need to set up a service control team, based in your organization's offices. The team needs a good understanding of the applications and technical environment used by your service provider and will, therefore, need to include in-house technical staff. Monitoring tasks rather than hands-on IT work is not to everyone's liking, so the service control team should have clear career development opportunities to help it remain well motivated for the critical outsourcing role it performs.

The responsibilities of the service control team include:

- carrying out formal service acceptance procedures when the outsourced services are first introduced;
- analyzing performance data from the reports produced by your supplier;
- assessing service management standards through the supplier's adherence to best technical management practices such as the Information Technology Infrastructure Library (ITIL) standards;
- monitoring the completeness and correctness of operations and system procedures such as contingency plans, back-up procedures and test procedures;
- resolving service issues and problems;
- reviewing invoicing procedures;
- analyzing new service requirements or changes requested and following them through the change control process.

The team can collect data from performance reports produced by your supplier, regular meetings with the supplier's service management team, visits to the supplier's premises and direct access to some of the supplier's systems. This data should be consolidated and analyzed for the contract manager and other senior managers in your organization. It may also be helpful to present a summary of the findings to liaison meetings with representatives from the service user community.

5.11 Service Users

To get the best out of your outsourcing arrangement, you will need to encourage the service users to develop a good understanding of the new, formal arrangement between your two organizations, how to request service changes, how to tackle problems and how costs are incurred. One of the advantages of outsourcing is that users should become more aware of the balance between quality and price, and should more critically examine the business benefits of system modifications and developments.

Promote understanding by sharing information with users as the outsourcing programme progresses. If there are a large number of service users you may find it helpful to ask for user representatives who have a good knowledge not only of business operations but also of business strategy and longer-term goals. These representatives can help you identify future service requirements and set appropriate performance standards. These representatives are sometimes known as "informed customers" or "intelligent customers". Their role is to:

- act as a point of contact between your service provider and a group of users, co-ordinating views and disseminating information;
- encourage constructive working relationships between your supplier's staff and the end users;
- interpret the users' requirements and concerns as necessary for the supplier;
- promote understanding of the outsourcing contract, the costs incurred for various IT services and the balance between quality and cost;
- help users understand and follow problem escalation and change request procedures;
- liaise with the contract manager and service control team to co-ordinate activities across your organization.

This role is especially important if there are a large number of service users, perhaps widely dispersed throughout your organization. In these circumstances it is not possible for all communications and other dealings with your outsourcing supplier to pass through a small team in the IT department. User representatives can then play a very helpful role in the success of the outsourcing initiative. You will need to be clear about whether their role is to control, co-ordinate or facilitate communication between business areas and your service provider and to what extent they are authorized to instruct the supplier. Do make sure that the role is fully developed, understood by all those working on the outsourced services and communicated to all users.

Contact with the service users helps your supplier to get a better understanding of user requirements and problems.

5.12 Contract Administration

You will need to implement a number of administrative procedures and clerical functions to support the outsourcing contract. Contract administration procedures include:

- contract maintenance;
- charges and cost monitoring;
- ordering procedures;
- payment procedures;
- budget management;
- performance reporting;
- asset management.

The procedures should be designed to reflect the scope and complexity of the outsourcing contract and your organization's policies and business processes. Clear administrative procedures ensure that everyone understands who does what, when and how.

5.12.1 Contract Maintenance

IT service requirements will evolve over the life of the outsourcing contract and must respond to changes in the business environment. The contract documents should be modified through formal change control procedures and by mutual agreement with your supplier. It is best to update contract documentation as changes occur rather than relying on informal arrangements. Even in the best outsourcing relationships, differences of opinion do occur and it helps to have up-to-date contract documentation.

Apply sound document management principles:

- Identify all relevant contractual documentation, for example contract clauses and schedules, service level agreements, procedures and manuals.
- Control all changes to documentation using version control and change control procedures, ensuring that no changes are made without proper authorization.
- Record the status of documents – current or historic, draft or final.
- Ensure consistency across all contract documents.

There are three types of contract change:

1. Changes to contract conditions, which should be processed as numbered contract amendments and formally accepted by both your organization and the supplier. Maintain a register to track the status of each amendment, recording the date the change was first proposed and when it is accepted. Remember that the amendment legally only comes into effect when it is formally accepted by both parties. The contract administrator should monitor the progress of all proposed amendments and chase outstanding responses from your supplier.

2. Contract changes made under an enabling condition. For example, service level agreements are usually included as contract schedules while the main contract clauses include a condition defining how changes to these agreements will be processed or a new agreement added. Records of such changes should be maintained. It can be helpful to add a record of the changes formally to the contract from time to time.

3. Changes to the interpretation or understanding of the contract, which are documented and agreed through separate letters, reports or minutes of meetings. These can be difficult to track but do need to be recorded. One solution is to make a note in the contract amendment register and annotate the working copy of the contract with a cross-reference to the relevant material.

Keep the master copy of the contract (the original, signed contract documents and amendment papers) separate from the latest working copy that incorporates agreed amendments. A back-up copy should be held in a separate secure location.

5.12.2 Charges and Cost Monitoring

The contract should specify cost formulae and charging mechanisms. Different approaches may be needed for the different services covered by the outsourcing contract. Types of service charge include unit costs, a flat service charge irrespective of usage, fixed price quotations and benefit sharing mechanisms.

In many cases the costs incurred by the supplier will not be visible to the customer organization and payment will be based on agreed service charges. But in some instances, contracts may operate on the basis that the supplier shares some cost information with the customer organization. This open book accounting approach gives the customer access to information about costs incurred and profit margins achieved. This degree of openness is important in benefit sharing arrangements.

Charges and costs incurred under the outsourcing contract should be monitored to help determine if the arrangement is delivering value for money. This information will feed into discussions with your supplier about possible changes to services or charging mechanisms.

If the contract provides for inflation by allowing price variation relative to an agreed index, the contract administrator will need to monitor price changes to ensure that they fall within agreed limits. Similarly, where contracts commit the supplier to reduce operating costs over a set period, this will also need to be monitored.

The contract manager will need to keep under review the overall cost of the outsourcing contract to ensure that the service costs remain within budget. Internal costs, including the costs of managing the contract, need to be taken into account.

5.12.3 Ordering Procedures

The outsourcing contract will specify requirements and costs for a core set of IT services. During the life of the contract new services or modifications to current services will be required. Processes for raising these requests and reaching agreement on charges should be incorporated in the outsourcing contract. Procedures should be introduced and clear guidance issued to determine:

- who in your organization may request and authorize service changes;
- whether and when there should be an internal technical or business review of service requests within your organization;
- responsibility for financial approvals;
- who in the supplier's organization may accept service orders and allocate resources to deliver them.

The contract administrator should record details of all service orders submitted to the supplier to ensure co-ordination and accountability. This helps identify any discrepancies, check orders and spot any opportunities to reduce costs through economies of scale.

5.12.4 Payment Procedures

The outsourcing contract should cover payment processes including:

- structure and content of invoices;
- submission of invoices;
- invoice approval process;
- payment terms.

Your organization probably has existing procedures for paying invoices. You will need to ensure that there is adequate co-ordination and liaison between service users, the contract manager and the finance department so that invoices are correctly authorized for payment.

If invoices are submitted centrally you may need to allocate or recharge costs to individual departments to meet your organization's internal accounting requirements. In this instance you will need to make sure that the supplier provides sufficient detail and presents charging data in a suitable format on the invoices.

Do not forget to monitor your organization's compliance with the agreed payment terms. In large organizations especially, there can be quite a delay between invoice authorization and actual payment to your supplier. The larger outsourcing suppliers understand this and some delay should not cause too many difficulties. But smaller suppliers may be more sensitive to any delay and their business will suffer as a result. Look into this before it becomes an issue. It helps to understand how your organization works and how many days will elapse between invoice authorization and payment to your supplier.

Service credits may be incorporated in the outsourcing contract to compensate your organization should the supplier's performance be poor. The credits should be clearly linked to specific services and agreed service levels. The contract administrator should monitor the calculation and payment of service credits.

5.12.5 Budget Management

Practice varies from one organization to another, some organizations retain budgets for outsourced IT services centrally while others delegate budget provision to the departments that use the services. In both instances, however, there is generally a need to monitor committed and proposed expenditure under the outsourcing contract to ensure that it does not exceed the allocated budget.

The contract manager will also participate in forward planning for the service, budget allocation and in defining forward commitments for future use of the outsourced services.

5.12.6 Performance Reporting

Requirements for performance reports and management information are defined in the contract. Information may be required about all performance measures or only about "exceptions" or instances where performance varies from agreed standards. Exception reporting helps focus on potential problem areas and reduces the volume of reports and hence time needed to review the data. But it can also hide trends and uninspiring (but not contractually inadequate) performance. Information about service performance may be disseminated to the contract manager and key user representatives, with summaries submitted to senior IT and business managers. There is further discussion about performance measurement and reporting in Chapter 6.

5.12.7 Asset Management

If ownership of any of the assets used in the delivery of the outsourced services, such as hardware, office equipment and premises, is retained by your organization, then you will have responsibility for these assets. If your supplier carries out the day-to-day management of these assets you will need to ensure that:

- your organization's asset register is kept up-to-date;
- any third party use of the assets is recorded (for example, if your supplier delivers services to other customers using your equipment);
- upgrades and replacements are planned and budgets identified;
- your supplier provides an audit trail of technical changes made to any systems.

If assets have been transferred to your supplier as part of the outsourcing deal but will transfer back at the end of the contract term, you will need to ensure that your supplier is maintaining an up-to-date asset register and recording upgrades and changes.

In some cases, charges will be based on the assets used, for example help desk service charges may be based on the number of PCs. Clearly in this instance it is essential to keep the asset inventory up to date as charges will be based on the information in this system.

5.13 Outsourcing Management Organization

In earlier sections we examined a number of new functions that need to be introduced to manage and monitor the outsourcing initiative once the contract is signed. These are summarized below:

- Contract management
  - Disseminating contract information
  - Negotiating interpretations and contract changes
  - Monitoring contract expenditure against budget, value and benefits

- Service management
  - Service performance monitoring
  - Service level agreement reviews
  - Maintenance of service quality and technology standards
  - Service planning
- Service control
  - Analysis of performance reports
  - Monitoring contingency plans, test procedures etc.
  - Resolving service issues
  - Analysing service change requests
- Informed customer
  - Co-ordinating user feedback and disseminating information to users
  - Promoting understanding of contract and procedures such as problem escalation
- Contract administration
  - Contract maintenance including document updates
  - Introduction and maintenance of various procedures such as charging, invoicing and payment procedures
  - Detailed budget monitoring
  - Collection and distribution of performance reports.

All outsourcing contracts need to be managed effectively if they are to be successful, but the size of the team required will vary depending on the scale and complexity of the IT services that have been outsourced. Small-scale outsourcing initiatives may require a small team of perhaps three or four members of staff who share responsibility for the various functions. Large complex outsourcing deals, on the other hand, may require very large teams of 50 or more staff with separate sections concerned with service control, contract administration and so on.

Your organization needs to plan at the outset how and when the outsourcing management team will be identified and trained. This needs to be done before staff transfers are discussed in detail with potential suppliers to ensure that your organization does not find that it has agreed to transfer all those with relevant expertise and business knowledge to the supplier.

The outsourcing management team needs to develop influencing and relationship management skills, the ability to co-ordinate and represent business requirements and negotiating skills that will be used informally in daily dealings with your supplier. Some technical skills need to be retained too so that proposals put forward by the supplier can be properly assessed and technical plans evaluated.

From the experiences of various organizations we can draw a number of lessons about outsourcing management:

- Establish unambiguous roles and responsibilities for the outsourcing management team, service users and the supplier. Develop a responsibility matrix that shows which party is responsible for each specific activity and whether that activity is within the scope of the core contract or subject to excess fees.

- Build a formal contract management structure into the contract and monitor your supplier's compliance with this structure.

- Define the supplier's point of contact in your organization for specific issues and ensure adherence. This will stop the supplier making unwanted advances to business managers and shifting the focus of the contract away from the main services to more lucrative opportunities.

- Regularly review the outsourcing management team numbers and skills – requirements will probably change during the life of the contract. Try to anticipate changes in requirements before any skills gaps have an impact on contract performance.

- Retain the right to veto the supplier's choice of key contract management staff so that the quality of outsourced services can be maintained and ensure that, whenever possible, your organization is given early warning of any such changes.

- Use secondments between your organization and your supplier to help build effective working relationships and greater understanding between your two organizations.

- Be aware that job titles can give a false impression and use descriptions that are meaningful in your organization. The function may be described as contract management, relationship management or alliance management. The team roles may be described as manager, liaison officer, advisor, administrator or support staff. There are many other possibilities. Everyone needs to know exactly what is expected of them and what they can expect from others.

- Maintaining adequate technical expertise in the outsourcing management team can be difficult. With the daily technology work on the IT services transferred to the supplier, the technically skilled staff that remain in your organization may not have the opportunity to update and practise their skills on a regular basis. It will also be difficult to develop this expertise in-house. Your organization will need to address this issue before problems occur. Some companies have found it useful to second these staff to the service provider from time to time for short periods; others have found it necessary to buy in technical specialists as and when required.

- It is useful to build into the contract management process a review of the process itself. This might be combined with an annual performance review.

5.14 Meetings

There will be plenty of informal contact and liaison between your service provider, the users and the outsourcing management team but a well-structured and planned series of more formal meetings will help you get the most out of the outsourcing deal and avoid unnecessary problems. The overall objectives of the organized meetings are to:

- ensure that the outsourcing arrangement is properly controlled and managed;

- promote the development of excellent relationships between the supplier and your organization;

- tackle issues before they become major concerns;

- derive maximum added value from outsourcing;

- provide a formal record of problems aired, which will be necessary should formal action be taken against the supplier or the contract prematurely terminated.

The number and frequency of meetings will vary according to the nature of the outsourcing initiative. Some examples are given below:

- Weekly operations meetings to discuss detailed service issues and problems.

- Monthly status meetings to review performance and monitor costs.

- Quarterly strategic meetings to discuss new directions or services.

- Quarterly service improvement meetings to review proposals from the supplier to enhance the efficiency or effectiveness of current out-sourced services.

- Twice yearly innovation forums in which ideas are brainstormed and the emphasis is on adding value to the outsourcing relationship.

- Annual meetings to review service performance criteria, overall contract value and other major issues.

Each meeting should have its own distinct set of objectives. Aim to avoid overlap: it is not uncommon for the same set of people to find themselves at several different meetings discussing similar topics, which can waste a lot of time.

It is a good idea to set down proposals for a structure of meetings, giving suggested membership, frequency and terms of reference for each meeting and explaining how the meetings interrelate. Preferably do this before the contract is signed and invite comments from colleagues in your organization and from potential suppliers. The aim is to have in place an agreed set of meetings when the contract is signed. Representatives should be nominated and dates fixed in diaries for the coming year as soon as possible – remember that you want to maintain the commitment and involvement of senior managers in the outsourcing initiative.

5.15 Change Control

If outsourcing is to succeed it is important that your organization recognizes that IT service requirements will change and is willing to accept appropriate costs. Enhanced or new services will attract higher charges, but IT should be an enabler not a constraint to business so encourage co-operative contract evolution to take advantage of developing technologies and other opportunities for service improvements.

The outsourcing contract should include change control mechanisms. A formal change request process ensures that your organization understands the value it will gain from the modified or additional services and the full costs that will be incurred. The change control process should prevent an enquiry about a possible change generating a considerable amount of investigation and analysis without proper review and authorization.

In the early days of a new outsourcing contract a large number of change requests may be raised:

● There may be a deluge of user demand for service improvements if these have been put on hold during the supplier selection process.

● In many outsourcing contracts, although the core set of IT services outsourced have been well defined, various IT activities are inadvertently overlooked or service use volumes have to be adjusted.

You will need to determine who can authorize various change requests and how this is done. This will probably vary according to the cost of the change and the impact on the overall outsourcing programme. If there are a very large number of change requests to be dealt with, it may be worth setting up a separate change authority group.

The change control process encompasses a set of procedures, which enable either your organization or the supplier to propose a change and define where the change will be costed, how other impacts will be identified and where the decision will be made to accept or reject the proposed change. The process is illustrated in Figure 5.1. A fast-track process should also be designed to handle urgent requests. In this instance the contract manager could be authorized to submit the proposal to the supplier for impact assessment. The IT Director or other senior manager could review the costed proposal.

The author of the change request allocates a priority rating on the following lines:

1. A necessity: the outsourced IT services will not function correctly without this change.

2. An important change: this is needed to meet business objectives.

127

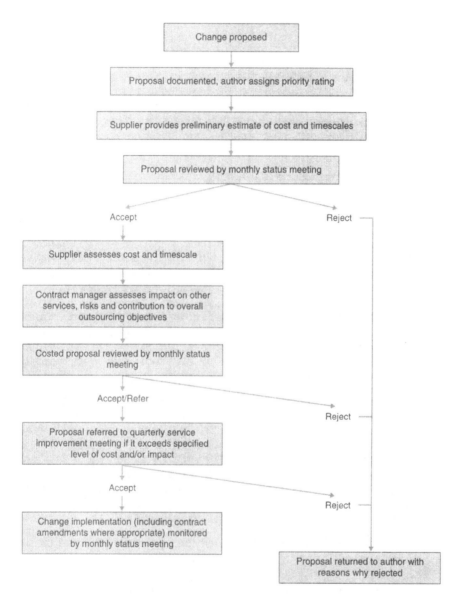

Figure 5.1 Change control process.

3. A nice to have, but not vital.

4. A cosmetic change, which would be welcome but does not deliver a quantifiable business benefit.

The last two categories of change are unlikely to be accepted unless costs are minimal.

To avoid unproductive but lengthy impact assessment work, the supplier is asked to give a preliminary estimate of cost and timescales. If these are significant the change will only be taken forward if it has a high priority rating.

A suitably authorized group such as the monthly status meeting will review the fully costed proposal. This group may have a limit set on the changes it can authorize. More expensive changes or those with a greater impact on your organization may need to be referred to a more senior management group.

The final step in the change control process is to monitor progress in the implementation of the change, including contract amendments where appropriate.

At any of the review points, the change proposal may be rejected for a variety of reasons such as being too costly or delivering insufficient business benefits. When this happens the author of the request should be notified and given the reasons for the rejection.

A register should be maintained to record details of all change proposals received, impact assessments, decisions and progress. A sample form that can be used to collect this information for each change request is given in Figure 5.2.

5.16 Issue Management and Problem Escalation

Inevitably every outsourcing programme raises some unexpected issues and problems occur. Rather than let disputes fester it pays to introduce procedures for bringing problems and potential difficulties to your supplier's attention. Your organization should not expect always to get its own way. Try to find a resolution that costs your organization little but

Reference No. (Assigned by contract administration office)
Change Proposal
Priority Rating (Assigned by author)
Preliminary Estimate (Prepared by supplier)
Initial Review Outcome (Authorization to proceed to full impact analysis where necessary)
Supplier Impact Assessment
Contract Manager Impact Assessment
Outcome of Review of Impact Assessment
Planned Implementation Dates
Date Author Notified of Rejection (where appropriate)
Implementation Completion Date

Figure 5.2 Sample change request form.

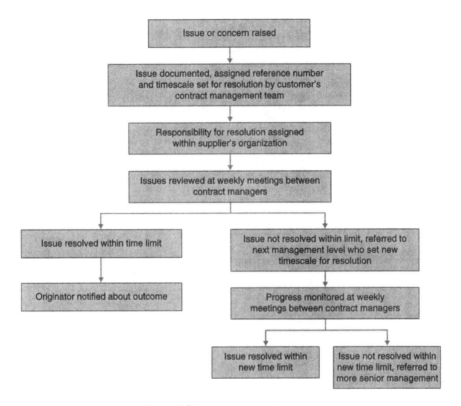

Figure 5.3 Issue management process.

gives your supplier a face saving way to agree with you. One solution is to aim for a written commitment to a timetable for resolving the problems. While your supplier has to make a sufficient profit margin to stay in business, it will want a satisfied customer as well. Generally suppliers price contracts in such a way that they make most profit towards the end of the contract term so they want the contract to last long enough to reach this stage.

Potential problems are best raised initially as issues, which may be questions or statements about concerns or difficulties with the outsourced services. Issues should be assigned to named individuals for resolution and reviewed regularly. Until the supplier has reviewed the issues, the severity of the problem is not always clear. Indeed it may be a misunderstanding rather than a service problem.

Introduce a well-defined, timed escalation process that includes a way to prioritize issues and allocates time limits for the resolution of problems. Define equivalent pairs of people at each level in your organization and the supplier; problem resolution can then be referred up through the various seniority levels in each organization. Make sure that you maintain order during the escalation process without either side going straight to the top and bypassing agreed procedures.

The issue management process is illustrated in Figure 5.3.

The goal of all those involved in issue management should be to resolve problems without the need to refer them to senior management levels. When major difficulties do occur, the time you have spent in escalating the problem through agreed procedures and the time spent by your IT managers trying to resolve the problem will illustrates the depth of concern to your supplier's top management.

Chapter 8 looks further at resolving difficulties when outsourcing fails to deliver.

5.17 Critical Success Factors

We conclude this chapter by summarizing the critical success factors that underpin effective management of outsourced services:

- Plan together with your supplier from the beginning. Focus on the underlying objectives of the outsourcing initiative to develop a shared vision of the way forward.

- Invest in building and sustaining excellent working relationships between the supplier, the outsourcing management team and service users. Aim to develop understanding and mutual trust through honest and open dealings with your supplier. Look for win–win solutions and know when to compromise.

- Nurture teamwork; put together teams from your organization and your supplier to tackle issues and use secondments to increase understanding between your two organizations.

- Try to understand the perspectives of different stakeholders in the outsourcing initiative and ensure that users and senior managers in particular have realistic expectations about the outsourced services.

- Recognize the importance of communication and introduce systems that ensure information is disseminated to all those involved in the outsourcing initiative.

- Introduce incentives and processes that encourage improved service performance and increased business benefits derived from outsourcing. Look for opportunities to add value to your organization from the outsourcing relationship.

- Retain in-house control over the strategic direction of the outsourced IT services by setting up a skilled contract management team.

- Define outsourcing management roles and responsibilities both for your organization and for the supplier's representatives. You also need a clear definition of the boundaries of the outsourced IT services.

- Monitor the performance of outsourced services against objective criteria and resolve problems as they occur.

- Schedule regular operational and strategic review meetings.

Measuring Performance 6

6.1 Introduction

It has been said that if you cannot measure an activity, you cannot control it and if you cannot control it, you cannot manage it. Without dependable measurements, intelligent decisions cannot be made.

These arguments can be applied to IT outsourcing initiatives and we will examine in this chapter ways in which performance measures for outsourced services can be derived and monitored. The definition of performance measures provides a common language for planning, identifying and reporting on service levels and benefits derived through outsourcing. The measures demonstrate whether your service provider has met the contractual service requirements and helps your organization achieve value for money through outsourcing. By tracking performance measures over time, you will be able to quickly spot divergences from plan or deteriorating service levels.

A good performance measurement system will:

- reflect your organization's overall business objectives;
- contain a balanced mix of financial and non-financial measures;
- collect performance data frequently enough for timely action to be taken to resolve issues and problems;
- encourage your supplier to provide the outsourced services your organization needs;
- help you predict what standard the outsourced services will reach in the future as well as enable you to understand what has happened in the past.

Traditionally, performance measurement has been seen as a technique for monitoring performance, checking progress and identifying areas that need attention. But outsourcing performance measures will also help your organization to:

● Improve communication as your organization works with your supplier to interpret measures and understand the implications of data collected. Measures affect behaviour and we can use this knowledge to influence the outsourcing supplier's performance.

● Assess the overall health of the outsourcing relationship with your service provider. In addition to measuring service outputs, your organization might measure user satisfaction, added value and innovation delivered through outsourcing.

● Stimulate learning by sharing best practice with other parts of your organization involved in outsourcing or working with other external service providers.

Note that your supplier will have its own business goals and metrics against which your outsourcing contract will be measured; typically the contract will be regarded as a profit centre. Depending on the business culture within your supplier's organization, the contract may need to be run at minimum cost with the emphasis on short-term profitability measures with the result that your supplier may appear reluctant to invest in activities for the longer term. Alternatively if the contract is seen within the framework of an ongoing relationship between your two organizations, your supplier may be more open to further investment and evolution of the contract and to sharing with you internal performance details and issues.

Performance measurement systems can be examined at three different levels, each of which raises issues that have to be tackled during the design and implementation of the system:

1. The individual measures of performance

   ○ Which performance measures should be adopted?

   ○ How much will it cost to collect the data?

   ○ What benefit does the measure provide?

   ○ Are the performance measures cost effective?

2. The performance measurement system

   o How many measures should the system contain?

   o What is the appropriate balance of financial, numerical and qualitative measures?

   o Are there any conflicting performance targets and how will this be resolved?

3. The wider context

   o Do the performance measures reflect the outsourcing objectives?

   o How do the measures fit with other business performance measures used by your organization?

Performance measures are generally required for all aspects of the outsourced services and standards should be specified in the contract. It is best to provide for a myriad of ways to monitor your supplier's performance, as it is hard to tell in advance which measures will be the most significant. The measures should cover:

● cost and benefits obtained;

● service volumes;

● service quality: timeliness, responsiveness, capacity, usability, accuracy, flexibility and reliability;

● service security and audits;

● service delivery improvements;

● added value and innovation;

● strength and responsiveness of your outsourcing relationship.

Once chosen, the performance measures will provide the framework for contract management activities such as performance reporting, monitoring and reviews. It is important that the performance measures selected provide clear and demonstrable evidence of the achievements of the outsourcing relationship. The measures and performance standards set will determine how challenging the contract will be for your supplier. Service levels help determine price and if performance measures are very demanding the price will be higher.

Bear in mind the reasons why performance data are collected:

● To identify whether the supplier is meeting contractual requirements.

- To ensure that decisions are based on fact, not subjective judgements.
- To identify whether the outsourced services are meeting their objectives.
- To show where improvements need to be made.
- To demonstrate where improvements have been made.
- To reveal problems that bias or prejudice might cover up.

You might find it helpful to test each proposed performance measure against the SMART criteria:

- Specific: is the measure clear and focused to avoid misinterpretation?
- Measurable: can it be quantified and used in meaningful statistical analysis?
- Attainable: is the measure achievable, reasonable and credible?
- Relevant: does the measure reflect your organization's objectives and is it cost effective?
- Timely: is the measure collectable within a given framework?

While the focus of performance measurement will be on the main outsourced services, don't forget the residual services such as systems analysts asked to set up desktop systems, disaster recovery testing, office relocation services and teleconferencing support. These residual services will, of course, vary between outsourcing contracts but most IT departments undertake a wide range of activities, some of which may be within the boundary of your outsourcing programme but may not previously have been monitored or measured.

Not all customer organizations will be ready to set binding performance standards when the contract is signed. Existing legacy systems may not be performing adequately, performance data may not have been collected or existing measures may be unsatisfactory. Though not ideal, the outsourcing contract may have to start with a limited number of high level, output-based service standards with provision in the contract for joint evaluation of a fuller set of performance measures and remedial work at an early stage.

In all outsourcing programmes it is a good idea to remember that performance measures and standards required will probably change during the life of the contract and procedures should be agreed for reviewing and changing measures at intervals.

6.2 Linking Performance Measures to Objectives

Defining a performance measure involves more that simply identifying a formula. The performance measurement process starts with the setting of objectives at the very beginning of the outsourcing programme. Business objectives need to be translated into service requirements and performance measures defined that relate to the business objectives. Each customer organization will have its own objectives and will need to measure different aspects of performance but all will include measures of cost and service quality.

Table 6.1 illustrates the performance measures that would be relevant to some common outsourcing objectives. Performance standards should relate to the achievement of the objectives but not beyond. There is no point – and potentially considerable cost – in providing "gold-plated" services when just a regular service will suffice. For example, if the service requires relatively few online transactions then response times may not be a good measure of performance. But if key managers must have certain business reports by 9am each morning then the timely and accurate delivery of these reports could be an effective performance measure.

Performance standards, particularly financial and other commercial measures, drive the behaviour of both customer organization and service provider. Hence it is vital that the measures contribute to the right business outcomes. Understanding what should be monitored and why will help your organization prioritize what needs to be done.

Think carefully about the impact on your supplier's behaviour. Supposing you introduce an incentive aimed at reducing the capital costs of IT. The supplier is offered an equal share of any discounts it can negotiate on your behalf with the aim of encouraging the supplier to drive harder bargains and deals on IT equipment. Your goal is to be fair-minded and share the benefits of decreased costs with your supplier. Unfortunately, the more equipment the supplier purchases, the greater this share of discounts will be and the net effect is likely to be that your organization will incur higher capital IT expenditure and will purchase equipment that, strictly speaking, is not necessary.

139

Table 6.1 Performance measures linked to specific outsourcing objectives.

Objective	Performance measures
To reduce operating costs.	Current costs of outsourced services should include not only the supplier charges but also contract management costs.
	Costs incurred must relate to an acceptable level of service. Minimum service levels should therefore be identified and measured to monitor any fall in standard.
	The initial cost baseline needs to be set during service specification. But in future years, continuing cost reductions may be required and performance measures need to take this into account.
To give access to additional skilled resources.	Performance measures will relate to the speed at which technical problems are resolved or new or modified services introduced.
To free up management time and energy to focus on core business issues.	This can be difficult to measure. If IT services have been outsourced successfully and there is a defined contract management structure in place, other managers should not need to become involved in service issues. One possible measure is to ask these managers if they are spending less time on service problems. You should also measure what they have been able to achieve with the time saved (drinking coffee is not a recognized business benefit!).
To provide access to world-class capabilities.	The target is to introduce new technology, tools and techniques into your organization and the performance measures might include projects delivered to time and budget, speed at which new technology is delivered, degree of innovation and contribution by outsourced services to business benefits.

6.3 Setting a Baseline

You will need to set a baseline for the level of service to be provided by the outsourcing supplier. The baseline is commonly identified over a period of several months while negotiations with the supplier are under-way (and before the outsourcing contract is finalized). The supplier will base the charges for the outsourced services on the performance recorded over this period. It is therefore very important to measure everything. The customer organization runs the risk of being charged excess fees if the supplier underestimates the resources required to provide the services. So remember to measure service availability, volumes, timescales, telecommunications performance, application development, support and maintenance, security, disaster recovery, report production and distribution, help desk services, training and so on.

Potential problem areas include:

- Length of the baseline period and time of year: if use of the outsourced services fluctuates during the year, this needs to be reflected in the baseline measurement. The supplier may suggest averaging performance over several months but, in terms of volume of service use, this could mean use exceeding baseline levels 50 per cent of the time. In this instance it would be better for the baseline to incorporate a volume range.

- Achieving 100 per cent service accountability: for example, if the baseline specifies that 90 per cent of the management information reports should be delivered in 3 days, remember to specify when the remaining 10 per cent should be available.

- Performance measure dilution: for example, if the supplier proposes that 95 per cent of the reports will be delivered on time and 95 per cent will be accurate, then only 90 per cent will be both on time and correct.

- Specifying world-class services: this is easy to say but more difficult to define in a measurable way.

Of course, we cannot assume that the baseline measures are sufficient for the outsourcing contract. The customer organization or supplier may wish to add, combine, improve or delete certain performance measures. It is still advisable, however, to assemble as much historic data as possible that demonstrates past performance before the start of the contract.

If you are aiming for service improvements or changes through outsourcing it might be helpful to agree with your supplier before the contract is signed that there will be a period of transition in which:

- initially there will be no fundamental changes to the performance metrics currently in use in your organization;

- performance data are collected for aspects of the IT services that have not previously been measured but need to be monitored for the outsourcing contract;

- services are improved as necessary so that by the end of the transition period they are fully compliant with the contracted standards;

- other service improvements are introduced where the opportunity exists and where they provide demonstrable business benefit;

- further historical performance data are collected;

- towards the end of the transition period the relevance and usefulness of all proposed new performance measures are reviewed and the final set of metrics to be used agreed.

6.4 Benchmarking

As we saw in Chapter 3, benchmarking enables you to compare the service quality and value for money achieved through outsourcing with standards and best practice in other organizations. The information gathered can be used to identify and prioritize possible areas of service improvement. Benchmarking can help your organization improve:

- economy, by demonstrating that others have achieved higher productivity and/or lower prices;

- efficiency, by comparing the costs of providing the outsourced IT services and the contribution these services make to your business with what has been delivered in other organizations;

- effectiveness, by comparing the business objectives achieved through the use of outsourced IT services against what was originally planned.

Benchmarking can initially be used in compiling the baseline for the outsourced services. Once the contract is operational, benchmarking can provide a basis for continuous improvement as markets and technologies evolve. Without such a measurement technique, your organization may become increasingly dependent on your supplier's judgement about reasonable service costs and knowledge of new technological opportunities.

Define a clear benchmarking process so that there is clarity about how the results will be used and what items are relevant, and you avoid personalities rather than facts dominating the evaluation or preconceived solutions being adopted. Ensure that your supplier participates in the benchmarking process and include provision in the contract for negotiations based on benchmarking results. Some organizations hire external experts in part so that the benchmarking findings can be shown to be impartial.

A typical benchmarking exercise might consist of the following steps:

1. A structured collection of defined performance data about service levels, pricing, user satisfaction, outsourcing relationships, contract management and benefits realized.

2. A report presented to customer organization and supplier.

3. Gap analysis carried out using a joint, structured workshop.

4. The creation of joint working teams commissioned to explore alternative solutions to raising service standards; solutions are generated, evaluated and prioritized.

5. The more promising proposals are then formally validated, refined and costed.

6. A formal decision-making process in which appropriate solutions will be adopted and integrated into the outsourcing contract.

6.5 Measuring Benefits

Measuring the benefits derived from outsourcing is a complex area because:

- simple measures of service cost reduction or quality improvements will become less meaningful over time;

- measuring benefits in comparison with the business case may not be meaningful if the business environment changes in a way that was not anticipated;

- the indirect benefits of outsourcing may require a comprehensive change programme across your organization in which outsourcing IT services is only one element.

Measurable

	High	Low
High	Reduction in service costs Increase in service revenue Reduction in capital expenditure	Improved management information Reduced risks Improved security features Access to additional resources and new technical skills
Low	Faster response times Faster problem resolution Faster report delivery Improved user satisfaction	Access to world-class capabilities Degree of innovation Improved management productivity (enhanced focus on core business)

(row header: **Tangible** — High / Low)

Figure 6.1 Example of IT outsourcing benefit matrix.

Nevertheless we must do our best to provide demonstrable evidence of the business value delivered through outsourcing. We begin by looking briefly at the types of benefits that can be delivered by outsourced IT services. IT benefits can be tangible, directly affecting a company's profitability, or intangible, having a positive impact on business but not necessarily directly influencing costs or income. Each benefit can also be classified into quantifiable (capable of objective measurement) or unquantifiable (precise, direct measurement is not possible). Some examples of the different types of benefit are shown in Figure 6.1. The different benefit types are measured using various techniques as illustrated in Figure 6.2. Perhaps the most difficult type of IT benefit to assess is the unquantifiable intangible benefit, yet some of the most significant and valued benefits of outsourcing IT services fall in this category.

Recognize that there may also be dis-benefits – not a failure to achieve anticipated benefits, but problems caused by outsourcing, for example:

● a loss of control over IT systems;

● an inability to respond sufficiently quickly to changed business requirements;

144

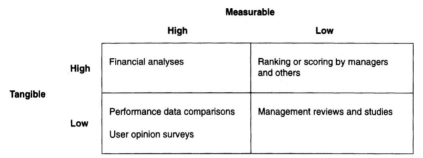

Figure 6.2 Examples of benefit measurement techniques.

- a fall in the standard of service because your supplier runs into problems meeting other commitments;

- your supplier goes out of business or is taken over by a company that is an unsuitable outsourcing partner for your organization.

These dis-benefits are risks that potentially jeopardize the outsourcing initiative. Risk management and countermeasures are discussed in Chapter 7.

6.6 Involving Service Users

Try to involve the users of the outsourced services in performance measurement and monitoring. They are best placed to determine whether the services are fulfilling business requirements and their views will give a more rounded picture of the overall performance of the outsourcing initiative. Your organization's contract manager should meet regularly with user representatives to review performance reports and remedial actions.

Where services are delivered to a large population of casual users or to your organization's customers, it is often easiest to frame performance measures in terms of what these users find acceptable. Reviewing the levels of reported incidents, help desk queries or complaints can help you assess this. Where specific problem areas are identified, deeper investigation will be needed to identify appropriate solutions.

Effective communications will be needed to ensure that users' expectations match their needs rather than historical service levels. Users need to understand that higher service standards are generally more expensive. If service levels can be reduced without damaging business value, then by all means reduce performance targets but do make sure that the users understand the justification and cost implications.

Many performance measures used in outsourcing are quite subjective. In the early stages of the outsourcing contract, users may be inclined to rate performance problems as serious to ensure that they get immediate attention and speedy resolution. But in time a more balanced view should emerge. Setting up joint teams of users and representatives from your supplier to tackle key issues of concern helps to foster shared understanding and identify a range of possible solutions.

6.7 Service Level Management

Service level management is the term used to describe the process of defining, agreeing, documenting and managing the levels of IT service required to meet business needs and provide value for money. Critically it is based on the performance measures and service level agreements that are incorporated in the outsourcing contract. The goal of service level management is to maintain and improve the quality of outsourced services through a constant cycle of agreeing, monitoring and reporting on service delivery and instigating actions to resolve service problems.

Effective service level management not only improves service quality but also can minimize service disruption and the time spent by users and managers resolving service failures. Other benefits of service level management in the context of outsourced services include:

- There are specific targets to aim for, and against which service quality can be measured, monitored and reported.
- Both supplier and users have a clear and consistent expectation of the level of service required.
- IT services delivered by your supplier are designed to meet set performance standards.
- More reliable service standards improve relationships with satisfied users.

- Contract management effort is focused on those areas that matter most to the business.

- Service monitoring identifies weak areas so that remedial action can be taken.

- Service level management helps demonstrate the business value derived through outsourcing.

Once the outsourcing deal is signed, performance levels that were agreed during negotiations must be delivered, reviewed and actions taken to ensure that corrections are made. Inevitably the expectation or perception of IT services where money is paid to an external organization is higher than when IT costs count as salary and other internal expenditure. Service levels will be more critically reviewed and demands for improvements made where standards are not maintained.

The service level management process should include an open and objective search for performance improvements. Commitments to specified improvements may be included in the outsourcing contract. Aim to motivate your supplier to pursue continuous improvements in priority areas, perhaps through benefit sharing arrangements or bonus payments. Your organization may wish to identify targets for the level of performance improvement sought over, say, the next year and develop a plan in conjunction with your service provider to achieve or exceed this level.

Performance improvements can be expressed in various ways, for example:

- improved user satisfaction as measured by independent surveys;

- more efficient ways of providing specified services;

- useful additions to the contractual service;

- eliminating aspects of the services that are no longer required;

- implementation of new technologies that can provide the services more economically or effectively;

- changes to the interface between your organization and the supplier.

Suggestions for improvements can come from users of the service, perhaps via the help desk, or from the outsourcing management team.

6.7.1 Monitoring

Performance measures are simply a means to an end. All the time and effort the outsourcing programme team will have spent, identifying and defining the measures and reaching agreement with the service provider, will have been wasted unless a proper monitoring system is established to ensure that action is taken when performance falls below standard. Monitoring is essential and performance review procedures should be an integral part of the outsourcing processes. Try to keep the procedures simple and as explicit as possible so that there is no doubt about exactly what is required. Everyone should be able to understand exactly what is expected of him or her. The easier the procedure is, the more likely it is to be carried out. Complex procedures, on the other hand, may lead to confusion and disagreements. Build automatic measurement and monitoring into the day-to-day outsourcing procedures whenever possible and avoid complex and costly manual data collection and analysis. Encourage self-monitoring by your service provider, using periodic checks to verify the accuracy and reliability of the data collection process.

Agree an agenda with your supplier for performance reviews. Once the performance measurement system has been developed, you will need to agree how to use the performance measures on an ongoing basis throughout the life of the contract. To do this you will need to address a series of questions:

- Who will collect and maintain the performance records?
- How can your organization get assurance about the consistency and quality of the performance data collected?
- How will performance be reviewed?
- How frequently will it be reviewed?
- In what forum will it be reviewed?
- Who will be responsible for organizing the reviews?
- Who will be involved, both from your organization and the supplier?
- What will the agenda be?
- When will the first review take place?

Not all aspects of performance are easy to measure and monitor. The service level agreement should clarify how performance standards are to be assessed to avoid misunderstandings that can result in disputes and a loss of confidence in the service management process or the outsourcing programme itself.

It is important that performance monitoring matches the users' perception of the outsourced services. Unfortunately this is often very difficult to achieve. Remember to focus on service outputs rather than inputs. For example, measuring the availability of various servers does not necessarily reflect the level of service delivered to users. Desktop or telecommunications failures also mean that the service is not available as perceived by users. Without monitoring all input components in the end-to-end service (a potentially difficult and costly exercise) a true picture of the service as experienced by users does not emerge.

Many organizations use data collected by the help desk to monitor the users' perception of service quality and availability. If this function has been retained in-house, you may need to review incident logging procedures and records to ensure that the relevant data are available for the outsourced services. The help desk should also monitor incident response times and resolution times. Some amendments may be needed to the applications used by the help desk to capture the relevant data.

For online or Web-based services, transaction response times (the time between sending a message and receiving a response) are also very difficult to measure and monitor. One solution that has been adopted requires users to report any delays above a specified number of seconds to the help desk when they occur. The performance measure is based on the number of such reported incidents. This also helps alert your supplier to potential underlying problems in the outsourced systems. Automated client/server response time monitoring tools are preferred by some organizations and these provide the opportunity to measure or sample actual or very similar response times to those experienced by users.

As we have seen, not all aspects of the performance of outsourced services can be measured with hard data. The users' perception of the standard of service is a very important factor that is not always directly related to the number of service failures. If users perceive that reported incidents are receiving prompt attention and that the service provider is committed to resolving problems without delay, then they may be very satisfied with the level of service they receive. Conversely if there are few service failures but users are ignored or met by an unhelpful response when they seek advice from the outsourcing supplier, then they are likely to be dissatisfied with the level of service.

You will need to monitor measures of user perception of the services through telephone surveys, questionnaires, survey handouts or user group meetings. Targets should be set and monitored over time just as for other performance measures. If users provide input to performance measurement, ensure that they receive feedback and evidence of action taken to resolve any concerns revealed by the surveys.

6.7.2 Service Level Reports

Service level reports should be produced as soon as the contract commences. Performance should be reported against all targets included in the service level agreement. Initially reports may be required daily, weekly and monthly, comparing actual performance to the agreed standards. As the outsourcing relationship develops you may find that you no longer need such frequent reporting but the option should be retained in case you hit a period of poor service levels. Few suppliers will complain about a reduction in reporting requirements, but may well baulk at a request for additional performance reports.

Reports summarizing service performance need to be produced and circulated by the contract management team to participants in the performance reviews a few days in advance of their meetings, so that any queries or disagreements about the results reported can be resolved ahead of the meeting. These summary reports should include details of performance against all key targets, together with information about any trends and actions being taken to improve service quality.

It is not unknown in large outsourcing contracts for 500 or more performance measures to be collected. Even in smaller outsourcing arrangements, the mass of performance data can be overwhelming, especially for users and business managers. Here are a few tips for presenting the performance data in a way in which it can be assimilated readily and used constructively as a tool for achieving higher service levels:

● Use colour coding to indicate areas of particular concern. For example, performance measures can be coded red for serious problems, amber to indicate the performance is heading in the wrong direction and green for perfectly acceptable.

- Focus on trends rather than examining every minor deviation from the required standard. The goal should be to ensure a positive trend towards improvements in those areas that are under-performing. In the reports highlight measures that are stagnating or declining below target.

- Pick out only the most important performance measures in the reports. Continue to collect comprehensive data and keep your selection of key measures under review.

- Be wary of accepting your supplier's standard performance reports. Check that they report performance against agreed service levels; give performance for the current time period; and provide for exception reporting for missed targets and a trend analysis of performance over several time periods.

- Use exception reporting to highlight missed performance standards.

- Produce graphical reports and illustrations whenever possible. While some people prefer to study lists of numbers, many more find it easiest to read pictures with significant elements picked out in colours.

- If reports are produced on paper, use different coloured paper for different sections of the performance report.

6.7.3 Performance Review Meetings

Performance measures are most valuable when they are used to instigate corrective action or service improvements. Performance reviews should be structured to make sure that this happens. The key to a good performance review meeting is to follow a process that enables participants not only to review historical performance achievements and the causes of problems, but also to produce and monitor an appropriate corrective action plan. The action plan should record the:

- service level that requires attention;

- description of the corrective action proposed;

- named individual who will be responsible for taking forward the action (this will usually, but not always, be a member of the supplier's team);

- target completion date (interim target dates are useful where major change is required);

- progress to date.

151

Occasionally it might be decided that the service level was, or has become, unachievable. In this instance it may be necessary to review and agree a modified target.

Review meetings are best held monthly and can usefully be combined with the status meetings described in Chapter 5. This is preferable to a separate meeting since performance monitoring is an integral part of outsourcing management. Attendees should include supplier representatives who "own" or take responsibility for the key performance measures. User representatives may also attend these meetings. The outsourcing management team will, of course, play a major part and will be responsible for preparing the agenda, preparing the action and implementation plans and other records and preparing minutes.

The typical agenda items for a performance review would include:

- review of previous minutes;
- review of progress as recorded in action and implementation plans;
- review of key performance measures and trends;
- proposed new corrective actions.

You will probably find that it takes two or three review meetings before the group begins to focus on the action plan rather than simply reviewing last month's performance. The meeting chair or your contract manager can help steer the discussion in this direction by asking, "What can we do to improve performance?" Do not be too disappointed if the process does not work very well at first. Generally what happens is that the group's understanding of the outsourcing arrangement and the performance review process evolves over time. Initially the supplier's representatives tend to use the meeting as a forum for reporting how well they are doing, while users may emphasize the seriousness of service issues to ensure that they receive urgent attention. If members of the contract management team were previously involved in the formal negotiations that led up to contract signature, they may still be operating in a hostile, adversarial manner. A different approach is needed once the contract is live.

To help the group learn how to get the best out of the performance review process, each owner of performance measure(s) that fail to meet the standard set in the contract should be asked:

- Are we on course to achieve the target?

- If not, what do you propose?

Separate sessions may be required to tackle problems in performance areas that are more difficult to quantify. Some organizations, for example, find that there is a period around the middle of the contract term when user perception of the service provider is poor, regardless of the evidence provided by the performance data. If this happens in your organization, try the following remedies:

- Organize separate performance review meetings to which a wide range of user representatives are invited as well as members of the outsourcing management team and the supplier's team. Explain that this is an opportunity to bring major issues not raised elsewhere to the attention of those working on the outsourced services. Exclude discussion on quantified performance data. A mediator will be needed to ensure that the discussion focuses on problem resolution and the generation of new ideas that are acceptable to all.

- Have both users and supplier teams meet separately to document their perceptions of each other. The teams should then meet to share these perceptions; it is important that each side listens to the other.

- Set up joint teams to address areas of concern or take forward ideas generated by these meetings. Set out a work plan to take these activities forward and add entries to the main performance review action plan.

6.7.4 Service Level Management Problems

Effective service level management will improve communications between your organization and the service provider and speed up resolution of service issues. It will also help your two organizations to share responsibility for problem resolution and to recognize that both parties will, on occasions, make mistakes. The process should also avoid a blame culture in which the supplier's reputation is tarnished at every opportunity. Never forget that the ultimate aim is to improve service levels. Most people want trouble-free IT services, not a poor service and service credits.

As with any other process, service level management does not guarantee success. Here are some of the possible problems:

- Users may have an over-inflated view of the services that were delivered in-house, especially if few performance measures were recorded.

- The supplier may be tempted to agree to service targets to win the outsourcing contract without checking that they are feasible.

- Contractual targets may be ill defined and unworkable.

- The customer organization may not invest sufficient resources and time into the performance review process – it may be seen as a marginal activity.

- The contract manager may have insufficient authority to set up adequate service level management processes.

- The responsibilities assigned to the customer organization and supplier may not be clearly defined, some tasks may not be allocated to either party and no one then takes responsibility for them.

- The performance measures may be IT-based rather than built on business requirements.

- The service level agreement may be too lengthy.

- The service level agreement may not be properly communicated.

- Some members of the customer organization may treat the service level management process primarily as a mechanism for agreeing penalties and service credits, to the detriment of the overall outsourcing relationship.

Recognize these potential difficulties in advance, plan and prepare carefully and make sure that your organization has sufficient resources committed to performance measurement and review.

6.8 Service Level Agreements

Service level agreements are one of the most important components of outsourcing contracts and are a powerful management and communications tool for both customer organization and supplier alike. Derived from the statement of service requirements and including performance measures and reporting requirements, the service level agreements are normally included as schedules to the outsourcing contract. The agreement defines the level of performance that the supplier has contracted to provide and gives the customer organization rights and remedies should the supplier fail to deliver this level of service. It can provide an effective incentive to encourage the supplier to meet the customer organization's objectives for outsourcing.

In defining service levels, the end-to-end performance as experienced by users is key. There is little value in having one excellent service component if another falls significantly below standard. For example, no matter how excellent an Intranet site, it will be viewed as a poor service if the network links are poor. In business terms, the service can only be as strong as its weakest link. Service level agreements are not so much about technology as about the business. The risk or cost of poor service needs to be assessed by the business users, not the IT department.

The specified service levels must be clear, unambiguous and precise. For example, is the Intranet service "available" if the server is operational but the local network links are not working? Is it "available" when some Web pages have been changed and are functioning incorrectly? Unless the service levels are defined precisely, you will not have a proper agreement: differences of interpretation and confusion could well lead to disputes with your supplier. Other reasons for preparing a comprehensive service level agreement include:

- It helps demonstrate the performance achieved by the outsourced services.

- Service levels are guaranteed as far as possible.

- By involving users in the compilation and review of the service level agreement, you can ensure that the outsourced services meet user demands.

- It aids the measurement and assessment of the outsourced services.

- The level of service that can be expected from the outsourced services is clarified and this helps foster realistic expectations.

- Compliance with external standards, such as the ISO 9001 quality management standards, can be specified.

Once service level agreements have been finalized it is important that the agreed service levels and targets are widely disseminated at operational level within your organization and in the supplier's organization. Without this knowledge throughout both organizations, the service level agreement cannot be used actively to maintain or improve service levels. All staff should be clear on what is expected of them so that they can work towards service targets and be made aware of any penalties that will apply should the standards not be reached.

Try to avoid a multiplicity of interrelated performance measures and service levels that only a few people fully understand. Remember that the service level agreement needs to be well understood by all those working on the outsourced services and to reflect business service needs. Keep things simple and focus on the core user requirements.

Service level agreements need to be kept up to date. They should be formally reviewed on a regular basis, such as annually, to ensure that they continue to meet business needs and the outsourcing objectives. Changes may be requested at any time and should be handled through the normal change control process.

6.8.1 Service Level Agreement Structure

Unless you are outsourcing one simple, self-contained IT service, you will probably find that you need a series of service level agreements covering different services or different uses of the same system. Begin by deciding how these can best be structured to make them easy to understand, to use and to modify. You may decide to have one service level agreement for each service – but remember that different users may have different requirements for response times, management information, problem resolution times and so on. An alternative approach might be to compile a service level agreement for each major group of users, which will probably be welcomed by the users but may be unworkable and confusing for your supplier.

Some organizations use a multi-level service level agreement structure that combines the service-based and customer-based formats:

- A top level corporate or framework service level agreement, covering generic performance standards and measures that are relevant to all users and outsourced IT services. This service level agreement is relatively stable and requires few changes.

- A customer level agreement that relates to all services provided to a specified group of users.

- A service level agreement relating to a specific group of users and covering one outsourced service.

This approach may be helpful if you are dealing with a range of outsourced services. But do aim for simplicity, keep all individual service level agreements to a manageable size and avoid unnecessary duplica-

156

tion so that the documents can be readily understood and do not all need frequent updates.

6.8.2 Sample Service Level Agreement Contents

Service level agreements should be clear and concise; there is no need for legal terminology. Have someone who is not closely involved review draft documents to help spot ambiguities. The list below gives examples of the main topics to be covered in a service level agreement:

- Introduction
  - Name of service and very brief description
  - Scope of agreement
  - Names of parties to the agreement
  - Start and end dates
  - Links to other service level agreements
- Description of service
  - Outline of service
  - Roles and responsibilities of users and supplier
  - Description of user groups
  - Role in business strategy
- Availability
  - Hours and days of the week
  - Holiday arrangements
  - Special extension arrangements
  - Availability targets such as maximum downtime permitted
- Levels of use
  - Anticipated volume of use
  - Volume ranges, where different charges apply to different volumes of use
  - Forecast trends during life of contract

- Support
  - Help desk and other support services
  - Support hours
  - Response time and clear up rate targets
  - Targets for reducing the number and severity of reported incidents
  - Problem escalation procedures
- Security and contingency
  - Security functions provided
  - Compliance with recognized standards such as ITSEC accreditation
  - Disaster recovery and contingency plans including testing arrangements
  - Contingency targets
- Outputs
  - General service products
  - Management information reports
  - Performance reports (content, frequency and distribution)
- Responsiveness
  - Transaction response time targets
  - Problem resolution targets
  - Targets for processing change requests
- Charging
  - Invoicing procedures and targets
  - Payment terms (note that actual charges may be listed in a separate contract schedule for ease of use and confidentiality reasons)
- Penalties and service credits
  - Criteria that trigger penalty payments or service credits
  - Procedures for making penalty payments or making service credits
- Interfaces

- ○ Specifications of links between this service and the services provided by other suppliers

- ○ Procedures for resolving disputes between suppliers over causes of service failures

- Performance review

  - ○ Schedule and targets for user satisfaction surveys

  - ○ Frequency and type of performance review meetings

  - ○ Timetable and procedures for reviewing the service level agreement

- Amendment sheet

  - ○ Record of agreed modifications with dates

6.9 Managing Multiple Suppliers

As the use of outsourcing in the provision of IT services has grown over recent years, an increasing number of organizations have chosen to outsource different IT activities to different computer services companies. There are three main reasons driving the trend towards the use of multiple suppliers:

1. Organizations are concerned not to become overly dependent on a single supplier to the extent that they lose flexibility and a degree of control over their IT activities.

2. Smaller, specialist outsourcing companies have emerged, often focused on new technologies. These suppliers are able to offer expertise and innovation that is not always readily available from the larger more established computer services companies.

3. Increasingly, globalization is leading many companies to set up operations in other countries. New business units need to be set up fast to keep pace with a rapidly changing market place. Even the larger outsourcing companies may not be able to offer services in all continents and organizations are finding that local or regional computer or telecommunications services companies can offer the best outsourced services to meet local business needs.

The management of outsourcing relationships with multiple suppliers, especially the measurement and monitoring of service levels, presents a number of challenges:

- Not all outsourcing suppliers are happy to work alongside other computer services companies. They prefer to act as sole supplier, sub-contracting activities as necessary to bring in specialist skills. Getting such companies to work together can be very difficult.

- Some customer organizations maintain a degree of competition between multiple suppliers in order to encourage innovation and competitive pricing for new project work. As a result, these suppliers will focus on achieving good results on "their" performance measures, potentially to the detriment of the service delivered to users.

- Supplier selection will need to take account not only of the culture fit between your organization and each supplier but also between the different suppliers that need to work together. This needs to be examined in the context of your organization's IT activities – outsourcing companies work well with each other in some instances and badly in others.

- The key concern above all others to your organization is the level of service provided to users. Too much time and energy can be wasted on resolving disputes between suppliers and arguments about who is responsible for service failures.

- You will need to provide users with a single contact for queries and problem resolution for each service. This generally means giving one supplier overall responsibility for managing the help desk; incident monitoring and reporting; and problem escalation.

Performance measures and service level agreements need to be developed for each outsourcing relationship. The techniques adopted to manage multiple suppliers include:

- Identify one service provider to act as lead supplier, responsible for co-ordinating the activities of all suppliers, operating the help desk and reporting on performance.

- Alternatively, structure the outsourcing deals in such a way that the suppliers are mutually dependent on each other for the success (or failure) of their business with your organization. For example, share benefits delivered through outsourcing between the suppliers and if services fail to meet targets share the penalty payments too. (This is likely to be very difficult to achieve in practice.)

- Set various IT standards and common processes (for example project management techniques, planning tools, change control process, systems analysis methodologies, quality management standards) with which all outsourcing suppliers have to comply. These will form part of all service level agreements.

- Encourage a shared understanding of the overall objectives and direction of your organization's sourcing strategy by holding quarterly meetings to which all suppliers are invited.

Developing excellent relationships and establishing effective performance measurement systems are probably more demanding where multiple outsourcing suppliers are used. The most practical approach is possibly to minimize the interfaces and dependencies between suppliers. In any event you will need to set up effective contract management processes for each supplier and recognize the resource implications of this activity.

Risks and Controls 7

7.1 Introduction

Outsourcing can be a risky business. Certainly IT outsourcing can deliver improved services, quicker adoption of new technologies and reduced operating costs. But it can also result in unforeseen charges that exceed any possible cost savings; it can lead to stagnation and delays in implementing new services; and it can result in a loss of control over IT activities.

Control and risk mitigation are therefore central concerns if IT outsourcing is to succeed. In Chapter 5 we looked at the role contract management plays in maintaining control over outsourced operations and managing potential risks. We now consider the other major control mechanism – the outsourcing contract. Your legal department or other legal advisors will clearly play a major role in the construction of the outsourcing contract, but in this chapter we provide a general overview of the contract contents to illustrate the topics that need to be covered and offer guidance on the issues that commonly arise in IT outsourcing.

We then look more generally at the risks commonly found in outsourcing initiatives, countermeasures that might be put in place and risk management techniques.

7.2 Outsourcing Contracts

A contract can be defined as an agreement enforceable at law for services (or goods) in return for a consideration. Outsourcing contracts should be structured to meet the objectives of both sides. The deal should be carefully balanced with neither side significantly disadvantaged.

One-sided contracts rarely last: customers will look for ways out of unfavourable deals and suppliers may lose enthusiasm and commitment if the agreement is heavily weighted in favour of the customer. Faced with an unduly demanding agreement, suppliers will look for ways of covering their financial risk or reducing their costs; they prefer no surprises and minimal risk.

The outsourcing contract should be expressed in clear and precise terms. It should unambiguously define the scope of IT activities to be outsourced, the roles and responsibilities of customer and supplier, dispute resolution procedures, remedies, targets and performance measures. It should specify payment terms and mechanisms for problem and issue management and change control. To create a truly effective contract you will need to bear in mind the way in which companies behave in response to formal agreements and how groups of people from different organizations work together and tackle problems. The customer looks to the supplier to meet its service expectations, while the supplier has to make a profit. Everyone needs to know what is being provided, at what cost and to what standard. Both sides need an acceptable mechanism for handling changes to existing services and the introduction of new services. The more carefully this is set out in detail, the less room there is for dispute and the more likely it is that the customer organization will remain in control throughout the life of the contract. The level of detail required in an outsourcing contract often results in very lengthy legal documents.

The word "partnership" is used frequently in discussions about outsourcing. In one sense "partnership" captures the flavour of the ideal relationship between customer organization and supplier in which the interests of both parties are equally balanced and there is mutual trust and respect. In this chapter, however, when we look at the legal outsourcing agreement, we will not use the term "partnership". The outsourcing deal is not a genuine legal partnership, in other words a business in which two or more partners invest, share the profits and risk losing their assets should the business go bankrupt.

The closest outsourcing model to a partnership is the joint venture initiative in which the customer organization and outsourcing service provider set up a new business. Both companies invest in the new business, both are at risk from an operating loss and both share any profits. Neither party can easily withdraw from the new business without suffering financially or commercially. Both organizations therefore need to be committed to its success. This arrangement is relatively rare.

Normal outsourcing contracts need to recognize that the two parties are separate, independent organizations. If the supplier is, for example, granted authority to negotiate software licences and hardware contracts, the outsourcing agreement should clearly state whether the supplier is doing so in its own name or on behalf of the customer organization.

We have referred to the outsourcing contract as a key control mechanism but there are other reasons for investing time and effort in preparing and negotiating a comprehensive legal agreement:

- The process of preparing, discussing and seeking agreement about the outsourcing contract with the service provider helps clarify expectations and develop true understanding between the two organizations. There will probably never be a better time to tackle and resolve tricky issues. Both parties are keen to conclude a favourable deal and will, therefore, be more likely to make concessions or consider alternative solutions. If your organization cannot reach an amicable deal with the service provider at this stage, how much harder it will be when disputes arise after the contract is signed. It is much better to discover any major hurdles before the deal is finally agreed.

- The contract framework provides a useful structure for the negotiations.

- Throughout its life, the outsourcing contract acts as a useful reference document, defining in detail agreed charging methods, payment mechanisms, reporting procedures, service level benchmarks and so on.

- The outsourcing contract is an important risk management tool. Effective issue management and dispute resolution processes, written into the contract, help both parties find solutions to problems relatively quickly and inexpensively. This also helps prevent small difficulties escalating into major issues.

- By defining rights and responsibilities when the agreement terminates, the contract provides helpful direction at what can be a difficult time. This is important to protect the interests of both parties, particularly if there have been major disputes.

- Ultimately the outsourcing contract protects your organization against loss and damage. If, despite your best endeavours, the services provided by the outsourcing supplier are poor and the relationship between your two organizations deteriorates, a good contract is vital to defend your organization's interests.

We have seen here that the outsourcing contract is critically important. It is far more than a dry legal document that is a burdensome necessity, which is put away and forgotten about the moment it is signed. While an outsourcing relationship that is working well will rarely need to refer to the detail of the contract, it would be a serious mistake to be lulled into a false sense of security before an outsourcing agreement is signed. Naturally, everyone will be aiming to please at this stage and some may suggest that a detailed contract is not needed or even that it can be discussed at a later stage once the main agreement is signed. Experience has shown all too often that this is not a wise move. Successful IT outsourcing depends on comprehensive, detailed contractual agreements.

7.2.1 Memorandum of Understanding

The first document to be signed by the customer organization and supplier, especially in large outsourcing deals, is known as a Memorandum of Understanding (MOU). This is a statement of intent rather than a legal document and it sets out in general, rather than detailed terms, broad objectives. Effectively it expresses both parties' commitment to proceeding to conclude a deal. It provides, therefore, a degree of reassurance to both organizations before they commit the resources required to negotiate and agree a detailed outsourcing contract. The MOU indicates the scope and length of contract envisaged and the broad principles that will apply to known difficult areas. Discussions at this stage may show that it will be impossible to conclude a satisfactory outsourcing deal – a much quicker and cheaper way of identifying this fact than more formal, legal negotiations.

Although it is not legally binding, the MOU should not be signed lightly. It should be drafted carefully to avoid inadvertent and unwanted commitments. The document is normally 4–20 pages long. It will usually indicate that it is "subject to contract" and also dependent on the involvement of third parties, for example to transfer software licences to the supplier. The MOU may also include a binding non-disclosure agreement to protect confidential data that might be exchanged during contract negotiations.

The MOU may alternatively be known as "heads of terms", "heads of agreement" or "letter of intent". It can be a useful device for keeping your management board informed, avoiding early misunderstandings, clarifying the way forward and identifying possible areas of contention. But do look out for the possibility that a MOU is requested simply in anticipation of the sales representative's commission.

7.2.2 Contract Structure

The outsourcing contract can be structured in a number of different ways. Which format you choose will depend to a large extent on the purchasing and legal policies within your organization. What follows describes one model format for an agreement covering the transfer of IT services to an outsourcing supplier with the associated hardware, applications and telecommunications and the transfer of staff who support the services within your organization.

The contract is structured into two major parts:

1. Main clauses that include general terms and conditions governing the rights, powers and obligations of both customer and supplier and general statements about the services to be provided, assets to be transferred and staff who will move to the outsourcing supplier.

2. Schedules (or annexure or appendices), which are discrete documents providing detailed information on specific topics. The schedules are legally binding and will include the service level agreements, detailed transition plans, information on asset sales and detailed employee information.

You will need to consider all the mechanisms, features, risks and skills that will be involved in providing the outsourced services and translate them into:

- commercial arrangements such as pricing, committed levels of use, benchmarking and indexation;
- contract terms including duration, change control, dispute resolution and liabilities;
- management processes such as contract management, auditing, open book accounting and benefits management.

The ability to cope with change is a vital feature. Obviously it is not possible to construct an infinitely variable deal, but you can identify principles and processes defining how your organization and the service provider will deal with change.

7.2.3 Contract Main Clauses

General Terms and Conditions

The contract terms and conditions set out the rights, obligations and duties of each party. They may be preceded by an introduction that identifies the contracting parties, describes the business context of the outsourcing deal and lists the objectives. Although these are not legally binding, they do provide a useful reminder about the background to the outsourcing initiative and its aims.

There will be a number of standard clauses, which your organization's legal department will probably provide. These will cover topics such as publicity; corrupt gifts (or illegal inducements); transfer and subcontracting (the supplier would not usually be allowed to assign the outsourcing contract to a third party). Other general terms and conditions are described below.

Contract Duration

You will need to specify the contract term and include a reference to any agreed break points. A termination date can be fixed or the contract can be specified to run continuously until a notice period (normally of at least one year) is served. It is common to specify a minimum period before which notice will not be served.

There are a number of factors to take into account when considering the duration of the contract:

- Longer contracts (5 years and more)
  - Provide stability and continuity.
  - Generally offer greater savings overall.
  - Encourage more innovation from service providers if they see a longer pay back period.
  - Can lead to a loss of flexibility and inability to respond to business opportunities as technology changes.
  - May make the supplier complacent and less responsive to your organization's needs.
  - Can make your organization over-reliant on the service provider.
- Shorter contracts (less than 5 years)

- Help prevent your organization becoming tied to one supplier.
- Enable your organization to respond more quickly to significant shifts in IT service requirements.
- May attract less commitment from suppliers.
- Provide less scope for innovation.
- Can be more costly, especially if transition costs are significant.

As a safeguard, the contract can provide for an extension to give your organization the option to purchase outsourced services on the same terms or at reasonable charges for a certain number of months beyond the specified termination date. The supplier should continue to respect your organization's security and confidentiality rights after the formal termination date.

Contract Termination

The outsourcing agreement should set down the procedures and rules for either party that wants at some point in the future to terminate the contract. In circumstances where the contract has satisfactorily run its full term (or the full notice period is served) it will be important that everything is in place to ensure a smooth transition to a new contract with the same supplier, a move to an alternative supplier or taking the IT services back in-house.

The outsourcing contract should cover the following:

- Roles and responsibilities during termination.
- Who pays what costs.
- Return of assets and updated documentation.
- Arrangements for your organization to purchase any new assets acquired by the supplier solely to support the outsourced services.
- Reassignment of associated contracts, leases, software licences and intellectual property rights.
- Support and assistance to be provided by the supplier during termination.
- Preparation of the exit plans.
- Access to the supplier's premises to ensure that service levels are maintained throughout a possible transfer to another service provider.

169

- Your organization's right to call for an independent audit.

- The supplier's agreement to provide without additional charge any information reasonably required by the auditor.

- Training for in-house staff or staff from the new supplier who will be responsible for the outsourced services.

- Agreement that, subject to certain constraints, the new supplier or your own organization can approach key staff working on the outsourced services at contract termination, and possibly recruit them.

In the UK, Intellect's (previously the Computer Software and Services Association's) Code of Practice requires suppliers to provide all reasonable assistance when a contract is terminated so that the provision of services can be transferred back to the customer organization or to any nominated third party. If your supplier is a member of Intellect, compliance with this Code of Practice should be specified in the contract.

There will be circumstances where either the customer organization or supplier will want, or need, to terminate the outsourcing contract before it has run its full term. For example, one organization might be acquired by another company or might go bankrupt; or the services may consistently fail to reach agreed performance levels; or service requirements might fundamentally change. The contract should describe the process to be adopted should either party want to unilaterally terminate the contract and will need to cover:

- Notice periods to be given in different circumstances.

- Period to be allowed for the supplier to remedy faults where service levels have fallen to an unacceptable level.

- Period to be allowed for the customer organization to remedy any failure on their side of the deal such as not paying for satisfactory services within agreed timescales.

- Who pays what transition costs (where this differs from arrangements for termination at the end of the contract term).

- Compensation payments to be made.

The detailed termination procedures should be negotiated and agreed at the beginning of the outsourcing relationship, preferably before the contract is signed and certainly before the end of the first year of the agreement, when both customer organization and supplier are confidently looking forward to the success of the outsourcing initiative. Should the relationship deteriorate at a later stage, the termination arrangements are already documented and in place to protect both parties' interests. Experienced suppliers should have little difficulty in tackling these issues. They will have been in situations both where they have won outsourcing contracts from another supplier and where they have lost a contract to one of their competitors. Inexperienced or new service providers may feel threatened by discussions about contract termination but should be encouraged to see that it is in their interests too to agree arrangements for the end of the outsourcing agreement.

Change Control

A key issue in outsourcing contracts is the need to ensure that the agreement is sufficiently flexible to be able to absorb changes in IT service requirements. This can be addressed in the contract in various ways such as:

- allowing for fluctuations in service volumes and performance levels over time;

- specifying minimum technology refresh requirements, particularly in contracts covering technical infrastructure;

- providing for access to resources and facilities in the wider supplier organization, beyond the scope of the initial service requirements;

- including costed options for possible future requirements (a balance needs to be made between the effort of agreeing precise contractual terms and the likelihood of taking up the option).

To be able to cope with unforeseen changes, the contract should define a change control process. A contract clause should specify that both customer and supplier are required to comply with the change control principles with details given in a contract schedule.

Change control should protect the interests of both parties and should ensure that the organization with the stronger bargaining position (usually the supplier) does not abuse this situation. The change control process should also define procedures and timescales for commencing and conducting contract change negotiations. Further information about the change control process is given in Chapter 5.

Watch out for "change of character" clauses that might be proposed by suppliers. These will state that customers will be charged for any substantial change in functionality. You will need to consider very carefully what amounts to a substantial change, what excess charges this might trigger and what is included in the supplier's baseline fee. Some organizations have found that they have incurred significant additional charges for what they regarded as straightforward changes in service requirements.

Audit Rights

Outsourcing is the transfer of an internal IT service function to an outside service provider but the customer organization is still obliged to keep track of its resources and how they are used. Audit rights are therefore included in the outsourcing contract to guarantee the customer's auditor access to the supplier's records. The contract usually requires the supplier to provide regular performance reports to the customer on a range of relevant topics such as service use and user satisfaction. These constitute a self-assessment by the supplier of its performance. To ensure that the customer can have confidence in the reports, the contract states that the customer has the right to audit the supplier's record-keeping and reporting procedures.

Where open book accounting has been adopted, the customer's auditors require access to sufficient financial records and processes to be able to verify the data.

The objectives of the audit are typically:

● to review the performance data integrity and validity;
● to verify the quality of services received;
● to review the assets supporting the outsourced services such as hardware, data, applications and documentation;
● to validate the supplier's billing data and practices;
● to verify general contractual compliance.

There may be difficulties negotiating and managing appropriate audit rights. One potential problem is that the customer's auditors may not have the technical expertise to provide independent observations on the supplier's IT environment. Another issue is the sensitivity of the data stored on the supplier's computers. It may not be possible to offer access to one customer without compromising the security of data belonging to other customers.

Confidentiality and Data Protection

The contract should ensure that any commercially sensitive information is protected. Outsourcing is a particularly close form of relationship between the customer and supplier organizations, which potentially gives either party access to the other's confidential information including:

- private details about the customer organization's staff, for example where the payroll system is outsourced;
- sensitive business information belonging to the customer;
- information that might affect the customer organization's share price, such as acquisition plans;
- sensitive commercial data from the supplier that the customer requires, such as future business plans and costs given in open book accounting arrangements.

The contract should require both parties to keep each other's information confidential and ensure that their staff, contractors and advisors do likewise. The information should be held securely whether held on paper or in electronic form. The only exceptions are information already in the public domain, such as company annual reports; and information that must be revealed by law, such as in a court case.

Special provisions relate to "personal data", which is defined as data held about living, identifiable individuals, and has to be treated with greater care than other kinds of data. In the UK, data protection legislation places obligations on "data users" who record and hold personal data. Data users have to be registered on the Data Protection Register and follow the principles set out in the legislation to ensure that personal data is held, processed and used properly, fairly and lawfully and that there are adequate procedures in place for keeping it secure. The data users should also ensure that those accessing data are authorized to do so, for legitimate purposes. Organizations whose business depends on personal data such as financial services, and any organization that outsources payroll or other personnel systems, needs to be confident that the contract contains sufficient security assurances to protect personal data.

Security Provisions

The supplier may be asked to give a contractual commitment to complying with the customer's security procedures. An overview of the security rules and regulations should be included in a contract clause with details given in a schedule. Clearly more rigorous security procedures can mean higher costs but companies must meet legal requirements for the protection of company data.

The outsourcing contract may also include a clause requiring the supplier to meet external security standards such as the purchase and use of security products certified under a recognized scheme such as:

- The ITSEC scheme (Information Technology Security Evaluation Criteria), which is recognized throughout Europe. The security features of these products are tested independently of the suppliers to identify logical vulnerabilities. This testing is known as security evaluation and is carried out against standardized criteria to a formalized methodology. The UK, France, Germany, Australia and New Zealand issue ITSEC certificates.

- The CC (Common Criteria) scheme, which has been ratified as ISO 15408. The USA, Canada, Australia, New Zealand, France, Germany and the UK issue CC certificates.

The outsourcing supplier should provide a statement on its security provisions for inclusion in a contract schedule. This document should set out the supplier's security policy and procedures for allocating responsibility for information security and for educating staff about security matters. The schedule should also detail contingency planning and disaster recovery procedures to ensure that normal services can be restored as soon as possible following a system failure. There should be provision for testing the contingency plans.

Managing Poor Performance

The contract should include financial remedies or penalties for poor performance. You should consider carefully how to address unsatisfactory performance and what remedies to seek. Such penalties can have an unforeseen negative impact on the outsourcing relationship, incurring high monitoring costs and leading the supplier to seek to cover the costs of potential penalties in their contract prices. There will be different kinds of IT service failure and the remedies need to take into account the nature and severity of the failure and its outcome, the speed and effectiveness of the resolution and whether this is an isolated incident or common occurrence. The overall aims should be to address minor faults without delay and encourage good performance so as to prevent major failures and the breakdown in confidence in the supplier. Clearly, terminating the contract is a drastic solution that should only be adopted as a final resort.

Penalties for poor performance can include:

- Cash penalties, which will motivate the supplier to perform satisfactorily as long as cost centre management within the supplier's organization links the cash payment to the section responsible for the poor outsourced services. These penalties do not necessarily fully compensate the customer for the consequences of the poor IT service.

- Service credits derived from the accumulation of points awarded for contract service level breaches. Points are allocated according to the severity and importance of the service failure.

The contract should also specify agreed escalation procedures so that faults can be remedied as quickly and as efficiently as possible. Problems should be referred to increasingly senior levels of management in both customer and supplier organizations where difficulties prevent fast resolution.

Be alert to the possibility that sometimes your own organization may be at fault and may cause the service failure. Suppliers may request that the responsibility for each missed service performance level is determined. This protects the supplier's interests. Since it is contractually bound to meet service requirements, it should not be punished for the customer organization's errors.

The general principles of the agreed penalties should be stated in a contract clause with detailed processes including the escalation procedures, covered in a schedule.

A standard contract clause, which will normally appear in all outsourcing agreements, relates to "force majeure". This term refers to causes beyond the reasonable control of either party, which result in failure to meet contractual commitments. Your organization's legal department probably has a standard form of words to be used in all contracts. In legal terms, a service delay or failure during the contract's operation due to reasons of force majeure does not constitute "frustration" (a contract is said to be "frustrated" if it becomes impossible for the contractual obligations to be performed). To protect either party from being liable, many contracts include a standard provision that suspends the agreement during force majeure conditions. The contract may also give either

175

party the right to terminate if the force majeure situation continues for a specified period, say 90 days.

You may find different opinions about which causes are force majeure, in other words beyond reasonable control. Most organizations would accept freak weather conditions and terrorist activities as outside the control of both customer and supplier. But can the same be said for industrial disputes, or staff absences through illness? If the supplier provides contingency planning and disaster recovery services, are there any causes that could constitute force majeure and that should relieve the supplier of the contractual commitment to continue to provide the outsourced services?

Warranties

Specific obligations made by customer or supplier to confirm their level of commitment to the outsourcing deal are included as warranties. For example, the supplier might commit to providing suitably skilled and qualified representatives to support the outsourced services while the customer might give guarantees about the standard of the computer equipment transferred to the supplier. Warranties are contract terms that are less important in principle than contract conditions. It is not necessary to specify in the contract which terms are warranties.

A contract condition is of primary importance and if not met the whole outsourcing deal is fundamentally affected. The contract is said to be "repudiated" and the injured party may claim damages. A breach of a warranty given by one party to the contract also entitles the other party to claim damages if they suffer a quantifiable loss as a result.

Limitation of Liability

When two parties have signed a contract, and one party breaches the agreement causing damage to the other party, the perpetrator is generally liable for these damages. This includes economic loss such as lost profits. The two parties can agree, however, to cap this liability contractually. We know that IT service failure can lead to significant economic loss. But the risk of liability for substantial damages effectively represents a cost to the outsourcing supplier and this is directly reflected in the professional indemnity insurance premiums it must pay. The supplier may therefore want to use the contract to limit its liability to a reasonable level compatible with the scope and nature of the IT services provided. In particular, the supplier will want to ensure that it is not held responsible for any service failures that it has not caused, such as errors made by users or other suppliers.

Normally the supplier aims to minimize liability for any of its activities while the customer looks for compensation for all its losses and liabilities arising from a breach of the agreement. Inevitably the contract must represent a compromise between these two extremes. The customer organization may have to look to its own insurance to cover losses over a certain level or it may consider sharing the costs of the supplier's insurance. Remember, however, that your organization as the customer should not be contemplating an outsourcing contract unless it is confident in its choice of supplier. A claim for breach of contract should only be made as a last resort.

The limit placed on supplier liability under the contract should be justifiable on the basis of the type of IT service provided, the level of risk to either party, insurance cover, the value and importance of the contract and the level of the supplier's turnover. It is not satisfactory simply to limit liability to the value of the contract – from the customer's perspective, the risk is not necessarily directly related to the price being paid.

Where the supplier has staff based permanently on the customer's premises, the supplier and customer may agree to split the liability for injury or illness caused by working at the site. A common approach to health and safety matters helps in this instance.

Indemnities

A contract indemnity defines the compensation payable for something lost or suffered and is particularly relevant to the purchase of strategically important services such as outsourced IT services. Either party may offer indemnities for specific circumstances and they are often subject to upper financial limits.

For losses to be recoverable by compensation, they must either arise naturally from the breach of the contract or must be losses that could reasonably be anticipated by both parties to occur if contract performance fails. The customer must advise the supplier during negotiations of probable losses should the contract be breached in various ways. It is up to the customer to recognize in advance what the risks would be if the contract failed and to communicate these to the supplier.

Note that the level of compensation payable may have significant consequences for the overall cost of the contract. The supplier has to recognize the risk that compensation payments may have to be made and take account of this factor in contract pricing.

Supplier's Financial Viability

The customer organization carries the risk that the chosen service provider might go out of business during the contract term. If the supplier ceases trading altogether, this can have very serious implications for the outsourced IT services. In the computer industry we have seen that this can happen with little warning and affects both large and small companies. It is worth remembering that many IT service companies own very few hard, tangible assets. Cash flow can be jeopardized if, say, two major contracts are terminated at the same time.

The contract can provide some protection by establishing procedures to help the customer spot possible future financial problems. The supplier can be required to provide copies of financial reports, business plans, details of any pending court cases or lawsuits. Prior knowledge of difficulties at least helps the customer to put contingency measures in place.

Dispute Resolution

The first objective should be to structure the outsourcing arrangement in such a way as to minimize the likelihood of disputes arising. Frequent liaison meetings, objective performance measures and realistic service levels all help. The contract should also include carefully structured dispute resolution procedures. Approach this topic as if you already had a dispute with the supplier and aim for clear responsibilities and remedies. There should be a number of steps to be taken before legal proceedings are contemplated. Taking disputes to the courts is inevitably expensive, can damage the reputation of one or both parties and is not guaranteed to give a satisfactory outcome for either organization.

Alternative ways of resolving disputes include service credits for poor performance, reference to external auditors and informal dispute resolution procedures. There is further discussion on this subject in Chapter 8.

Experienced legal advisors can draw on past events and draft contracts to help devise appropriate dispute resolution processes. Senior management in both customer and supplier organizations should endorse the procedures.

7.2.4 Service Provision

Service Description

The main contract clauses should give an outline of the IT services to be provided with detail included in schedules. The services should be described in output terms where possible, giving the supplier the flexibility and opportunity to be innovative in the way in which the services are delivered. This section of the contract can be based on the statement of service requirements prepared earlier in the outsourcing programme (see Chapter 4).

The following topics should be addressed in the contract:

- service outputs required;
- optional, but fully specified services, for which prices have been negotiated;
- additional, unspecified services, which should be kept to a minimum and should require written authorization from the customer before the supplier incurs costs;
- transition plans;
- quality plans;
- timescales for the implementation of new technology;
- plans for infrastructure upgrades during the contract term;
- back-up procedures;
- complaints procedures and problem management processes.

Contract Management

The agreement needs to genuinely empower the staff who are responsible for making outsourcing work. The contract should specify:

- agreed performance measures;
- the performance reports to be delivered by the supplier;
- the contract management teams to be set up by both customer and supplier and their locations;
- the structure and frequency of contract management meetings involving both organizations;

179

- roles and responsibilities, identifying appropriate levels of authorization for various activities.

Charges and Charging Structure

Precise charging formulae, tax issues and detailed invoicing procedures should be included in a schedule with a general statement in the main contract. The supplier may require certain guarantees – remember that the contract will have been priced on the basis of the statement of service requirements and other information provided by the customer organization. The supplier may want to check the accuracy of information including financial statements it has been given either before the contract is signed in a due diligence exercise or through a post-contract verification review.

Keep in mind that suppliers often make most profits in the later years of the outsourcing contract.

Invoicing and payment procedures should be clearly laid out in the contract. The customer organization will want to ensure that it is properly charged only for those services that have been satisfactorily delivered. The customer will also look for a smooth, orderly process with minimum invoice handling costs. The contract should prescribe the invoice format and frequency; define where invoices should be sent and deadlines for invoice issue each month or quarter. Procedures should be set down indicating how the customer will deal with valid invoices, specifying a set period for invoice queries and describing how disputes will be handled.

You will need to anticipate likely growth (or reduction) in demand for the IT services and how this might impact on the outsourcing contract. Larger service volumes might reduce unit costs and the customer could share this benefit with the supplier. Similarly unit processing costs generally decrease over time and this could be reflected in contract prices. Conversely, a decrease in service volumes could lead to higher unit charges. Note that experienced service providers might have a more detailed understanding of these unit cost fluctuations than your organization.

Charges may also need to be adjusted to reflect business changes. The contract should include a clause covering major volume adjustments caused by company acquisitions, mergers or the sale of business units. The supplier may seek a substantial notice period and transition fee for a significant service volume change.

7.2.5 Asset Transfers

All assets that form part of the outsourcing deal, including computer hardware, telecommunications equipment, third party contracts and software licences, must be identified and listed or described in the outsourcing contract. Details should be included in contract schedules. IT services often depend on external providers such as hardware leasing companies, maintenance contractors, leased circuit providers and software companies.

Obtaining the agreement of each of these third parties before the IT service is outsourced can be a lengthy and tricky job so it pays to start as early as possible in the outsourcing process. Third parties will not have the same commercial incentives or sense of urgency as your organization and the outsourcing supplier. If it proves impossible to complete this process before the contract is signed, it may have to be finished during transition. The contract will then be implemented in stages, each step subject to gaining agreement from the appropriate third parties. This is clearly not an ideal approach and runs the risk of never being completed.

Since your organization has all the relevant information about third party contracts, you are probably in the best position to take the lead. You will need to decide with your supplier who is going to pay the costs of obtaining consent from the third parties and what might be done if one or more of these organizations legitimately refuse to give their consent.

From the supplier's perspective, they cannot assume that all existing agreements between your organization and third parties are satisfactory. Before the assets are transferred, therefore, the supplier should undertake a due diligence exercise, closely examining the third party contracts, identifying risk and potential future costs such as insurance premiums.

Hardware Transfers

The contract should specify hardware assets that will transfer to the outsourcing supplier and those that will be retained by the customer organization. The two parties need to agree and set down in the contract which of their organizations carries the risks associated with equipment renewal and fitness for purpose. These factors will be important when it comes to dividing up the assets when the agreement is finally terminated.

181

The assets can be sold to the supplier and then leased back to the customer organization. The structure of such leases raises significant legal issues and has complex tax and accounting implications. Alternatively, the charges raised for outsourced services can be formulated to cover the costs of hardware used to support the function.

Software Developed by Your Organization or the Supplier

Software is a form of intellectual property – it cannot be seen or touched and it comes into existence through creative effort. The right to own and use software in support of IT services is valuable but can easily be overlooked.

A licence should be granted formally to the supplier to use any software created by your organization and used to provide the outsourced services. The licence should be included in the outsourcing contract. Your organization needs to decide whether to protect its intellectual property rights in the software once the supplier starts to enhance, modify or otherwise change the application to meet future requirements. Care is needed, since copyright law can give ownership to the originator of the changes regardless of who pays for the modifications to be made. Special provision must be made in the outsourcing contract if your organization is to retain ownership of the updated software.

An alternative approach is to leave the ownership of the updated software with the supplier in return for other benefits such as reduced contract prices. In this instance it would be important to retain the right to use the software either within your organization or to transfer this right to a different outsourcing service provider should you decide to change suppliers in the future.

If your supplier's own proprietary software is used to support the outsourced services, over time this is likely to become indispensable. The outsourcing contract should include a clause licensing your organization to use the supplier's software, ideally permitting use of the software beyond the end of the current outsourcing contract and by a future service provider.

To provide access to software once the outsourcing is terminated and to protect your organization's interests should the supplier go out of business, an "escrow" (or source code deposit) agreement can be negotiated. A copy of the source code is deposited with a neutral third party custodian for release only in certain situations as defined in the "escrow" agreement. The supplier's proprietary software and software developed specifically for your organization should be covered by "escrow" agreements incorporated in the outsourcing contract.

Software Developed by Third Parties

You will need to be sure that software transferred to the supplier with the outsourced services is correctly licensed for use and that ownership is clearly defined. Commercial software developers and distributors do not rely on basic copyright law in marketing and supplying their software. They expect customers and end users to enter into contractual arrangements for the use of the software via licence agreements. The licence gives the software owner the opportunity to impose conditions in an effort to control and prevent unauthorized use of this valuable asset. As the customer of any third party software used for the IT services to be outsourced, your organization would be breaching the terms of the software licence agreement if it allowed the supplier to access the software without proper authorization.

Prepare a comprehensive inventory of existing software. Start negotiations with third party software providers as soon as practical. The analysis of rights and restrictions in existing third party software licences is often a major exercise. You will also need to review support and maintenance contracts. Third party licensors will probably want to novate or transfer the licences formally and may want to renegotiate terms. Some will see this as an opportunity to increase their income and will charge relatively high fees to assign the licences to the outsourcing supplier.

7.2.6 Staff Transfers

The outsourcing contract should define the terms under which staff currently working on the IT services will transfer to the supplier at the start of the contract term. Detailed personnel information for the individuals transferring is given in a schedule. In Chapter 3 we saw how many countries have employment protection legislation that applies to any staff transferred to a new employer as a result of outsourcing. Your organization's legal advisors and personnel department should be closely involved with all aspects of this section of the contract.

Your organization may look for some say in the appointment, or replacement, of key individuals in the service provider and the contract should cover any agreement on this point. Your organization may also seek other contractual reassurances aimed at maintaining the quality of the outsourced IT services:

- A guarantee that a sufficient number of suitably qualified and skilled staff will be available at all times to support the outsourced services.

- Defined minimum periods during which key personnel will not be moved to new assignments within the supplier's organization, together with arrangements for giving notice of changes.

- The right to veto the appointment of any member of staff working on the contract on reasonable grounds such as security concerns.

- A reasonable level of continuity, avoiding the need to educate and train new staff about your organization's business processes and policies on a regular basis.

- Agreement that the supplier will provide specified information about the staff working on the outsourced services to any other potential service provider at the end of the contract term.

Additionally, both organizations may agree not to actively recruit staff employed by the other company during the contract term.

Remember that staff who transfer to the supplier will have a new career structure and may be promoted or move to new jobs to widen their experience. It would not be reasonable to try to maintain control over all staff working on the IT services; a degree of turnover is inevitable. Employers are not entitled to impose restraints on ex-employees merely to protect their own competitive position.

7.2.7 Contract Schedules

The schedules to the outsourcing contract contain detailed information and copies of relevant documents supporting the main contract clauses. The subjects covered include:

- Termination procedures and exit plans
- Change control procedures
- Customer's security policy and procedures
- Supplier's security policy and procedures
- Penalties for poor performance
- Escalation procedures
- Dispute resolution procedures

184

- Service requirements definition
- Service level agreements
- Transition plans
- Performance report specifications and timetable
- Supplier's quality management plans and procedures
- Infrastructure upgrade commitments
- Back-up, contingency and disaster recovery plans and procedures
- Contract management organization structure
- Contract management meetings; purpose, attendance and frequency
- Detailed charging formulae
- Invoicing and payment procedures and timescales
- Comprehensive asset listing
- Third party licences and letters of transfer or novation
- Escrow agreements
- Personnel information for those staff transferring to the supplier.

While your legal department or other legal advisors will probably draft the contract main clauses, the IT department will need to prepare and co-ordinate much of the material that is included in the contract schedules.

7.3 Outsourcing Risks

Every outsourcing initiative carries a number of risks that need to be identified, their severity and likelihood recognized, and countermeasures put in place and monitored. Many organizations find that concluding an outsourcing deal takes longer than they expect. If you want to ensure that proper controls are in place and increase your chance of success, the outsourcing process cannot be rushed.

The risks inherent in outsourcing can be viewed in two categories:

1. Pre-contract risks arising in the creation of a supplier short list, the evaluation of proposals, the selection of preferred bidder, the development of the contract and the negotiation process.

2. Post-contract risks that apply during the life of the contract and are linked to service management and controls, performance monitoring, contract change, termination arrangements and so on.

By way of illustration, we look below at some of the key problems and issues experienced in outsourcing initiatives and consider steps that can be taken to counter the risks these difficulties pose.

7.3.1 Unrealistic Expectations

Outsourcing is sometimes portrayed by sales representatives and publications as a cure all – the solution to all those IT difficulties that hold an organization back from achieving its business goals. The first point to recognize is that IT outsourcing is not the same as contracting out functions such as postal services, restaurant facilities or advertising. The IT function has different features:

● It is not a single, unified function but comprises a wide variety of activities.

● Technology continues to develop at a rapid pace and it is very difficult to forecast with any certainty IT service requirements in future years.

● It is not easy to assess the economic benefits of IT services.

● It is expensive and time consuming to switch between outsourcing service providers.

Secondly, recognize the true value of the promises made by suppliers. They may offer access to technical expertise, but in many instances the outsourced services will be supported by the same IT staff that were previously employed by the customer organization. The best staff are sometimes moved on to win new contracts for the supplier. Large service providers may also quote significant savings on IT purchases, but large customer organizations can often achieve the same discounts. Smaller organizations can make economies by negotiating low prices on slightly older technology.

Make sure that your evaluation of the supplier's proposals is objective and compared against the best that could be achieved in-house. If senior executives or users have unrealistic expectations they will inevitably be disappointed with the outsourced IT services (and may blame the in-house IT department, not the supplier). Plan a communication and education programme to run alongside other outsourcing activities so that your organization understands what it will get and what it will not get from outsourcing and is able to exploit the benefits and minimize the disadvantages.

7.3.2 Inadequate Contracts

Earlier in this chapter we have seen that incomplete contracts, negotiated too quickly, can have serious consequences for the customer organization. A failure to define poor performance remedies, dispute resolution procedures or termination arrangements can make it very difficult if not impossible to maintain service levels and may make moving to an alternative supplier or bringing the function back in-house complex and expensive. Good contracts need careful drafting and sufficient time to negotiate fully.

7.3.3 Poor Relationship with Your Supplier

Like any other relationship, your organization and the supplier need to continue to work together closely, clarifying expectations, co-ordinating goals and sharing successes and failures throughout the life of the contract. A good working relationship with your supplier goes a long way towards solving the problems that inevitably will arise in an outsourcing initiative. Conversely, failure to develop a truly collaborative relationship greatly increases the risk of unsatisfactory service levels, more frequent disputes, increased contract management costs and difficulties introducing new or modified services.

Jointly review the contract and outsourcing relationship with your supplier. Set and stick to regular reviews, even if everything seems to be going well. This will demonstrate to the service provider that your organization continues to be committed to the outsourcing initiative and is keen to invest in developing the relationship. These sessions give both organizations an opportunity to focus away from detail and to raise key issues and concerns that affect the overall relationship. Involve senior managers and users in these reviews so that they can play their part in directing and shaping the relationship.

Take care that no one in your organization abuses the escalation procedures. If some people address their problems or complaints direct to senior executives within the supplier's organization, this can sour the overall relationship. Give those actually working on the outsourced services an opportunity to correct faults and resolve issues in line with

187

agreed escalation procedures. Solve problems at the lowest level possible, with minimum fuss. An open and honest approach helps to build trust between the organizations. When problems are referred up through the escalation process and reach the supplier's senior management this will carry weight, as it will be apparent that you only raise very serious concerns to this level.

7.3.4 Supplier Lock-in

It is generally best not to outsource all IT functions to one supplier. Over dependence on one service provider can make costs and risks of moving to another supplier unacceptably high. It is much easier to negotiate contract changes or the introduction of new services if the supplier can see that your organization has an alternative option.

Locked in to one supplier your organization is at risk not only of the service provider becoming complacent and services deteriorating but also of potential bankruptcies and other financial disasters. The financial scandals that came to light in 2002 called into question the financial strength and viability of companies such as WorldCom. The ability to switch suppliers can be critical in such circumstances.

Remember to include contract clauses that commit the supplier to provide information and assistance when the contract terminates. Re-tender contracts at defined intervals and make it clear to your suppliers that this will happen. Take the opportunity to review and confirm the outsourcing objectives. Test your current supplier against the market both in terms of value for money and quality of service.

Monitor escrow procedures to make sure that you have ready access to software and documentation should it be needed. Keep detailed records of licence agreements and transfer arrangements. Update the outsourcing contract when new software is implemented.

Business risks are greater if the outsourced service is provided by a competitor organization or your chosen supplier is the target of a takeover by such a company. In these circumstances, your organization's competitor could gain access to confidential and sensitive business information.

7.3.5 Loss of Flexibility

It is not easy to construct and modify an outsourcing deal to take account of rapidly changing technology and business imperatives. Take care not to let the service specifications stagnate and fall behind current requirements. Never stop negotiating with your supplier for enhancements and changes. This helps to keep the contract alive and both supplier and users can see that there are always opportunities for implementing improvements. Separate service level agreements from the main contract clauses and include them as schedules. Ensure that the contract is written in such a way that these schedules can be amended relatively easily and new ones added as required.

7.3.6 Loss of Control

Once the contract is signed, there is a danger that the balance of power swings too sharply in the supplier's favour. The customer organization needs to ensure that it has suitable monitoring and management systems in place. Skilled staff need to be retained to manage the contract and an allowance made for the fact that some key individuals might decide to leave, taking with them valuable business experience.

It is important to retain and exercise the right to conduct IT audits at the supplier's premises and we have seen that this should be incorporated in the outsourcing contract. Set a timetable for regular audits and stick to it. Without this rigour, the supplier might be tempted to ease off and adopt unacceptable working practices without your organization's knowledge.

Make sure that you have defined clear escalation procedures, responsibilities and levels of authority. Your organization should co-operate with the supplier to ensure that problems are identified and then resolved quickly and efficiently. Allow for referral to different levels of authority, depending on the nature of the problem and the outcome of action taken so far. Aim to resolve problems at the lowest practical level within the supplier's organization.

Ensure that everyone who uses the outsourced services in your organization is familiar with the change control procedures. Instruct the supplier not to respond to informal change requests without approval from the contract management team. Work closely with the supplier to ensure that the change control process works efficiently and responds promptly to requests, especially from users. Communicate regularly to keep everyone well informed about progress.

Regulations influence outsourcing in some industry sectors. For example, in the UK the Financial Services Authority issued guidelines governing banks that outsource significant or material areas of their business. Where a bank outsources services that are material to its operations, reputation or risk, the bank must ensure that appropriate contractual arrangements are in place including the right to audit data and contingency plans covering the termination of the contract. The key concern is to ensure that regulatory control over bank services is not lost.

7.3.7 Risk Management

The information required to describe, classify and effectively manage each outsourcing risk is substantial and potentially complex. Unfortunately there are no short cuts; monitoring the risks and putting countermeasures in place is very important if you are to succeed in outsourcing. The analysis of risks is also a useful technique to illustrate to senior managers the potential impact of outsourcing and to engage their support and commitment, which are also vital elements of success.

Begin by devising a structured risk management process, clearly documenting your proposals and inviting comments from the IT department, users and business managers. The risk management system should be visible and supported by your organization. The process should cover a number of steps:

1. *Risk identification.* You will need to identify all the possible risks that might damage or halt the outsourcing programme, both before and after the contract is signed. Invite contributions not only from the outsourcing programme team members but also from others in your organization, such as auditors and the personnel department. It is a good idea to introduce a simple procedure for recording new risks that may be identified during the course of the outsourcing programme.

2. *Potential causes.* Next consider the underlying causes of the potential risk, documenting the circumstances that could trigger damage to the outsourcing programme.

3. *Risk assessment.* Each risk needs to be evaluated to determine its importance or significance to the outsourcing programme. Two criteria should be recorded:

   - The likelihood of the risk occurring, rated high, medium or low; or alternatively on a scale of 1–10.

- The impact of this event on the outsourcing programme, also rated high, medium or low; or alternatively on a scale of 1–10.

4. *Countermeasures.* Devise actions to be taken to manage the causes and consequences of each potential risk. What can be achieved depends on the nature of the risk and the extent to which the factors that cause potential problems can be controlled by your organization. The actions fall into various categories:

  - measures that stop the risk or problem from occurring or prevent any impact on the outsourcing programme;

  - actions that limit the impact of the risk or reduce the likelihood of it posing a threat to the programme;

  - contingency plans, which describe actions to be take should the risk materialize;

  - penalty clauses or insurance policies, which in effect pass the risk to the supplier or to a third party.

  A few risks will have no countermeasures at all, either because it is simply not feasible to influence the occurrence of the risk or because the identified countermeasures are judged to be too expensive. In these instances, senior management in your organization will need to recognize the potential impact of the risks and accept the possibility that they might occur.

5. *Risk management responsibilities.* Each risk should be assigned a risk owner or manager from within your organization, whose role is to plan, resource and monitor the actions being taken to counter the risk. The risk owner is responsible for assessing the risk and aims to have sufficient measures in place to reduce the likelihood and impact of the risk to minimal levels.

6. *Risk monitoring.* A small group should be set up to review the risk likelihood and impact ratings and to monitor progress in developing countermeasures. The group should have sufficient authority to challenge ratings assigned by risk owners and to direct activities. It should represent not only the IT department, but also business managers who rely on the IT services that are to be outsourced. The group should prepare a summary report, highlighting risks assigned a high likelihood of occurring or a high impact, for submission to an appropriate senior management group within your organization.

Risk Register

The descriptions and analyses of the risks, the countermeasures and progress reports are all recorded in a risk log or register, which may be divided into pre-contract and post-contract risks for ease of reference. The role of the risk register is to:

- facilitate identification of all outsourcing programme risks and their potential impact;

- provide the main source of data used in the management review of risks;

- help assess the overall risks to the outsourcing programme by consolidating risk management information;

- provide a basis for recording and monitoring the risk management actions.

Sample pages from a risk register are illustrated in Figure 7.1.

Reference no.	1234
Description	Unrealistic expectations.
Causes	1. Sales representatives over sell benefits of outsourcing. 2. Publication of outsourcing success stories but little sharing of problems.
Likelihood	Medium
Impact	High
Countermeasures	1. Educate users about performance of current services and improvements that can realistically be expected from an external service provider. 2. Include representatives from different departments on evaluation panel. 3. Run communication programme alongside outsourcing initiative to educate users and business managers about pros and cons of outsourcing.
Owner	Fred Smith
Progress	As at end September: 1. Column started in company magazine giving key performance measures and improvement targets. 2. Finance department have nominated representative, awaiting response from personnel. 3. Communication proposals submitted to senior management for their endorsement.

Reference no.	5678
Description	Supplier lock-in
Causes	1. Too much outsourced to one supplier. 2. Inadequate termination clauses in the contract. 3. Duration of outsourcing contract too long. 4. Supplier believes it will not be replaced.
Likelihood	Low
Impact	High
Countermeasures	1. Only outsource limited number of IT services to one supplier. 2. Negotiate detailed termination procedures and mechanisms for reassigning assets. 3. Avoid outsourcing contracts longer than 5 years. 4. Prepare and publish re-tendering programme.
Owner	Rosemary Jones
Progress	As at end September: 1. Sourcing strategy, introduced in January, defines potential boundaries for outsourcing initiatives. Payroll and personnel systems outsourced to supplier XYZ in April. Current outsourcing initiative relates to package of customer management services. 2. Termination procedures included in draft contract and accepted in principle by all short-listed suppliers. 3. Contract duration 5 years with optional extension to 6 years. 4. Re-tendering programme agreed by senior management in June and this information shared with all short-listed suppliers.

Figure 7.1 Sample pages of a risk register.

When Outsourcing Fails to Deliver

8

8.1 Introduction

Outsourcing is a complex business and difficult to get right. If your organization is dissatisfied with the service it receives from your outsourcing supplier, it is not alone. In the UK, a survey of senior IT staff by *Computing* found that nearly half were unhappy with the quality of service they received from outsourcing contracts. A Dataquest study in the USA revealed that just over half of all outsourcing customers had renegotiated their contracts and in nearly one-quarter of these negotiations, the supplier lost the account (www.computerworld.com). This has resulted in significant growth in arbitration and litigation in this area of computer law.

It is difficult to get a full picture of the extent to which outsourcing deals have failed to deliver. We all like to talk about successes, and suppliers welcome good publicity about their achievements, but it is not easy to discuss the things we have not got right and share lessons learnt. Few organizations are willing to talk openly about costly mistakes, unwise contracts or failed relationships. There is the added commercial sensitivity of the outsourcing relationship. The customer organization will not want to aggravate the position by open discussion of the supplier's flaws and both customer and supplier will have a vested interest in keeping the matter private. Aside from the audits and reviews of large public sector outsourcing deals and limited research into outsourcing failures, there is little published practical guidance to help us understand why some contracts fail to deliver and how we can best tackle failure.

This chapter sets out a road map to help you challenge perceived failure in an outsourcing relationship. You may have been appointed to a key contract management role only to discover that no one in your organization has a good word to say about the outsourced IT services. Or perhaps you worked on an outsourcing programme, selecting a supplier in whom your organization had great confidence. As time has passed, missed performance targets have become the norm and increasingly senior business managers are questioning the wisdom of continuing with the outsourcing partnership.

We begin by reviewing some of the main reasons why outsourcing fails to deliver and the warning signals of problems ahead to which you should be alert. A programme of tackling poor performance and a failing outsourcing relationship is then described. Finally we examine the options of taking formal action against your supplier and bringing the IT services back in-house.

Two principles underlie this chapter and should be stressed:

1. There are always two sides (at least) to every story. It is rarely, if ever, the case that all causes of failure lie at the supplier's feet. Internal discussion within your organization may suggest that you are dealing with the world's worst supplier! Be alert to different perspectives and viewpoints both in your organization and in your supplier.

2. Ending an outsourcing contract prematurely, changing suppliers or bringing the IT activities back in-house are costly, disruptive and lengthy exercises and are not guaranteed to deliver success. Be wary of adopting one of these options. It is usually far more cost effective to resolve the difficulties you are experiencing with your current outsourcing supplier.

There is no one easy solution that will fit all circumstances. The best way forward for your organization will depend, not only on the difficulties experienced in outsourcing, but also on the business environment, future business strategy and objectives set for outsourcing. This chapter will help by setting a framework for the corrective action to be taken and explaining the options available to your organization.

8.2 Reasons Why Outsourcing Fails

Suppliers are better at selling outsourcing services than customers are at buying. Customers are inclined to expect too much from their outsourcing supplier and not enough from themselves. In this section we will examine the reasons why outsourcing can sometimes fail to deliver or meet business requirements, illustrating this by examples taken from press reports of difficulties, lawsuits and contract termination. The discussion in this section is not of minor faults or contract targets missed occasionally. The examples represent major business upheavals or years of inadequate service standards, increased costs or unfulfilled objectives.

8.2.1 Unsatisfactory Outsourcing Relationships

Research by Gartner has shown that most major failures in outsourcing deals are due to a breakdown in the overall relationship between the stakeholders in the outsourcing agreement, and that the business pressure to reduce short-term costs is not a good foundation for a long-term outsourcing relationship.

Problems can also arise through the loss of a shared vision. At the outset of the outsourcing relationship, both customer organization and supplier may have a clear view on the objectives and future direction of the relationship. Once the outsourcing arrangement is underway this can become blurred as new people who do not share a common understanding become involved. Operational concerns may dominate the relationship with little attention given to service improvements or deriving added value from outsourcing.

Communication breakdown can occur where the reasons for implementing an outsourcing solution, its scope and goals are not properly shared throughout the customer organization. Outsourcing may then be perceived as a threat, not only by IT staff but also by users and business managers, and people may not willingly work productively with the outsourcing supplier.

Some customers complain that it is difficult to get sufficient time and attention from the supplier's managers. Outsourcing service providers need to invest time and effort into understanding their customer's business and be clear about the value proposition they are offering. The supplier's account manager needs to have sufficient authority and seniority within the organization to be able to deliver speedy resolution to service problems.

Outsourcing relationships may also fail where financial and legal considerations have dominated the supplier selection process with insufficient attention given to the supplier's total capabilities, including its ability to form a successful relationship with the customer organization.

It is not always the customer organization that makes the first move. CSC filed a lawsuit against Saks, a retailer based in Alabama, accusing it of misappropriating trade secrets and violating the terms of an IT services contract.

CSC alleged that Saks agreed to let it take over contract negotiations with telecommunication suppliers and computer hardware and software vendors, claiming that savings of about $2 million in annual costs were anticipated. Saks' telecommunications contracts were reviewed to see what savings might be possible by purchasing through agreements CSC had with suppliers. CSC alleged that Saks used this confidential information as a bargaining ploy in its own negotiations with telecommunication service providers.

8.2.2 Changes in the Business Environment

There is evidence to suggest that the majority of outsourcing contracts do not have the built in capability to accommodate the inevitable changes to business that will occur over the life of the contract. Given today's pace of change it is near impossible to predict future company structures, mergers or acquisitions, let alone forecast the impact of new technologies on the development of the market place. Outsourcing contracts may well be out of date before negotiations are completed. The agreements need to be built for continuous change.

Market and technology changes are not the only factors affecting the requirements of outsourced services. Corporate politics such as a series of top level appointments within an organization can lead to significant changes in business strategy and direction, in effect rewriting the objectives for IT services within the company.

Example

The financial services group Halifax Bank of Scotland (HBOS) was formed from the merger of the Halifax Building Society and the

Bank of Scotland, with a target to achieve IT cost savings of £150 million a year. HBOS decided to use the Bank of Scotland system for business banking and the Halifax system for retail banking. All outsourcing agreements across the two companies were reviewed.

An outsourcing deal with Xansa was terminated 18 months early. This contract, agreed by the Bank of Scotland before the merger, set up a joint venture known as First Banking Solutions and covered application development work, which HBOS decided to take back in-house. This work was previously centralized within the Bank of Scotland, but HBOS decided to adopt the Halifax decentralized model in which smaller computer services companies are used for regionally based packages of work. The joint venture was estimated to have lost £91 million in potential revenue. Xansa received £9 million in compensation for early termination of the contract.

Example

CSC signed an 11-year outsourcing contract worth $1.1 billion with Enron Energy Services. The business process outsourcing agreement covered billing and collection for retail gas and electricity customers, including the application of e-business technology to Enron's retail markets. As part of the deal, 300 IT staff transferred to CSC.

The contract is jeopardized by the collapse of Enron. If Enron is taken over, the buyer may retain the outsourcing deal – clearly billing is a crucial function. The buyer, however, would be in a strong position to negotiate a favourable deal and this may not prove adequate compensation for CSC's investment in the outsourcing arrangement. Bankruptcy law in the USA usually overrides any clauses written into contracts between a company and its supplier.

The New Orleans-based energy services and engineering company, McDermott International, decided to terminate a 10-year global outsourcing deal with AT&T after just 2 years. The outsourcing contract had given AT&T responsibility for 10,000 PCs and 350 servers, local area networks, end-to-end network management and some business applications. The deal included the transfer of 280 staff from McDermott to AT&T.

The two companies were in the process of renegotiating the contract when McDermott decided to end the arrangement, quoting efficiency reasons. The change in sourcing strategy followed a series of new top management appointments at McDermott, including the arrival of a new chief executive officer, chief financial officer and a new head of IT. These corporate leadership changes led to the decision to bring at least some IT operations back in-house.

AT&T continues to manage wide area voice and data networking for McDermott under a separate agreement.

8.2.3 Unsatisfactory Outsourcing Contracts

A sound contract is critically important to the outsourcing relationship. A clear, financially viable and practical contract defines the parameters of the outsourced services, performance measures that facilitate effective monitoring and procedures for processing changes and resolving problems. There are a number of pitfalls that can lead to unsatisfactory contracts, fundamental disagreements about the provisions of the outsourcing arrangements and a breakdown in the outsourcing relationship:

- Getting a deal that is simply too good. Customer organizations need to recognize the point at which they have struck a fair deal that represents a proper balance between the organization's interest in achieving value for money and the supplier's need to make a sufficient profit margin. Push too hard and some suppliers will over-commit themselves in their eagerness to win the deal. They will accept unjustifiably low profit margins and promise high levels of service. Once the contract is signed, the supplier will look to reduce its costs at every available opportunity, which usually results in an unacceptable level of service and minimum support and service development.

- Rushing through negotiations can prove a short-term economy. A full discussion not only helps clarify service expectations but also helps build understanding between customer organization and supplier. Baseline data used for performance measures needs to be comprehensive and a true reflection of current requirements.

- Major outsourcing deals are often sponsored by top management but it is a great mistake to think that outsourcing contracts can be developed by senior business managers and company legal departments alone. IT outsourcing contracts require knowledge of this specialist field. At a minimum, the customer organization should ensure that it is on an equal footing with the supplier during contract negotiations. Outsourcing suppliers are experts at designing outsourcing contracts and have comprehensive technical expertise to hand whenever it is needed. Customer organizations should employ specialist legal advice (from external experts if necessary) and it is vital that the IT department support the negotiations and help develop the contract using their knowledge of technology and the current IT services and infrastructure.

Example

Software AG sued British Nuclear Fuels Limited (BNFL) in a disagreement over an outsourcing contract. BNFL was accused of breaching its software licensing agreement by outsourcing IT operations to CSC. BNFL used Software AG's Adabas database and Natural 4GL programming language to develop an application used for tracking nuclear materials.

Software AG claimed that, by outsourcing IT operations, BNFL disclosed proprietary information to a third party and CSC, as part of its role as outsourcing supplier, made copies of the software.

8.2.4 Lack of Flexibility

Some customer organizations have found themselves locked in to long-term inflexible outsourcing deals. Lack of flexibility is a key reason why some outsourcing agreements break down. The contract should allow for both supplier and customer to instigate changes and both parties need to recognize that they cannot forecast every development and service modification required during the life of the contract. Difficulties arise when customer organizations experience substantial additional charges for new services required to meet business needs that develop during the life of the contract.

> **Example**
>
> Less than 2 years after signing an IT outsourcing agreement with CSC, Oxford Health Plans Incorporated, a Connecticut-based healthcare provider, decided to cancel the deal. The outsourcing agreement covered data centre operations, help desk services, desktop systems and network operations and was reported to be worth around $300 million. Oxford Health decided that it would be more cost effective to bring the outsourced IT functions back in-house. The scope of the original outsourcing contract was limited, the company was entering a growth phase and bringing the services back in-house provided more flexibility to re-deploy staff from one department to another and was expected therefore to be more cost effective. Oxford Health had hoped to save money and upgrade its technology infrastructure through outsourcing.

8.2.5 Higher Costs than Anticipated

Within any organization, payments made to external companies tend to be much more closely scrutinized than internal costs such as salary expenditure and overhead charges. Outsourcing IT services therefore highlights IT costs that may previously have been much less visible to senior managers. Increases in the costs of the outsourced services, as use increases or requirements change, will also be closely reviewed. Some organizations perceive that the costs of the outsourced services have risen to such an extent that outsourcing can no longer be justified and bringing the IT activities back in-house would be more efficient. Particular problems arise when customer organizations find that they are paying excess fees for services they believed were covered by the out-sourcing contract.

Example

The Bank One Corporation, based in Chicago, launched a major IT recruitment programme to speed up and expand internal technology projects aimed at moving the bank holding company away from outsourcing initiatives. An additional 600 IT employees were hired to join the technology department to integrate increasingly sophisticated systems without any customer disruption. This approach was regarded as more cost effective than outsourcing activities and provided the opportunity to develop greater historical knowledge of Bank One's IT infrastructure. Bank One is moving from a number of different online customer service platforms that are maintained through outsourcing agreements, to a single proprietary system that will let customers view account information and make deposits and money transfers. The single platform will provide a comprehensive national view of customer and product relationships.

Example

The Metropolitan Police reviewed its £125 million outsourcing contract with Sema Group (now ThunbergerSema) after 3 years, in the light of criticisms about excessive charges. The agreement covers the management and support of 14,500 desktop computers; help desks and local and wide area networks. Research by a member of the Metropolitan Police Authority claimed that high charges were being made for simple tasks such as changing a PC password and connecting a printer to a computer's hard drive.

8.2.6 Poor Service Levels

Customer organizations should monitor their supplier's resource levels and business knowledge so as to be able to spot potential problems in advance. There is always a risk that, having won the outsourcing deal with the "A" team, the supplier will transfer in the "B" team, which is barely competent to deliver the contractual service levels.

Some outsourcing deals suffer from delays and protracted difficulties resolving service issues. It is not always easy to unravel the causes of the problems, but the service fails to reach a satisfactory standard.

Example

The Lord Chancellor's department decided to end its agreement with Fujitsu Services for the development of office automation applications to be used in magistrates' court IT systems. Fujitsu Services had attempted to renegotiate the contract because of delays in the delivery of the system and increases in the development costs, but no agreement was reached. The Lord Chancellor's department stated that it had not been possible to reach an agreement on the specialized software at an acceptable price that would deliver value for money for the taxpayer.

Fujitsu Services continues to deliver and run the infrastructure services for magistrates' courts through a revised £232 million contract.

8.2.7 Unsatisfactory Performance Measures

Performance measures used for outsourcing contracts need to reflect business objectives and assess the service delivered to users rather than the technology components that support the service. The chosen performance measures become the focus of monitoring activities and have a strong influence on the style of contract management. Adopting unsatisfactory or inappropriate measures can therefore have a very damaging impact on the overall relationship:

204

- Concentrating on service delivery mechanisms and technologies used leaves little scope for the supplier to innovate and introduce efficiency changes. The focus should be on service outputs to get the best out of outsourcing.

- Failing to collect information about perceptions through devices such as user satisfaction surveys misses a critical angle on the performance of outsourced services.

- Measuring aspects of the service that are of less importance to users may mask more serious performance concerns.

- Collecting an excess of performance data can hide trends and particular issues of concern.

Example

At Johns Manville Corporation, a building materials supplier based in Denver, there had long been complaints about the financial and logistics mainframe services outsourcing contract with (i)Structure. Two years before the contract was due to expire, (i)Structure proposed a renegotiated contract that would increase from $3.8 million in the first year to $4.17 million in the fourth year.

When the services were reviewed in detail it became clear that although most of the performance levels were in fact being met, there were concerns about how they were being delivered. Staff at Johns Manville produced a new set of service levels on the basis that if (i)Structure met these standards it should be able to deliver the services in whichever way it saw fit.

Johns Manville then negotiated with (i)Structure with revised provisions for new performance levels and penalties as well as a more competitive price. Benchmarks listing the prices of similar IT outsourcing contracts were used and (i)Structure was informed that a new outsourcing competition would be launched if it was not possible to reach agreement on the new proposals put forward. As a result, (i)Structure agreed to negotiate and was pleased that its outsourcing contract, with clear and detailed service levels, was extended for a further 4 years.

8.2.8 Inadequate Contract Management

If IT outsourcing is to deliver benefits it must be carefully monitored and managed. Without proper governance structures in place, supported by sufficient resources, there is a real risk that the customer organization will lose control of the outsourced IT services. Poor contract management arises when:

- The outsourcing management team does not possess the right blend of skills to enable it to develop successful supplier relationships, negotiate service changes, resolve problems and monitor performance.

- The team is too small to support the range of managerial and technical skills required and resources are spread too thinly trying to resolve the issues raised by outsourcing.

- The supplier's account (or contract) manager does not possess sufficient seniority or authority within the organization to take the actions necessary to maintain service levels, introduce agreed improvements and resolve problems.

- A marked imbalance of power arises between the customer organization's and supplier's contract management teams.

Effective contract management is generally estimated to cost around 5–10 per cent of the total value of an outsourcing contract.

8.3 Warning Signals

We have looked at a number of examples in which outsourcing has clearly failed to deliver the anticipated benefits, with serious consequences. There are relatively few instances where significant action against a supplier (or a customer organization) receives publicity. Problems in outsourcing relationships arise much more frequently than the number of press reports would suggest and are resolved more or less successfully by the individuals working for the customer organization and supplier on the outsourcing arrangement.

When problems in outsourcing relationships do occur, it is clearly preferable to spot the difficulties before they escalate into major issues that require drastic action. Here are the warning signals to look out for if you are working on an outsourcing contract:

- If key individuals fail to turn up at contract liaison meetings on a regular basis, you are probably heading for trouble. The involvement of key managers from your organization demonstrates to the supplier the importance of the outsourcing relationship to your business strategy. If the supplier is convinced that your organization remains committed to outsourcing then it is much more likely to invest in the relationship for the long term. The absence of key supplier representatives suggests that your supplier does not attach great importance to the quality of outsourced services provided and there will not be an emphasis on resolving issues with minimum delay.

- Do you hear a constant stream of criticism about the outsourcing supplier, with no one in your organization able to find a good word to say about the outsourced services? This might be a problem of perception if the performance measures show that the services are, at least in general terms, meeting the required standard. It may alternatively suggest that the wrong performance measures are being monitored.

- Your supplier should readily and willingly inform you of any company changes or appointments that might have an impact on your outsourcing relationship. If you read about such changes in press reports or hear the news on the grapevine, you should consider why your supplier saw no need to inform you direct or did not regard this as especially important.

- If formal meetings are required to resolve differences or reach agreement on minor changes, then the relationship is not working well. Where suspicion and doubt exist so that little can be achieved informally, the outsourcing relationship will be slow to respond as business needs develop and will stultify rather than grow.

- When minor service problems prove difficult to resolve and are presented as major concerns, consider where outsourcing relationships are failing. Is there insufficient liaison with service users or is your supplier giving insufficient attention or priority to service problems?

- If the supplier dominates the outsourcing process you will find it hard to establish a relationship in which power is balanced and both parties' interests are protected. Be wary if your organization has adopted your supplier's performance measures and reports, problem escalation and change control systems. It is unlikely that these will adequately meet your organization's specific requirements.

- An over-emphasis on short-term benefits with little regard for the longer-term health of the outsourcing relationship is not a good sign.

- Where the initiative is dominated by financial, purchasing or legal considerations, then the business objectives that should underpin the outsourcing initiative may be lost. Outsourcing is a strategic decision that should involve business managers.

- Outsourcing decisions should be driven by rational, objective analysis. The consequences of any major sourcing decision are too fundamental to be based on emotion or individual preferences. Although personal working relationships are an important element of the outsourcing arrangement, they should not be the single overriding factor. Deals reached informally by one or two individuals are not a good foundation for a long-term relationship between two organizations. Processes and structures need to be well established and operating effectively, so that the success of the outsourcing arrangement can outlive the involvement of individuals.

- Finally, be alert if your supplier frequently fails to return telephone calls, breaks promises about service issues or delays action with no reason given.

8.4 Challenging Failure

In this section we look at the way in which a failing outsourcing relationship can be turned into a successful one. Any outsourcing initiative can hit a difficult patch, but all is not lost. Many outsourcing programmes have tackled problems, found solutions and eventually strengthened the outsourcing relationship.

Changing suppliers or bringing IT activities back in-house are disruptive and costly exercises. Here we describe a process for challenging outsourcing problems and improving the outsourcing relationship without taking legal action. At the end of the process, if you have not been able to retrieve the outsourcing programme, you will at least be in a much stronger position should legal action become necessary.

When things are going wrong in an outsourcing relationship there is a tendency for both customer organization and supplier to look inwards, to stop talking to each other and to see the other party as the cause of all the problems. If you are to challenge failure and turn it into success you will need to:

- recognize that there are different perspectives on service problems and you need to be objective at all times;

- make sure that you are part of the solution, not a contributor to the problems;

- set a series of achievable milestones along the way – it is rarely possible to jump straight from a failing outsourcing relationship to a successful one;

- be clear about roles, responsibilities and ownership of issues and make sure that everyone else is too;

- sit down, talk and listen to your supplier, business executives, users, IT managers and staff;

- collect information and refer to facts, not hearsay or rumour;

- do not threaten your supplier – this approach does not fit well with the open and honest outsourcing relationship that you are trying to build;

- remember that if the situation deteriorates you are still dependent on your supplier for service provision in the short term and you will need to work closely with your supplier should it be necessary to transfer the services to another provider. You cannot simply walk away and have no more dealings with your supplier.

8.4.1 A Ten Step Programme for Turning Failure into Success

Step 1: Establish Channels of Communication with Your Supplier

You will need frequent and effective communications with your supplier throughout the process. This will be a critical factor in turning around the outsourcing relationship, so begin by reviewing how and when you can best communicate, and with whom, at your supplier. Here are a number of points to consider:

- You will need a balance of informal and formal meetings; neither is sufficient alone. The complex issues raised by outsourcing cannot be resolved over a pint of beer nor can they be sorted in a formal meeting with 20 or more attendees.

- Review the meetings that currently take place between your two organizations. If the relationship is failing it is very unlikely that these meetings are successful. Consider why they are not tackling the real concerns. Do they focus on performance issues that are not relevant to business users? Do key individuals from either your organization or the supplier fail to turn up on a regular basis? Is action not followed through?

- Identify an opposite number in your supplier with whom you feel you can work productively. This does not necessarily have to be a senior manager but will need to be someone who commands the respect of his/her colleagues and has sufficient authority to make things happen within the supplier. Meet with this individual and explain the concerns about the outsourcing relationship being expressed within your organization. Do try to do this without attaching blame to anyone – at this stage it is far too early to be confident that you have all the facts and know where all the faults lie. Arrange to meet regularly with your contact.

- In liaison with your supplier contact, set up a series of meetings that will be dedicated to analyzing the crucial outsourcing issues, developing an appropriate action plan and monitoring progress. The emphasis should be on solutions to problems and service improvement, not attaching blame and extracting the maximum penalty payments. Bear this in mind when naming the meetings and drawing up terms of reference. Select a small group of attendees who can represent a wide range of stakeholders and take a positive and constructive approach to problem solving.

Remember throughout this exercise that communications are vitally important. It is easy to lose sight of the need to communicate when you are absorbed in various actions, but without much improved communications between your organization and the supplier you will not be able to deliver a successful outsourcing relationship.

Step 2: Review the Contractual Arrangements

You will need to investigate carefully within your organization the exact nature of the contractual agreement with your outsourcing supplier. It is not a good idea to rely on views expressed by others – you will need to

210

actually see the contract for yourself. If this seems an unusual approach, note that it is not unknown for otherwise well-organized companies to have inadequate contracts with some of their suppliers and to have instances where proper procedures were not followed.

Carefully examine the contract checking the following points:

- Did both parties properly sign the contract at its inception?
- Has it been regularly updated? When was the last update? Did both parties sign the latest version?
- Does the contract contain a service level agreement, is this up to date and have the modifications been formally incorporated?
- Are the service standards and performance measures in the contract the same as those in daily use in the outsourcing arrangement?
- What is the scope of the contract and does this reflect the outsourced services actually provided?

It is helpful to have a sound knowledge of these contractual matters as you begin to take action forward to improve the outsourcing relationship. Hopefully the contract will define the required levels of service and specify appropriate penalty payments. If improvements cannot be made despite your best efforts, more formal action may need to be taken against your supplier and you will be well informed about steps that can be taken and penalties that might apply within the terms of the contract. If, however, you find that the contract is defective in some way you will at least know where your organization stands and you can avoid empty threats or groundless claims made against the supplier if the outsourcing relationship deteriorates further.

You may be able to take the opportunity to tie up any loose ends. There may be contract amendments that have been agreed but have not been signed and formally incorporated into the contract. Use this exercise to demonstrate your organization's continued commitment to the outsourcing relationship and make sure that there are proper procedures in place to keep the contract up to date in the future.

Step 3: Research the Problems and Perceptions of Problems

Before the first meeting of your new problem-solving group, carry out investigations into the problems existing in the outsourcing arrangement and the perceptions of those problems:

- Schedule a series of interviews with key stakeholders including some users, business managers and IT staff to gather views and opinions about the outsourced services. The aim is to gather perceptions rather than facts. Use a standard list of questions covering all the areas you believe are causing difficulties, but also providing an opportunity for observations about any aspect of the service. Not only will these sessions provide helpful information to you, they will also demonstrate to colleagues in your organization that positive action is being taken to tackle the outsourcing problems.

- Analyze performance data collected over the previous 6 months or a year. Is the trend towards improving or reducing service levels? How many service targets are missed and how frequently? Do the performance measures used give a satisfactory indication of the aspects of service that are giving rise to complaints within your organization?

- Collect benchmarking data so that you can compare the performance of your outsourced services and processes with best practice achieved by other outsourcing programmes.

- Identify a set of performance measures that would accurately reflect improvements that you hope to achieve by resolving the perceived and actual outsourcing problems. Consider also any indicators that will demonstrate when the overall outsourcing relationship has improved.

- Speak to other customers of your supplier to see if they have experienced similar problems and learn from their experience and any solutions they have implemented.

Bring together all your research findings into one report and have a group of colleagues in your organization review it and validate your overall conclusions.

Step 4: Informal Discussions with Your Supplier

You have established your organization's formal contractual position and gathered performance data and opinions about the outsourced services. The next crucial step is to explore the perception of the quality of the outsourced services with your supplier.

Starting with your main contact, work through a standard set of questions, similar to those you used when you interviewed colleagues in your own organization. Try to understand how they perceive the services and

212

where they think improvements could and should be made. Do they believe that your organization is satisfied with the service it is receiving?

Crucially, explore how your supplier perceives your organization's performance as a customer of outsourced services:

- Are requirements always clearly stated?
- Does your organization always deliver on promises and agreed actions?
- Are invoices queried promptly if there is any disagreement about the charges raised?
- Are cleared invoices paid promptly within contractually agreed time limits?
- Are performance review meetings well organized and constructive?
- Are the agreed problem escalation procedures followed?
- How do they rate the overall outsourcing relationship?
- What lessons might your organization learn from the supplier's other customers?

Taking advice from your contact, try to interview a number of the key players in the supplier organization. Remember that it is important to be open to the fact that your organization might not have performed very well. Your job at this stage is to listen, not lecture or justify the actions of your organization. You will need to be sensitive to the fact that some of the supplier's representatives might have assumed that all was well in the outsourcing relationship and may feel very threatened. Keep talking and involve them in the action programme as it develops throughout this process.

Step 5: Develop Proposals for Remedial Action

Bring together the results of your supplier interviews with the findings of your study of the performance data and perceptions within your organization. Analyze the information to determine the actions that could be taken to resolve problems and improve the overall relationship between your organization and the supplier. In particular, look for opportunities to:

- deliver some quick wins that will demonstrate to both organizations that you are committed to improving the situation and will take action where necessary;

- devise more appropriate performance measures and cut out performance data collection that serves no useful purpose;

- improve service levels visibly in ways that will help your organization but have minimal cost implications;

- publicize what is working well but might not be fully appreciated within your organization;

- improve communications and understanding between your two organizations, for example by using joint workshops, action teams or projects;

- instigate action that will benefit your supplier without incurring additional service expenditure, for example offer to act as a main reference site once certain service improvements have been made;

- pursue opportunities to extend the outsourcing contract (either in scope or the length of the contract) in ways that would benefit your organization subject, of course, to sustained improvements to the overall standard of service.

Aim for a balance of activity that tackles performance in a number of different areas and has the potential to offer something to both your organization and the supplier. These are only preliminary proposals and others will offer further suggestions as you work through the process.

Step 6: Agree an Action Plan with Your Supplier

Sit down with your supplier contact and work through your ideas for remedial action. Take his/her views on the likelihood of the various ideas working and being acceptable to the supplier. Encourage contributions and additional ideas for activities that will help improve the outsourcing relationship.

Produce a jointly agreed draft action plan with your contact. Each of you should be responsible for ensuring that you have the endorsement and support of your respective senior management. Without this neither of you can be confident that the other will deliver.

Once you have this authority, take your proposals to the newly formed problem-solving group that was set up in Step 1 of this process. You will need to explain that the draft plan is based on the findings of your investigations and takes account of the diversity of views expressed about the outsourced services. It has been endorsed in principle by senior management in both organizations. The aim now is to refine the proposed activities and finalize the action plan. Invite views on the best way forward to tackle the various tasks, who needs to be involved, who should take lead responsibility and what the timescales should be. (Note that the aim is not to rewrite the proposed plan, which could result in a programme that is heavily biased towards one side or the other and may give precedence to someone's pet project rather than the outsourcing problems in the round.)

Following this discussion, you can complete the action programme in liaison with your supplier contact. The problem-solving group now becomes the outsourcing improvement task force.

Step 7: Launch the Outsourcing Improvement Programme

The action programme that you are about to launch is a significant milestone in the life of the outsourcing contract. The achievements of this exercise could make or break the outsourcing relationship. So you need everyone involved in the outsourced services both in your organization and in the supplier to be aware of the programme of activities and to be supportive of the overall aim.

Plan to launch the programme at the start of the remedial work. Present the actions positively and constructively – you are laying down a blueprint for the future, seeking service improvements and enhancing the value your organization derives from the outsourcing relationship, problem solving and taking corrective action. While you should not be over confident of success, the programme should not be presented as a last ditch attempt to get the supplier to improve its performance before legal action is taken.

You might like to think up a catchy name for the action programme. Consider producing leaflets giving an overview, start a newsletter to report on progress and add details to your organization's Intranet. Any published material (on paper or on the Intranet) will have to be carefully vetted for commercially sensitive information. It would be very unfortunate, especially while the outsourcing relationship is at a low point, if confidential data got into the public domain.

Step 8: Monitor Progress

You will need to monitor progress carefully and frequently. The outsourcing relationship has been judged to be poor so we can safely assume that the normal mechanisms for reviewing performance and introducing service improvements are not working effectively. The new outsourcing improvement task force has been set up to give a fresh start, untainted by the problems that may have bogged down other contract management meetings. The outsourcing improvement programme should have a clear beginning and end, so the new task force (which will monitor progress) has a limited lifespan.

Reference number: 1234

Action:

Arrange short-term secondments for members of sales support application development team to supplier. Returning secondees to prepare report on their experiences and propose changes in Marketing Department's processes to enable them to get more out of the outsourced IT services.

Action owner: Kate Shearing

Timescales: Three secondments to be completed by end September.

Progress as at end April:

Bill Carter's secondment completed. Proposals for new ordering processes accepted and to be implemented by end June.

Amy Jones' secondment completed. Report due by end May.

Felicity Johnson's secondment yet to be arranged.

Reference number: 5678

Action:

Review membership and terms of reference of the monthly contract management status meeting to ensure that:

(i) The group has sufficient authority to instigate required corrective action.

(ii) The supplier's representatives can speak for all relevant sections working on the outsourced services.

(iii) Users' views are properly represented.

Action owner: Alan George

Timescales:

Revised terms of reference to be agreed by end May, new members in place by end August.

Progress as at end April:

New terms of reference proposed and sent to senior IT strategy group for approval.

Marketing, Sales and Legal Departments support proposed new representation but Finance contacts have raised queries. This will be discussed with the Finance Director in May.

Figure 8.1 *Sample action records.*

Prepare records for each agreed action; examples are given in Figure 8.1. Your task force should meet regularly – fortnightly is about right – to review progress, agree additional actions and modify the programme where it is not producing the desired outcome. As services are brought back in line with agreed standards, ongoing monitoring should be handed back to the normal contract management mechanisms.

One of the potential problems in this process is the possible conflict between actions started within the outsourcing improvement programme and actions arising out of the normal contract management process. You will need to keep a close watch on this potential difficulty. The task force should report into the contract management status meeting. Given the seriousness of the failing outsourcing relationship, however, it is important that both your organization and your supplier recognize the significance of the outsourcing improvement programme, giving it priority and not overriding its activities. Support from your senior management will be important in this matter. It may be helpful for the IT Director or another senior IT manager to lead the task force.

Step 9: Communicate Achievements

As progress is made, make sure that it is effectively communicated to a wide range of people in your organization. You need to change not only certain aspects of the performance of the outsourced service but also, critically, the perception of the performance. Use newsletters, give presentations, and arrange road shows for your organization and your supplier to explain the performance improvements that are being made. Be prepared for more problems to surface as you begin to make progress. You will have made a significant step forward if others have confidence that you will be able to resolve their concerns.

Also provide feedback when difficulties prove hard to resolve. Explain what you are doing and how you hope to be able to make improvements. Give timescales where you can for planned action.

Step 10: Celebrate Successes, Continue to Work on Failures

Avoid dwelling on continuing problems all the time. Take time out to celebrate when you have made real progress. Thank those in your organization and, importantly, at the supplier for their hard work. This is often forgotten, but much appreciated.

If you have a large programme of remedial work, you may find it helpful at set intervals – say, once a quarter – to review all the achievements to

217

date and summarize progress to remind yourself and others how much has been done.

Continue to work at those areas that stubbornly refuse to show improvement. You have demonstrated your commitment to the outsourcing process and worked hard to make it a success. If, despite your best endeavours, your supplier still proves unresponsive and unwilling to make the effort necessary to improve the standard of outsourced services, your organization will need to consider more formal action. This will be a lengthy, expensive process, which does not guarantee success or the delivery of excellent IT services. You will, however, be able to feel confident that you have tried all reasonable means to resolve problems in the outsourcing relationship short of formal, legal action.

8.5 Formal Action Against Your Supplier

If the outsourcing relationship deteriorates beyond an acceptable level, your organization may decide to take more formal action to resolve the difficulties. At this stage specialists from the legal and purchasing departments are likely to become much more closely involved with the outsourcing arrangement and senior management will want to tightly control and direct action.

During the process, outsourced IT operations may need to continue either because they provide IT services on which your business depends, for example desktop e-mail facilities, or because the system needs to be available in order to identify problems and clearly articulate them to the court, should litigation prove necessary.

Negotiating a good contract at the outset is the best safeguard against disputes arising that cannot readily be resolved. The aim, as we have seen, is to deal with difficulties before they harden into disputes. Outsourcing contracts may include provision for a final escalation procedure, which requires an extraordinary management meeting to be set up with the aim of resolving differences and maintaining the outsourcing relationship. This meeting would be attended by a small number of senior representatives from both customer organization and supplier. Another technique, sometimes incorporated into outsourcing contracts, is to bring in an agreed external independent technical expert to resolve disputes about technical issues. This means, of course, that both customer organization and supplier must be able to agree on the expert to be used and must both be prepared to accept his/her judgement.

If all negotiations fail, then formal methods of dispute resolution need to be implemented – arbitration, alternative dispute resolution or formal legal proceedings. While these formal means of dispute resolution are in progress, the customer organization may be unwilling to pay the supplier. The contract may set out terms for a deposit account to be set up in the names of both parties so that the customer organization can continue to comply with its obligations under the outsourcing contract with payments made into the deposit account. Once the dispute is resolved, payments can be made out of the account with accrued interest as determined by the formal proceedings.

8.5.1 Arbitration

Arbitration is an important form of formal dispute resolution that avoids costly legal proceedings and delays. It is an adversarial process with an impartial arbitrator who adjudicates by making binding decisions or awards. The City of London is world famous as a commercial arbitration centre of excellence.

In the UK, the Arbitration Act 1996 sets out the scope of arbitration proceedings and the powers of the arbitrator. The Act aims to facilitate impartial dispute resolution, avoid delay and unnecessary costs while giving the parties concerned freedom to decide their own methods and approaches to arbitration. Arbitration arrangements should be agreed as part of the outsourcing deal and included in the contract before any disputes arise. A common approach to arbitration involves each party establishing a position from which they will be prepared to negotiate. Pendulum arbitration is an alternative and requires one party to work out what their minimum settlement would be and the other to put their maximum offer on the table.

The advantages of arbitration are:

● The arbitrator can be an acknowledged authority on outsourcing and computer services.

● The evidence can be submitted in writing beforehand, so that all viewpoints have been formally expressed and witnesses do not need to give oral evidence. The arbitrator will thus be fully briefed before the meeting and will only need to hear the personal views of the main parties involved.

- The hearing can be at a time and place convenient for the various parties, often outside normal working hours. (There are no special arrangements for hearing court cases outside business hours, and litigants are often kept waiting around for a previous case to conclude so that the court's time will not be wasted.)

- Arbitration is private and the press are not entitled to be present as they would be in a court trial.

- Disputes involving companies based in other countries can be resolved by arbitration, which avoids conflicts of law.

The arbitrator has no power to insist that anyone not party to the original agreement about the use of arbitration attends the arbitration hearing. If third parties are likely to be involved in an outsourcing dispute, litigation is probably a more practical means of dispute resolution.

Arbitration is not a cheap alternative to litigation. The arbitrator's fees must be paid and in the majority of disputes there will be an oral hearing with each side usually represented by lawyers. Not all organizations favour the use of arbitration, some preferring to rely on litigation to settle disputes.

8.5.2 Alternative Dispute Resolution

Both litigation and arbitration can be costly and the adversarial nature of the process can cause views to harden, making it more difficult to resolve the dispute. This can lead the outsourcing relationship to deteriorate further. As a result, other methods of resolving disputes have become increasingly popular. Alternative dispute resolution (ADR) is an umbrella term for formal but non-binding forms of dispute resolution – mediation, conciliation or mini-trial. (In the USA the term ADR usually includes binding arbitration.) The Centre for Dispute Resolution (CEDR), created to promote ADR in the UK, offers many possibilities.

Mediation is used in the majority of cases. A neutral independent mediator will be appointed by, or on behalf of, the customer organization and supplier. This advisor will not be a decision-making adjudicator but a facilitator who acts with the full consent and backing of the two disputing organizations. The mediator helps the parties to define their differences and helps them identify a solution that is acceptable to both sides. Procedures are informal and the mediator cannot force either party to accept a particular solution. The process helps to focus on the most important issues and to avoid adopting entrenched positions. The representatives involved in mediation are usually senior managers who were not involved in the initial dispute and it is important that they have the authority to settle on behalf of their respective organizations. Even if mediation is not successful, it may reduce the number or complexity of the issues concerned.

ADR is voluntary so the parties do not have to agree in advance to be bound by the outcome. The outsourcing contract might, however, include the provision that the parties will treat any agreement at the end of the mediation process as binding. It should also specify how mediation costs will be apportioned. To avoid any information gleaned by either party during mediation being exploited in later litigation, the outsourcing contract should specify that these negotiations will be conducted in confidence, without prejudice to either party's rights in any future legal proceedings. A named organization such as the British Computer Society or CEDR can be appointed to select the mediator.

ADR has the advantage of speed, lower costs and responsiveness to the needs of both customer organization and supplier. Either party can halt it without further obligation or commitment. ADR may be used as an alternative to litigation or to run alongside legal proceedings. It may be worth considering in outsourcing deals where the continuation of the outsourcing relationship is the aim. How much ADR is used is unclear because successful outcomes are not publicized. ADR will not be the best route in all instances – it would not, for example, be appropriate if there were concerns about alleged fraud.

8.5.3 Litigation and Contract Termination

All outsourcing customers need to plan at the outset for the whole life of the contract to ensure that it runs well, meets its objectives and can be terminated or renewed effectively. There are various reasons why an organization may wish to end an outsourcing agreement:

- The contract runs its full term and comes to a natural end.

- Termination for breach; for example, the supplier persistently misses service targets or the customer fails to pay bills even though they are accurate and reasonable.

- Termination for convenience, which may be included in the outsourcing contract and allows the customer to end the contract early for a fee.

- Termination for special circumstances such as company mergers or acquisitions.

Customer organizations need a contract termination plan, which addresses the following issues:

- How and where will the IT operations be carried out the day after the outsourcing relationship ends?
- Is there an option to remain with the supplier after contract termination and what would this cost?
- If the outsourced services will transfer to another supplier, how much conversion work is required and how long will the transition be?
- If the services are to be brought back in-house, what resources are needed and how long will the transition be?
- Is there provision for the supplier to return third-party contracts, licences and equipment purchased to support the outsourced services?
- Can the current supplier be compelled or encouraged to co-operate with its successor?

Where contracts are terminated by giving the agreed contractual notice period, then the customer organization is under no obligation to give reasons. But if the termination is because of contract breaches, a dispute is almost inevitable and it is likely that the reasons given will be challenged. Termination is the final sanction and should not be exercised lightly.

To succeed in a civil case at court, the plaintiff must prove that, on a balance of probabilities, they have suffered damage caused by the defendant's breach of the contract. Proving the breach and quantifying the damages caused by the breach can be difficult and complicated. Several years can elapse between the start of legal proceedings to the court hearing. During this period the parties will have many opportunities to reach a settlement out of court, and most do so. Under English law, the risks for litigants if their case proceeds all the way to the court hearing include an obligation for the loser to pay a large percentage of the winner's legal costs as well as their own. This risk needs to be carefully assessed – and adds to the incentive to settle out of court.

As well as awarding damages, the court may issue an injunction or decree compelling one of the parties to undertake an action or stop an activity. An injunction will be a more appropriate remedy than damages in some circumstances. For example, if confidential information has been misused or software copied in breach of a licence, then the damage has been done and there is a need to prevent a repeat of this wrongful action. The court will issue an injunction to this effect.

Legal action must normally be initiated within 6 years of the alleged breach of contract. Some outsourcing suppliers will seek through negotiation to limit this to 2 or 3 years to make forward planning and insurance assessment easier.

Termination, for whatever reason, is costly and disruptive. It requires careful planning and close monitoring. Where contractual disputes have grown, litigation may seem inevitable, but any organization contemplating legal action will want to review its chances of success and will need to be confident that the end result will be worth the time, effort and cost.

8.6 Backsourcing

Having previously decided that the most profitable way to achieve IT service improvements or cost savings was through outsourcing, some organizations subsequently decide to bring operations back in-house. This process is sometimes referred to as backsourcing.

Various reasons lead organizations to consider backsourcing:

- Dissatisfaction with the quality of outsourced IT services.

- Escalating costs of outsourced services and analyses that demonstrate that the services could be provided more efficiently in-house.

- Having experienced outsourcing, the customer organization comes to realize that too much control has transferred to the service provider. Responsibility for developing IT strategy and applications that are core to the organization's business are transferred back in-house.

- Where outsourcing is used to give access to new technical skills at short notice, IT services may be backsourced when new expertise and resources have been developed in-house. Outsourcers often undertook early e-commerce projects, but much of this work has now been taken back in-house.

- Company mergers and acquisitions or new top level appointments bring different views and approaches to IT sourcing strategies.

Organizations commonly aim to achieve a balance between insourcing and outsourcing and look to develop a sourcing strategy that exploits the benefits of both. Rebuilding the IT function takes time and resources and will require senior management commitment and support. It may not be economical to transfer all outsourced services back in-house and the contract management function will need to be maintained to monitor ongoing outsourced services. Renegotiations may enable the customer organization to derive greater value out of the services that remain outsourced.

For those activities that are backsourced, new IT facilities and processes will need to be set up. It will not be acceptable simply to replicate the function that was originally outsourced. Business requirements will have changed and the new IT function needs to take a fresh look at practices and processes to make sure that it continues to compare favourably with the services that could be purchased from external service providers. Cost control is often an important element and a number of tactics can be used to reduce costs including:

- Introducing more automated service management tools such as network monitoring, problem management and help desk applications.

- New IT charging systems, which encourage users to take responsibility for their level of resource consumption. Two examples illustrate the principle:

  o For desktop facilities, users pay a standard fee per desk for a modest set of standard software. For additional software, the user pays the cost of the software licence and maintenance. If two business units want to use the new software, they negotiate between them how the costs will be split.

  o Each business unit commits to a certain volume of use and the IT department has a budget fixed to deliver these volumes. Regular usage reports are distributed to senior business managers. When use by a business unit exceeds the forecast to the point where additional IT resources need to be purchased, the business unit (not the IT department) must make the case for additional IT funding.

- Data centre consolidation, which has the potential to significantly reduce IT costs but often needs a strong drive by senior management to overcome political opposition.

- Purchasing used equipment or upgrading existing equipment can achieve hardware economies. A specialist IT purchasing expert can achieve good deals through knowledge of the IT market and equipment.

- Service levels can be reduced where management values the cost savings more than the service quality lost. For example, reductions in system testing and paper printouts and an increase in response times.

Once the necessary resources, skills and commitment are in place to backsource the IT services, a smooth transition is needed. This requires a good working relationship with the outsourcing supplier and agreements on transferring assets such as software licences. Effective support from the outsourcing supplier will be needed throughout the transition. Some IT activities commonly remain with the supplier and it is important that the split between insourced and outsourced services is well understood, with a clear boundary between the two.

If backsourced IT services are to be supported by current IT staff, training may be required and sufficient priority assigned to the backsourcing project to ensure that it does not get pushed to the bottom of the pile by more pressing business requirements for new services.

Example

Four years after Continental Airlines outsourced nearly all IT functions to EDS, the IT department had been reduced to a dozen staff. A review of EDS's particular competencies was carried out and the strategic implications of each IT and business function considered. Much of the IT was brought back in-house, resulting in roughly half of the IT operations remaining with EDS. The in-house IT department grew to 400 staff.

Continental Airlines continues to outsource commodity services while keeping IT activities that support the airline's future development in-house. Data centres are managed by EDS; application development, online reservations, customer service and supply chain management are supported in-house.

ASPs, WASPs and the Future of Outsourcing

9

9.1 Alternative Supply Models

A new range of outsourcing supply companies has emerged since the late 1990s, based on new business models that deliver selective outsourcing services. In the space of 4 years over 1,000 new outsourcing companies were set up in the USA – many did not last, but the market continues to expand with a high level of merger and acquisition activity.

We can identify a number of key influences that led to this surge in the growth of outsourcing companies:

- The new technologies that developed in response to the potential for e-commerce opened up by the Internet; browser technology, Java, broadband networks, networked storage and virtual private networks (VPNs).

- The new dotcom businesses for whom speed was the essence. These companies did not have time to develop IT functions, choosing instead to buy in services as needed. This opened up a new, rapidly expanding market for IT outsourcing.

- The concept of the virtual organization, pioneered by the dotcoms, in which companies could be set up almost overnight on the basis of outsourcing all but a small core of strategic activities.

- The potential for growth in the outsourcing market represented by small and medium-sized businesses. Just as larger companies were exploiting the Internet to offer global services and to market to smaller organizations, so small and medium-sized businesses were looking to develop their own Web-based services and to compete internationally. They needed an economical way to buy in software and infrastructure services.

Whole new ranges of outsourced services developed and continue to develop. Many new names and acronyms have appeared, and some have disappeared too. The shape of this emerging market continues to evolve. Some of the early predictions for market growth have proved to be over-optimistic, rather like the dotcom phenomenon, but a solid core of new outsourcing companies continues to flourish. Major players from the more traditional computer services, software and telecommunications sectors are also developing services along these new business models.

The new outsourcing model supplies services in a different way but many of the principles, developed over the last two decades and based on experiences of outsourcing, still apply:

- The advantages of competitive tendering in the selection of a supplier and the need for an effective RFP.

- The use of service level agreements and the need to express requirements in terms of the services delivered to the users rather than the technologies used.

- The need for effective contract management.

- The importance of good customer support services and an effective relationship between customer and supplier. The quality of service support is a particular concern among customers of the new outsourcing companies.

9.1.1 Application Service Providers (ASPs)

ASPs offer centrally managed applications to remote customers over broadband networks on a leased or pay-as-you-go basis. The ASP business is often built on a partnership of organizations with expertise in hardware, software applications and vertical markets. The services offered may include a package of applications, system integration, e-commerce functionality, customer relationship management, financial packages and e-mail facilities.

Like a more traditional outsourcing service, ASP services offer a number of advantages over software purchases:

- there is no need to purchase the software up-front;

- the ASP is responsible for daily operations, software maintenance and upgrades and infrastructure management;

- the ASP employs the technical specialists that are required to support the applications;

- the customer organizations have access to more applications of a higher standard than they would have been able to purchase for the same outlay;

- implementation is rapid;

- simplified pricing and billing;

- predictable costs;

- flexibility to scale up as use of the service grows or cut back if service use falls.

ASPs that offer applications which support e-commerce or other financial transactions are sometimes known as Business Service Providers (BSPs), while those that offer a range of value added services may be called Full Service Providers (FSPs).

ASP Service Components

The ASP systems operate on powerful servers capable of serving hundreds or thousands of users, installed in a data centre. The servers can be dedicated for use by one customer or shared where several customers use both servers and the applications running on them. Clustered rather than stand-alone servers are commonly deployed since this is more affordable, robust, reliable and scalable. When used with storage area networks, clustered servers allow faster data transfer and reduce delays experienced by users. Load balancing software shares the processing across servers to prevent one server becoming overloaded. Web server caching is used to store Web pages that are commonly accessed by users. As a general rule, ASPs find that a larger number of small servers are preferable to a few large servers or mainframes. The small servers can be put to different uses and offer greater flexibility. They can also be packed into small spaces at the data centre.

The connection to the remote ASP data centre is made over a standard open Internet service or via a secure VPN, which creates an encrypted tunnel between the user's PC and the ASP servers, thus safeguarding data in transit. Users access applications through a terminal service or browser-based connection linked to the remote servers, rather than accessing systems held on a local PC drive or server. Since all processing is done at the remote server end, only modest PCs are needed on the desktop. Network reliability is critical. Most ASPs offer a minimum 99.5 per cent availability, with set hours of service and scheduled down time for maintenance work. Service level agreements define details of service availability. The network needs to be scaleable so that network capacity can be rapidly increased as new customers are added. Some ASPs set up their networks to be able to offer different standards of service to different customers at different prices.

ASPs use one or more operating systems and databases in addition to various types of middleware to support the hosted applications. The applications are sometimes referred to as 80 per cent or generic application services because they only meet about 80 per cent of the customer's requirements. The ASP provides the remaining 20 per cent or software customization when each customer signs up for the service. Client management software needs to be installed on the customer's desktop systems to allow remote management of some hosted applications. The software hosted by ASPs invariably has a Web browser interface; it is capable of scaling up as new users are added; and is easily simplified to form the generic version of the application.

Data centres used by ASPs should be reliable and secure. Rigorous back up and disaster recovery procedures should be in place and regularly tested. Many ASPs use virtual tours to promote their data centre facilities but prospective customers are well advised to visit the site themselves to review the set up and processes. Different levels of customer service are provided, some ASPs have support staff on hand to answer queries during service hours, while others deal with queries by e-mail or phone messages left with an automated help desk facility.

As well as the hosted applications, ASPs offer a range of additional services to help differentiate them from the competition and attract more customers. These services include fast track implementation, IT specialist staff to work at the customer's site, additional data storage facilities and data back-up services.

ASP Service Partners

A feature of the ASP industry is that services are typically offered by a coalition of companies with expertise in relevant areas such as software and network technology. In effect the ASP outsources its own functions, using the skills of other companies to enable it to start in business as soon as possible and scale up as the customer base grows.

Hardware providers such as IBM and Hewlett-Packard not only supply equipment but may also offer data centre services and will partner the ASP through an equity stake in the company.

Network providers are generally international voice/data carriers, Internet Service Providers (ISPs) or system integrators. A large ASP offering multiple applications to a large customer base will need a reliable and robust network that has a solid track record and is well financed for future developments. Smaller ASPs with a niche market may be able to strike a good deal with an efficient, more cost conscious smaller network provider.

Software suppliers, system integrators and re-sellers all act as service providers to ASPs. They may offer hosted applications for various reasons:

- to sell their applications down market to customers who could not afford to buy licences and install the software themselves;

- in competition with other cheaper hosted software with similar functionality offered by other ASPs;

- as a first affordable step or pilot run before a potential new customer purchases and installs the software for themselves;

- as a demonstration of an installed application to prospective buyers.

Some ASP services offer applications that have been customized for specific industry sectors such as banking or manufacturing. Software vendors may work with value added resellers or trusted business advisors (a company with excellent business knowledge of the target industry sector) to simplify and customize the software and promote the ASP service.

As the ASP industry has developed, infrastructure service providers have emerged, offering different combinations of services, for example access to and management of broadband wide area networks, data centre space, back-up facilities, servers and storage. The ASP can lease any or all of these services to get up and running fast without the need for large up-front investments. A variety of services and combinations of services are available. Some infrastructure service providers offer services to many different ASPs.

Pricing Structures

The ASP model is based on simple pricing structures and predictable costs. Prices can be flat leasing rates, tiered leasing rates and per click charges:

- Flat leasing rates are fixed charges for certain periods of time, often regardless of levels of use. They may be based on the number of software user licences the ASP needs to purchase to serve a particular customer.
- Tiered rates are fixed prices charged for different levels of use over a certain period of time.
- Per-click charges reflect actual use of the applications and are calculated on activity levels such as the number of e-commerce transactions completed.

These pricing structures can be combined to suit different customers. Large customers with high levels of use tend to prefer flat rate charges. Tiered rates can be fixed in advance based on estimated usage. To encourage business, the ASP might prefer to charge a tiered rate based on the number of transactions, with a rate that reduces in each tier as more transactions are carried out.

Additional fees will be payable for extra services such as consulting, storage facilities, initial set up costs and premium support services.

Security Issues

Alongside performance and reliability, security remains one of the key concerns for ASP customers. Remote processing of commercially sensitive data adds a new dimension to the potential vulnerabilities and security risks that need to be addressed by any organization. Security policies and services need to be agreed and implemented not only by the customer and ASP but also by any supporting service providers (hardware, network, software or infrastructure).

Customers need periodically to carry out an audit of the security techniques and devices used by ASPs, checking access controls, data integrity and confidentiality, the use of authentication and/or encryption, firewall and VPN deployment and physical security mechanisms.

ASP Market

Rather like the dotcom boom, many companies were caught up in ASP mania in 1999 and 2000 when this supply model looked set to dominate the software applications market. Since that time, there have been many bankruptcies, mergers and acquisitions. Many of the early ASP services failed to offer the right combination of applications, services and infrastructure. The small and medium-sized business market for ASP services has not taken off as anticipated.

With the hype surrounding the ASP model, many companies jumped on the bandwagon, using the name to describe any software or IT service provided remotely. There is an ongoing problem in defining precisely what constitutes an ASP service and this impacts market data and forecasts. But it is clear that market forecasts have significantly reduced since the early days. There is some evidence to suggest that the initial shake out is near complete, and software suppliers, traditional outsourcing companies, system integrators, telecommunications operators, network providers and Web hosting companies are now collaborating – and competing – in ASP operations. Slow but steady progress is being made towards the availability of hosted applications anytime, anywhere.

One of the less helpful features of the ASP market is the lack of experience and success in delivering hosted application services over a number of years. Few companies have managed a multi-year ASP contract to the end of its term without either the customer organization or service provider going through a major reorganization or going out of business altogether.

Example

The flower delivery specialist Interflora, outsourced its e-mail system to ASP Interliant in a 25-month contract. The florist's 2,000 UK shops use the messaging application in Lotus Notes to send and view orders to and from Interflora. Orders are placed over the telephone, via the Internet and through member florists who access the service and enter order information.

> **Example**
>
> The London Stock Exchange rents space on its electronic trading system. Using the ASP model, it provides the trading platform for the Johannesburg Stock Exchange in a 5-year £11 million deal. The service exploits spare capacity resulting from a £12 million upgrade to the London Stock Exchange trading system that tripled capacity.

> **Example**
>
> National Gypsum is a North Carolina-based manufacturer and supplier of building and construction products throughout the USA. Corio was selected to upgrade and improve the performance of National Gypsum's PeopleSoft Financials environment, which was dependent on legacy systems that caused considerable performance problems. Under a fixed price bid, Corio transferred the Financials applications from the existing mainframe environment to a Corio hosted environment built on Sun servers and an Oracle database. The applications were restructured and tuned to improve overall performance. Corio introduced its own development methodology, documentation standards and change management process.

9.1.2 Managed Service Providers (MSPs)

MSPs remotely manage hardware, software and network resources, providing services both to ASPs and direct to customer organizations. They establish operational procedures such as change control, upgrade and back-up procedures. Services offered include performance monitoring and reporting, performance load testing, desktop management and service level tracking. Real time information on the availability, security and performance of the IT infrastructure is provided. Data is collected and analyzed to enable customers to trouble shoot systems problems and to optimize system performance. MSPs also run tests that mimic live transactions to measure the ongoing performance of applications.

As the MSP market has developed, different providers have defined the service in different ways and the breadth of services offered by MSPs varies considerably. Hundreds of providers now describe themselves as MSPs. Three types of MSP can be identified:

1. The first group tend to describe themselves as Management (not Managed) Service Providers. They generally limit their services to remotely monitoring the performance of the network and the applications running over the network. Some may also offer security, storage and testing services. These MSPs tend to be small companies and their customers are small or medium-sized organizations.

   This category of MSP takes little responsibility for the business services delivered to the customer organization. If service level agreements exist they will relate to the performance of the monitoring process rather than the IT service.

2. The second group describe themselves as Managed Service Providers and offer a broader range of services, with a greater involvement in the customer's business. Adding to network monitoring and reporting, these MSPs may implement software patches and install upgrades. Web-hosting MSPs in this group will work with their customers if the site goes down to restore functionality. A wide range of services will be offered and reflected in the service level agreement.

3. The final category of MSP offers customers the potential to outsource all IT operations if required. They offer a full range of managed services plus systems integration and even remote application hosting. The service is customized and each service level agreement reflects an individual customer's requirements.

   In this group there are both large and small MSPs. The smaller service providers serve niche markets. The larger players include some of the major computer services companies and management consultancies and serve large multinational companies as well as medium-sized businesses.

The MSP industry is currently growing fast as organizations move beyond the early e-commerce projects of setting up a Website, online catalogues and e-mail contacts towards exploiting Web technology to reconstruct business processes. The infrastructure needed to support these systems is complex and requires staff with the new technology skills. The MSP model offers customers the opportunity to selectively outsource new Web-based IT functions, as an alternative to investing in new equipment and network monitoring tools, and hiring new staff or retraining current employees.

9.1.3 Storage Service Providers (SSPs)

The growth in e-business and Web-based services has created a vast amount of data that needs to be stored. Increasingly, organizations need to be able to access new storage facilities on demand. Given the reduced cost of broadband connections over recent years and the increased costs of paying staff to manage storage (especially since Web services operate on a 24-hour basis), the remote storage of data by SSPs is now a viable option.

SSPs lease both storage infrastructure and staff resources to organizations that want to outsource storage equipment management and/or infrastructure. They typically design, implement and operate the storage solution. This might include loading customer data into storage devices in a remote data centre, periodically backing it up and creating archive copies that are securely stored. SSPs will adopt storage strategies that minimize costs by storing frequently used data on faster, more expensive storage media and infrequently retrieved data on slower, less expensive devices. Storage area networks help improve performance, linking storage devices with broadband connections so that any server can access any storage device, and enabling the SSP to manage different data stores centrally.

An SSP may own and maintain several data centres or storage centres that contain storage equipment. Alternatively they may own a central storage facility but lease additional storage, network facilities and data centre space from network and infrastructure service providers. Some SSPs also manage customer's in-house storage infrastructures in a traditional outsourcing arrangement. Others provide warehouses where companies can store hard copy documents that legally must be retained for fixed periods.

As with other remote, hosted services, dotcom businesses generated much of the early business for SSPs. Dotcoms had limited funds and expertise yet needed access to large storage infrastructures fast. The concept of storing confidential data remotely, under the management of an external organization, still causes concern to more traditional companies but outsourcing the back-up and restore function may be an acceptable first step. In any event, not all data generated within an organization is sensitive. The Internet, of course, generates huge amounts of data. Most companies need access to new storage regularly, simply to archive company e-mails.

The SSP market continues to evolve, providing flexible managed storage services and increasingly developing customized services.

9.1.4 Managed Security Service Providers (MSSPs)

MSSPs specialize in managing the security threats inherent in Internet operations, providing services to small and medium-sized businesses, dotcoms and ASPs. They provide a wide range of security services:

- vulnerability assessments that highlight potential weaknesses in infrastructure, policies and procedures;
- security audits, meeting various industry standards as required;
- installation, maintenance and operation of security management technology at a remote data centre to monitor firewalls and other security devices;
- intrusion detection services that alert customers if any unauthorized access to their systems is attempted;
- investigation of security incidents, defining any security breach that occurs, implementing corrective actions and gathering evidence;
- preparation of security policies;
- training and education in security matters.

Different MSSPs offer different combinations of these services. The newer, smaller MSSPs provide specialized security services and an alternative to the major accountancy and management consultancy companies in this area. The market for managed security services is growing as a result of skills shortages and the complexity of managing new organizational security environments.

The focus in many of these outsourcing arrangements is on protecting against viruses and malicious hackers rather than tackling the business risk such as security breaches leading to financial loss or loss of market share. MSSPs can offer security services that protect the perimeter of an organization's infrastructure but firewalls and other security devices are also needed within the infrastructure. Guidelines for the use of out-sourced security functions are given below:

- Outsource only tactical or temporary tasks. Security of strategic assets, such as the firewall protecting a core database, needs to be kept in-house.

- As with traditional outsourcing, take care over contract terms and conditions and service level agreements. Check out potential suppliers both in terms of their specialist expertise and their long-term viability.

- Before outsourcing the function or commissioning audits or security tests, make sure that anti-virus software is up to date, passwords are properly applied and regularly changed and open ports are closed.

- Avoid conflicts of interest; for example use separate suppliers to install firewalls and carry out penetration tests.

9.1.5 Wireless Application Service Providers (WASPs)

WASPs offer services based on remotely managed wireless applications to ASPs, network service providers and direct to customer organizations. They also modify existing applications for use by wireless devices for software suppliers, integrators and other customers. There are two main categories of WASP:

1. Those that sell general purpose wireless applications to other service providers and portals that resell the service to consumers. These organizations re-brand the services for their own customers and pay usage fees to the WASPs.

2. WASPs that develop and lease specialized applications designed for organizations that want to offer wireless services to their customers or support mobile staff. These WASPs earn revenue from application development, licensing, usage and professional fees.

WASPs generally depend on infrastructure service providers for data centre and network infrastructure. Wireless coverage and data communication speeds are key factors in the delivery of mobile solutions. With their specialist skills in this fast moving technology, WASPs are well placed to supply wireless applications to other service providers.

9.1.6 ASP Application Aggregators (AAAs)

As the ASP market has developed and the different types of service provider proliferated, an opportunity opened up for services that consolidated offerings from a number of service providers so that customers would not need to establish separate arrangements and negotiate multiple service level agreements with different suppliers. AAAs combine diverse applications from various providers and software suppliers behind a common interface through which customers access all the applications. The customers receive one unified bill for those services. Most AAAs charge an initial set up fee plus a monthly leasing fee.

The AAA usually integrates each customer's chosen applications and guarantees they will interoperate. It will also maintain, troubleshoot and upgrade the applications. In-house IT staff also access the applications via the common interface.

To be profitable, AAAs need to buy in hosted services at a discount and be able to readily integrate the various applications. Accelerated integration is a key competency. In addition to hosting multiple applications, some ASPs integrate hosted applications with their customers' legacy systems and offer general IT consultancy services. The line between AAAs and ASPs may become more blurred as the market develops.

9.1.7 xSP

xSP is a generic term covering any of the new service provider models such as MSPs, SSPs and MSSPs. Some commentators exclude ASPs from the definition of xSP.

As we have seen, it is difficult to distinguish between the many types of service provider in the market today and there is a good deal of overlap between the different categories. New companies and new versions of the service provider model continue to appear alongside consolidation, mergers and company failures in the industry.

Partnerships are more important than ever in the industry. Most xSP companies are virtual organizations, heavily dependent on services bought in from other specialist service providers. The xSP model delivers value by centrally managing services remotely using broadband connections, whether Internet, leased line or wireless, to connect to its customers. Service charges are based on a per usage or per seat model. A centralized pool of skilled IT staff and expertise in niche markets or specific business areas supports the services. Benefits to the customer organization are similar to those for more traditional outsourcing arrangements; increased ability to focus on core business and cost savings compared to the investment in implementing and maintaining equivalent services in-house.

The ASP market has not delivered the quality of service initially promised and the industry was considerably over-hyped. As experience has developed, the newer xSP companies have an opportunity to offer secure services and realistic and reliable service levels to demonstrate the validity of this supply model. Service level agreements continue to play a vital role in the management of these service providers.

One factor seldom mentioned by xSPs is that it is rarely possible for a customer to make an immediate switch to using a service provider, especially where e-business is involved. Current business processes need to be reviewed and modified to get the most out of the new outsourced service delivery models and to maximize savings.

9.1.8 Utility Computing

Many organizations purchase and maintain a considerable amount of redundant computing resource to cater for peaks in system use and anticipated growth in use over time. The new concept of utility computing would deliver computing power on demand on a pay-as-you-go model. Some see this as a possible future development of the xSP model.

The utility computing supplier would have a pool of resources that are automatically and transparently allocated to customers when they need them; and monitoring systems that would measure use and trends for billing purposes and capacity planning. It is far from clear that this is a practical proposition for the future since it would require greater standardization between manufacturers, super fast network connections and ubiquitous broadband.

Utility computing would allow disk, server and network capacity to be added from anywhere in the data centre. It would, for example, allow resources used for applications that only run in the day to be additionally used to support other systems at night. Current IT architectures are generally too rigid for flexible reallocation. Utility computing would link computers over a network to pool processing power.

Data processing and applications would not be linked to any specific hardware but would link to a massive network of computer resources, with payments made only for the resources consumed when the service is used. Sophisticated load management techniques would make it possible to create virtual servers on demand. If it works, utility computing offers the potential for making much more efficient use of computer resources on the basis of shared services, resulting in more economical access to computing power for customers.

9.2 Other Outsourcing Trends

9.2.1 Business Process Outsourcing (BPO)

No organization is entirely self-sufficient. The extension of outsourcing to encompass entire business processes, including underpinning IT systems, fits well with the concept of the virtual organization. The ability to buy in business processes such as payroll and accounting functions as and when needed enables companies to expand (or contract) fast, focusing on their core competencies to grow their business. Using Web-based services and broadband connections, BPO services can be delivered efficiently to customer organizations.

In order to deliver Web services and become involved in e-business as the market took off, many companies looked to external service providers to support commercial functions that at one time would only have been carried out in-house. A pattern may thus have been established of using external service providers in order to be able to react fast to market developments and new business opportunities.

The BPO market is expanding rapidly. In Europe, it is the fastest growing segment of the IT services market, with most deals signed in the UK, Ireland and the Netherlands. Gartner predicts that the European BPO market will grow from $38.3 billion in 2002 to $64 billion by 2005 and that the global market will be worth $301 billion by 2004 (www.gartner.com). Ovum Holway predicts that the UK BPO market will grow from £3.5 billion in 2001 to £10.3 billion in 2005 (www.holway.com).

This is not yet a mature market and a number of concerns remain – the integration of BPO processes with in-house functions, risk, liability, service levels and regulatory compliance. BPO best practice is only slowly evolving, with little information available on performance measurement and the business benefits derived.

The major IT outsourcing suppliers are getting involved in BPO, but the potential growth of the market has also encouraged many new organizations to enter the field. Some of these are small specialist companies. Some unfortunately have adopted the BPO description as a sales ploy. It is far from clear that all these new companies have realistic business plans and there are likely to be consolidation and company failures in this field over the next few years. Any organization considering BPO will therefore have to pay special attention to the longer-term viability of their supplier.

9.2.2 Offshore Outsourcing

Offshore outsourcing, now a well-established outsourcing model, continues to grow rapidly with India as the prime location for offshore software development work. Political instability poses a potential threat in several offshore locations, although to date the offshore outsourcing market does not appear to have been significantly damaged by recent world events.

Software projects have been outsourced to developing countries for a number of years. A recent trend has been to outsource more time critical projects with short delivery targets such as Web hosting, design and other related e-business work. These require tight project control and more active management by the customer organization.

An increasing number of countries provide offshore outsourcing services. Eastern European countries are now beginning to make their way in this market. The Moscow-based company, iDeveloper Network, is one of the first Russian offshore developers to work in the UK. It employs a number of developers who are based in the provinces but paid at Moscow rates, which are still considerably lower than UK rates. The documentation and quality culture is strong. As well as cheap development costs, Russia offers a history of mathematical expertise and good English language skills. The Bulgarian company, iConcepts, undertakes offshore Web development projects, delivering to short timescales and offering good English language skills.

Not all offshore outsourcing is undertaken by far away, developing countries. Some companies in the USA prefer "near-shore" application outsourcing, in other words the service is provided by nearby countries such as Canada. A favourable currency exchange rate and lower pay levels in Canada still offer savings over USA software development with the added advantage of ready accessibility.

9.2.3 New Sourcing Strategies

As experience with traditional outsourcing initiatives has developed and new supplier models have emerged, customer organizations are refining their sourcing strategies. As competition in the outsourcing market has increased, customers have gained more power to bargain for selective, shorter outsourcing contracts with better financial packages. Many more niche players now offer specialized outsourcing services and customers are beginning to combine best-of-breed solutions from multiple suppliers. While this helps to avoid the risk of over dependence on any one supplier it increases the complexity of managing supplier relationships. The challenge for IT managers is how best to exploit the developing outsourcing market to achieve strategic business advantage for their organizations.

Traditional outsourcing contracts with suppliers selected through competitive tenders, specifying services to be delivered throughout the life of the contract are still very much the norm. But some customers are developing new contractual arrangements:

- Some new outsourcing contracts, in recognition of the near impossible task of defining future IT service requirements, are based on governance processes (change control, pricing formula, performance management and so on) rather than on service solutions. The aim is to give complete service flexibility and avoid the need for major contract renegotiations as business requirements change and new technology develops. Gartner has described this approach as "co-management". Maintaining excellent outsourcing relationships between stakeholders is fundamental to the success of such an approach. Given the pace of change in the business environment, customers are looking for ways of simplifying negotiations and contract documentation so as to be able to conclude outsourcing deals more quickly, while still protecting their interests and maintaining control over their suppliers. The co-management approach is one possible solution.

- Some customers are setting up shared outsourcing services. The impact of e-commerce and possibilities opened up by Web-based services have led some companies to conclude that it is not profitable to compete on all functions – this is a very different approach to a decade ago when competitive independence would have been much more jealously guarded. The new economy has made many companies recognize afresh the benefits of collaboration and interdependence. The shared services provide a range of IT services for non-core functions in specific industry sectors. Some are set up as joint ventures to market services to other companies in the sector.

• Various types of joint venture are becoming more popular and new forms develop as customers seek an outsourced supply of world-class IT services with added business value. Although a joint venture arrangement has the potential to offer greater control to the customer organization and the possibility of earning additional income through equity investment in the venture, these deals are also much more complex than traditional outsourcing contracts. In many cases the joint venture still earns the major part of its revenue from the original customer and may experience a conflict of interest as it expands into other business opportunities. Applications developed for one customer generally require considerable further enhancement before they are sufficiently generic and capable of maintenance as a service offered to other customers.

• The scale and complexity of some customer requirements, particularly in the public sector, often lead a group of suppliers to set up as a consortium to bid for a specific outsourcing deal. In the past, the major IT outsourcing companies would have expected to meet the total package of IT outsourcing requirements. Now this is not always the case. Outsourcing initiatives may include an element of business processing and may require access to specialist skills such as wireless technology. Consortia commonly come together for one outsourcing deal. It is not at all unusual, therefore, for outsourcing company A to find itself competing against company B in some circumstances and working with them in a consortium elsewhere. The relationships between outsourcing companies has become more complex and there is a much greater management challenge in ensuring commercial confidentiality at the appropriate interfaces. From the customers' perspective, it increases problems in identifying roles and responsibilities; in the diagnosis of service failures; and identifying accountability for problem resolution.

9.2.4 Computer Services Industry

Over the last decade, the computer services industry has grown dramatically to meet the expanding market for outsourced services. With increased competition, service providers have had to reduce margins and accept more selective outsourcing deals. They have also had to offer more customized services and consider alternative supply models such as hosted services. The smaller outsourcing companies often serve niche markets, offering specialized services to specific market sectors. In response to these market trends, the major outsourcing companies have developed in various ways:

- Some of these companies are developing their own hosted application services.

- There have been several major acquisitions, which enable greater depth of expertise and breadth of skills to be offered to customers. These include Schlumberger's takeover of Sema, CMG's acquisition of Admiral, Cap Gemini's takeover of Ernst & Young, and IBM's acquisition of PwC Consulting.

- Alliances between specialized service providers and major outsourcers have increased. Smaller service providers are in a better position to meet the demand for more limited short-term deals than the larger outsourcing companies, and the major players are outsourcing work to these specialist suppliers.

- Other partnerships with niche service providers enable the major outsourcing companies to offer a range of specialist expertise to their customers.

- The major outsourcers have found it useful to source some of their services from offshore units.

- The computer services industry continues to suffer from bad publicity when high profile government projects and e-business initiatives fail. Outsourcing companies are becoming more wary of pursuing every business opportunity. Submitting bids for potential outsourcing deals can be an expensive, high-risk process.

Example

General Motors' Saturn Division uses retail applications that are accessed by 8,500 users daily for sales, services, parts, accounting and reporting. These were previously run on servers owned and maintained within General Motors but are being transferred to a remote EDS systems management centre where the applications will be consolidated onto several midrange servers. EDS will provide services to Saturn Division on the ASP model. As well as retail applications, e-mail facilities and managed Internet access services will be offered.

Example

Oracle is actively pursuing the possibilities opened up by offering their software in outsourcing arrangements based on the ASP model.

The commercial division of the Co-operative Group outsourced the operation of the company's new Internet portal to Oracle. The division comprises travel, funeral, farm, engineering, building and property services. The new portal allows the 5,000 employees of the commercial division to access all internal systems through a single personalized portal. The hardware is based at the Co-operative Bank's secure data centre, but managed remotely by Oracle.

Example

Services Anywhere, offered by IBM, helps customers manage their corporate Internet environments by remotely accessing and managing Web servers on site at the customer location. IBM technicians build a remote operations console at the customer's offices. This console uses a VPN to connect with customer sites and an IBM hosting centre. While management and monitoring services are provided remotely, the customer maintains control of the site where information is stored and processed.

IBM's alliance partners add to the value that can be delivered through Services Anywhere. Virtela Communications provides secure, high-speed private network communications between

IBM facilities and USA-based customer locations. Advanced network and systems monitoring services are provided by siteROCK, Keynote Perspective and SurfAid Analytics.

Example

Mi8 was the first ASP to become an EDS alliance partner. EDS resells Mi8's messaging service and the two companies collaborate on other sales and marketing projects. Mi8 offers Microsoft Exchange as an outsourced service over public and private networks. The software runs on Mi8 servers deployed in remote data centres and may be accessed by users via PCs or Web-based or wireless interfaces. Provisioning and administration systems give customers control over their user accounts.

The alliance's first customer was the International Association of Athletics Federations (IAAF), which is based in Monaco and organizes various events including the World Championships for Track and Field, the World Cup and the International Grand Prix Circuit. A globally structured e-mail system is provided for 700 users.

9.3 The Impact of Outsourcing on the IT Department

Any organization that chooses to source a substantial proportion of its IT activities from external service providers changes the balance of skills and abilities needed in the IT department. To get the best out of outsourcing, this transformation needs to be carefully planned and implemented. The new emphasis will not suit everyone but it is better to recognize this than to persevere with the status quo regardless of the fundamental shift that outsourcing requires. Each IT professional will need to decide for themselves how they can best develop their own careers and increasingly we should expect to move between service

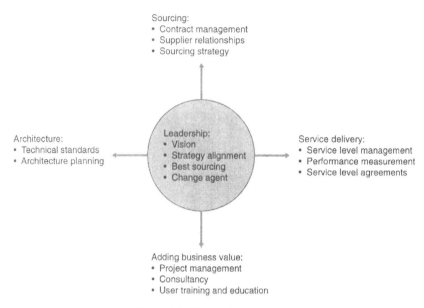

Figure 9.1 The new IT department.

provider companies and customer organizations as our careers develop. Experience working on IT services from both perspectives enriches our skills and ability to deliver the best from outsourcing deals.

We can identify five major functions in the new IT department:

- sourcing;
- service delivery;
- adding business value through IT;
- strategy and architecture;
- leadership.

This is illustrated in Figure 9.1.

1. *Sourcing.* IT is not a simple commodity service that can be bought in like a post room, restaurant or advertising service. It is ubiquitous and impacts a broad sweep of business functions. IT evolves at a very rapid pace in a way that is very difficult to predict. It is difficult to

measure the value derived from IT, but it is clear that moving between suppliers, outsourcing or backsourcing are expensive and disruptive exercises.

The development of an IT sourcing strategy is an increasingly important function within the IT department. Many larger organizations have centralized purchasing departments but it would be a mistake to leave all IT outsourcing decisions and activities to this department alone. IT sourcing needs a good understanding of systems integration, architecture and emerging technologies, as well as knowledge of the complex outsourcing service provider market. The risks inherent in IT outsourcing can lead to excessive extra charges if sourcing decisions are not well informed. The sourcing function will include responsibility for:

- contract management;
- contract administration;
- supplier relationships;
- identifying sourcing options and selecting service providers;
- monitoring computer services market developments;
- developing and maintaining IT sourcing strategy.

2. *Service delivery.* IT services are today commonly delivered by a portfolio of service providers, some in-house and others external to the customer organization. Performance measurement and problem escalation systems need to be co-ordinated so that problem areas can be readily identified and resolved. Service delivery functions include:

- service level management;
- benchmarking;
- establishing co-ordinated performance measurement systems;
- preparing and maintaining service level agreements;
- collecting performance data and monitoring service levels;
- problem and issue management.

3. *Adding business value through IT.* Simply delivering technology is not enough; IT must be effectively exploited in business processes if it is

to deliver value. To do this we need to establish a partnership between the IT department and business users, each contributing their respective skills and expertise. The IT department needs to encourage business areas to become constructively engaged in IT issues and help them identify where technology can add value. This includes:

- programme and project management;
- user liaison;
- change management;
- consultancy services;
- user training and education.

4. *Technology strategy and architecture.* Each organization needs to determine its own technology strategy and to define the standards and architecture underpinning the services delivered by disparate suppliers. The strategy should be precise enough to ensure interoperability between systems delivered by different suppliers but sufficiently flexible to allow suppliers to be innovative in the way in which they deliver services. The architecture needs to be capable of meeting present and future business needs. The IT department monitors technology developments, identifying opportunities to improve IT services and reduce costs.

5. *Leadership.* Finally, the IT department provides technology leadership in an organization. IT managers create a vision of the potential of IT to drive new business opportunities and the possibility of maximizing value delivered through IT. Increasingly IT managers are becoming change agents, initiating and progressing programmes that will fundamentally change business processes and outputs. IT leaders ensure that the IT strategy is aligned to the business strategy and seek out new ways of sourcing IT services that better serve their organization.

Each of these functions in the new IT department requires a different set of skills and expertise. Training programmes need to recognize these requirements and address any skills gaps. Compared to a more traditional IT department concerned solely with in-house IT activities, the new IT department with multiple service providers needs a greater emphasis on business knowledge and "soft" skills, such as relationship management.

9.4 Conclusion

IT outsourcing has been with us in one form or another for several decades. Unlike some other management trends, the concept of contracting out IT functions to external service providers has stood the test of time. It has become a complementary, routine method of sourcing IT services. Undoubtedly outsourcing has caused disruption and has proved more costly than anticipated in some circumstances. It has also led to low morale and disappointment for those IT professionals required against their wishes to transfer to a new employer. Nevertheless the outsourcing market continues to grow strongly, currently buoyed up by the economic downturn that is forcing many companies to look for ways of cutting costs.

Although some commentators have suggested that the end of the era of total IT outsourcing deals (contracts that cover more than 80 per cent of an organization's IT activities) is near, there is little evidence of this. Press reports of substantial new deals or extended contracts continue to appear on a regular basis. Meanwhile the outsourcing industry is developing into a rich mix of service providers able to satisfy a wide span of IT requirements, a combination of business processes and supporting IT systems, or specialized niche requirements. The growth of the Internet and availability of broadband connections have opened up new ways of supplying services.

Five major themes can be identified as we look forward to the future of outsourcing:

1. An increased use of selective outsourcing, exploiting best-of-breed services from outsourcing suppliers in a portfolio approach to sourcing IT activities.

2. New pricing models, with greater emphasis on payments linked to value delivered, benchmarking and open book accounting in large outsourcing deals and charges based on rates of use in deals with xSP companies.

3. Increased competition in the outsourcing market, with more traditional major outsourcing companies competing against the maturing xSP market. We are likely to see more consolidation and new alliances announced as the different players try to position themselves for market growth.

251

4. An emphasis on speed, to meet rapidly changing business environments. Customers will look to use their outsourcing experience to complete tendering and contract negotiations in shorter timescales. Fast implementation is a key feature of the xSP market.

5. Shorter outsourcing contracts, which customers can achieve because of increased competition in the outsourcing market. These deals offer flexibility to move between service providers or change service requirements rather than be locked into one supplier for, say, 10 years.

The lessons learnt from years of traditional outsourcing deals will continue to be relevant whenever external service providers are used:

● Recognize the importance of the outsourcing relationship and contract management in the overall success of the initiative.

● Negotiate an effective contract and appropriate service levels.

● Appreciate the total costs of outsourcing and recognize that, once contract management costs are taken into account, savings may not be as significant as it may first appear.

● Identify and manage the risks inherent in outsourcing.

Outsourcing has had, and continues to have, a fundamental impact on the working lives of IT professionals. It affects the work we do, our choice of employer, our career development, and even our pension arrangements. Many thousands of IT professionals now work in the computer services industry where IT is the core business. Looking ahead we can see that many specialized technical roles will be found in outsourcing companies, including the xSP industry, in future years. IT roles within other organizations, whose core business is not IT, will increasingly focus on deriving business value from IT investments, selecting the best sourcing option to meet various IT requirements, managing supplier relationships, and service level monitoring. Based in customer organizations or outsourcing suppliers, IT professionals will continue to seek ways of exploiting technology to deliver business benefit.

Glossary

Alternative Dispute Resolution (ADR)

An umbrella term for formal but non-binding forms of dispute resolution: mediation, conciliation or mini-trial. (In the USA the term ADR usually includes binding arbitration.)

Application Service Provider (ASP)

A hosted application service in which customers access applications operating on a remotely managed server using broadband networks. ASPs are commonly formed by a coalition of companies with expertise in hardware, networking, software applications and vertical markets.

Arbitration

A type of formal dispute resolution that takes the form of an adversarial process with an impartial arbitrator who adjudicates by making binding decisions or awards.

ASP Application Aggregator (AAA)

A service provider that combines diverse applications from various hosted service providers and software suppliers behind a common Web-based interface through which customers access all the applications. The customers receive one consolidated bill for these services.

Backsourcing

The process of re-establishing an IT function to take responsibility for services that have previously been outsourced.

Baseline

A statement of service performance levels against which service improvements or deterioration in performance by the outsourcing supplier will be measured. The baseline is measured before outsourcing by collecting current performance data over several months and identifying areas of known weakness where the outsourcing supplier will be expected to make improvements. The baseline reflects the minimum acceptable service level and will be specified in the outsourcing contract.

Benefit-based Outsourcing

An outsourcing arrangement in which both parties invest up-front in the IT services and share benefits as they accrue. If the benefits previously forecast and agreed do not materialize the supplier may not be guaranteed any income for its effort or input.

Benchmarking

A management process used to investigate, study, measure and enhance performance by comparing IT services against industry standards and best practice in other organizations. It can be used in the development of the service baseline or as a standard against which to measure suppliers' proposals and to gauge the supplier's performance in the later years of the outsourcing contract.

Business Process Outsourcing (BPO)

The transfer of responsibility for the planning, management and operation of an entire business process (including any supporting IT systems) to an external service provider.

Business Service Provider (BSP)

BSPs are ASPs that offer applications which support e-commerce or other financial transactions.

Change Control

An established process that ensures that all changes are properly controlled, including the submission of change requests, impact analyses, approval procedures and implementation.

Common Criteria (CC)

Internationally recognized accreditation scheme for security products. Compliance with the CC scheme has been ratified as ISO 15408.

254

Contract

A legally binding agreement between two or more parties that can incorporate documents such as security policies and technical specifications.

Countermeasure

An action that is designed to limit the impact of a risk which threatens the success of the programme; or to reduce the likelihood of the risk occurring; or to help recovery from the damage caused by the risk.

Customer Organization

The organization that purchases the outsourcing service from an external service provider.

Dotcom

A company that exists largely as a virtual organization, able to respond very fast to new and changing business opportunities using e-commerce technologies because it buys in business infrastructure services as and when they are needed.

Due Diligence

Literally, appropriate careful and persevering work. In purchasing, the term is commonly used to describe a process that takes place after the main contract terms are agreed but before the contract is signed, in which the supplier reviews and confirms details about the services and assets to be transferred in the deal.

Escrow Agreement

An agreement covering the deposit of source code with a neutral third-party custodian for release only in certain situations as defined in the agreement.

Facilities Management

The transfer of responsibility for the planning, management and operation of IT systems to an external service provider, with ownership of the computer assets remaining with the customer organization.

Force Majeure

This is a concept in French law, but is used in English law to mean in broad terms 'acts of God'. The specific events included as force majeure are defined in the contract, together with the consequences for the parties involved.

Full Service Provider (FSP)

An ASP that offers a wide range of added services for specific business functions or market sectors.

Impact

A measure of the effect or significance of a problem or a change requested. For example, a measure of the damage caused to the customer organization should a risk materialize; or a measure of the costs and amount of technical work necessary to implement a change requested to the outsourced services.

Informed Customer

An individual or team with responsibility for disseminating information about the outsourced services; educating users about processes such as change control; representing a group of users in liaison with the outsourcing supplier; and helping a specific business area derive maximum value from the outsourced services. The informed customer will often contribute to the purchasing process and help define service requirements; and play an ongoing role in performance monitoring once the contract is live. Where IT budgets are decentralized, the informed customer may also authorize orders for additional outsourced services.

Insourcing

Insourcing is the formal adoption of the internal IT department as service provider. Responsibility for planning, managing and operating the IT services is retained by the in-house IT department and governed by a service level agreement, against which performance is monitored. Spare capacity may be used to develop additional business, possibly outside the customer organization.

Invitation to Negotiate (ITN)

See Request for Proposals.

Invitation to Tender (ITT)

See Request for Proposals.

ISO 9001

The international standard that specifies requirements for a quality management system where an organization needs to demonstrate its ability to provide products that fulfil customer and regulatory requirements and aims to enhance customer satisfaction.

ISO 15408

See Common Criteria.

Issue

Area of concern that may affect the achievement of the programme's objectives.

IT Infrastructure Library (ITIL)

Produced by the UK's Office of Government Commerce, the ITIL is a set of guides on the provision and management of operational IT services.

IT Security Evaluation Criteria (ITSEC)

Accreditation scheme for security products, recognized throughout Europe.

Joint Venture

A separate company with its own management team set up by outsourcing customer and supplier to provide outsourced services. Both organizations provide staff to work in the joint venture and share any profits made by it.

Managed Security Service Provider (MSSP)

MSSPs specialize in managing the security threats inherent in Internet operations, offering a range of security services to small and medium-sized businesses, dotcoms and ASPs.

Managed Service Provider (MSP)

A service provider that remotely manages hardware, software and network resources, providing services both to ASPs and direct to customer organizations. The degree of involvement in business services and range of additional services varies between different MSPs.

Management Service Provider

A type of managed service provider whose services are generally limited to remotely monitoring the performance of the network and the applications running over the network, although some also offer security, storage and testing services.

Memorandum of Understanding (MOU)

A statement of intent rather than a legal document, which sets out broad objectives in general rather than detailed terms. Common in large outsourcing deals, this is the first document to be signed by customer organization and supplier.

Novation

The transfer of rights and obligations from one party to another.

Official Journal of the European Community (OJEC)

The journal in which all EC public authorities place notices about all purchases of products or services over a set threshold.

Offshore Outsourcing

The transfer of responsibility for any IT function, but especially application development, to an external service provider based in another continent.

Open Book Accounting

An arrangement between supplier and customer organization in which the customer will typically be given full details of the direct and indirect costs of the services provided by the supplier so that the profit margins achieved are visible and understood.

Outsourcing

The transfer of responsibility for planning, management and operating services to an external service provider.

Preferred Bidder

The supplier that submits the proposals that offer the best combination of quality of service and value for money and with whom the customer will enter into detailed negotiations.

PRINCE2

The standard UK government method for project management.

Programme

The group of activities and projects that collectively implement a business initiative or new corporate requirement.

Public Finance Initiative (PFI)

Introduced by the UK government, the PFI transforms government departments and agencies from owners and operators of assets into purchasers of services from the private sector. Under PFI, commercial companies assume responsibility for designing, implementing, financing and operating assets such as IT systems to deliver public services.

Public Private Partnership (PPP)

A term used to describe the relationship between public sector and commercial company working together to provide public services, including partnerships developed under the UK government's PFI.

Request for Information (RFI)

Request for preliminary information and indicative costings from potential suppliers.

Request for Proposals (RFP)

Request for detailed proposals and service costs; in outsourcing initiatives commonly from a short list of suppliers all of whom are capable of meeting the service requirements.

Risk Management

The process of identifying, describing, assessing and effectively managing each risk to the programme. The aim is to reduce exposure to risk to an acceptable level by putting appropriate countermeasures in place.

Selective Outsourcing

The practice of selecting some IT activities to outsource while retaining other IT functions (not less than 20 per cent of the total) in-house.

Service Control Team

A team set up to monitor and analyze performance data; service issues and problems; and compliance with service standards, contingency, back-up and security procedures.

Service Level Agreement (SLA)

Documents the standard of performance that the supplier has agreed to provide and gives the customer organization rights and remedies should the supplier fail to deliver this level of service.

Service Level Management (SLM)

The term used to describe the process of defining, agreeing, documenting and managing the level of service required to meet business needs and provide value for money.

Service Provider

An external company that supplies outsourcing services to the customer organization.

Stakeholder

An individual or team that sponsors a programme or service, is a major user of the service or otherwise participates in the programme.

Statement of Service Requirements

The term used to describe a detailed specification of service requirements in a purchasing exercise. The statement covers service level targets, service volumes, interfaces to other systems, user support, training, performance measures, security, change control, charges and respective responsibilities of customer and supplier.

Storage Area Network (SAN)

A robust storage network that operates independently of primary networks for better performance, comprising storage devices linked by broadband connections to servers so that any server can access any storage device.

Storage Service Provider (SSP)

This service provider leases both storage infrastructure and staff resources to organizations that want to outsource storage equipment management and/or infrastructure. They typically design, implement and operate the storage solution.

Strategic Sourcing

Decisions about what to outsource or insource in strategic sourcing are put into a wider business context. The aim is significant improvement in business performance rather than simply a short-term cost saving.

Tactical Outsourcing

Outsourcing that is adopted as a rapid and often short-term solution to a particular need or problem.

Total Outsourcing

The outsourcing of at least 80 per cent of an organization's IT activities to one or more external service providers.

Transfer of Undertakings (Protection of Employment) Regulations (TUPE)

UK regulations, based on a European directive, which protect employees from redundancy when a company is restructured, merged with another business, acquired by another company or a function is outsourced.

Transformational Outsourcing

Combines the outsourcing of an IT department with a comprehensive reorganization.

Transition

A term used to describe the implementation of the outsourcing contract or transition from in-house to outsourced IT services.

Transitional Outsourcing

Companies use transitional outsourcing to introduce major change such as moving from one technological platform to another. The outsourcing supplier may support legacy systems while the in-house IT department transfers applications to the new technology, or the supplier may implement the new systems.

Utility Computing

The concept of pooling computer resources (including hardware) and automatically and transparently allocating these resources to customers as and when they need them.

Virtual Private Network (VPN)

A high capacity secure network that is often less expensive to build than a private wide area network because the Internet provides much of the physical connectivity.

Wireless Application Service Provider (WASP)

WASPs offer services based on remotely managed wireless applications and modify existing applications so that wireless devices can access them. Their customers include ASPs, network service providers, software suppliers and integrators.

xSP

A generic term used to cover virtual service providers such as MSPs, SSPs and MSSPs.

Useful Websites

A number of Websites provide useful information and news about outsourcing and these are listed below. There are many sites covering ASP services; a selection of the sites is given.

www.allaboutasp.org

The ASP Industry Consortium site, providing news and information primarily aimed at ASP companies. The Consortium is a global advocacy group promoting the ASP industry by sponsoring research and articulating the benefits of this supply model.

www.asp.com

Site promoting ASP services; includes news, an ASP directory and a section for service providers.

www.aspnews.com

News and analysis of the ASP industry.

www.computerworld.com, www.computing.co.uk, www.cw360.com

Articles about outsourcing and news items about the latest deals, from *Computer World*, *Computing* and *Computer Weekly*.

www.iitug.org

Site belonging to the International Information Technology Users' Group, which is comprised of senior IT executives from organizations who are significant consumers of purchased IT services. A key goal of the group is to exchange technical information and best practice.

www.itaa.org/asp

The Information Technology Association of America's ASP Website, giving access to reports, articles and guidelines.

www.mspassociation.org

The Strategic Sourcing Advisory Council's (SSAC) site, providing access to information about the managed service provider industry. Formerly the MSP Association, the SSAC is a global, non-profit organization supporting service management quality standards based on ITIL.

www.nao.co.uk

The National Outsourcing Association's (NAO) site providing information about outsourcing developments, forthcoming events and news items. The NAO is an independent body that promotes best practice, lobbies the UK government and disseminates information about outsourcing.

www.outsourcing.com

The Outsourcing Institute's (OI) site, giving access to papers and information about outsourcing events. OI is a neutral professional association dedicated solely to outsourcing.

www.outsourcing-experts.com

The OutsourcingCenter Internet portal, providing access to information, research findings and the monthly online *Outsourcing Journal* and *BPO Outsourcing Journal*. OutsourcingCenter is the publishing and research division of the consulting firm Everest Group.

www.webharbor.com

An ASP industry portal, providing access to information about the ASP marketplace.

Bibliography

Aalders, R. (2001) *The IT outsourcing guide.* John Wiley & Sons, Chichester.

Boyce, T. (1992) *Successful contract administration.* Hawkesmere, London.

Burnett, R. (1998) *Outsourcing IT: The legal aspects.* Gower Publishing, Aldershot.

CCTA (2000) *IS management guides: Managing services.* Format Publishing, Norwich.

Fenn, D. (ed.) (2002) *Key Note market review: UK computer market 2002.* Key Note Publications, Hampton.

Financial Times. Outsourcing: the way ahead. *The Banker,* September 2001.

Gay, C.L. and Essinger, J. (2000) *Inside outsourcing: The insider's guide to managing strategic sourcing.* Nicholas Brealey, London.

Harney, J. (2002) *Application service providers (ASPs): A manager's guide.* Pearson Education, New Jersey.

Hirschheim, R., Heinzl, A. and Dibbern, J. (eds) (2002) *Information systems outsourcing: Enduring themes, emergent patterns and future directions.* Springer-Verlag, Berlin.

Johnson, M. (1997) *Outsourcing: In brief.* Butterworth-Heinemann, Oxford.

Kakabadse, A. and Kakabadse, N. (2002) *Smart sourcing: International best practice.* Palgrave, Basingstoke.

Kern, T. and Willcocks, L. P. (2001) *The relationship advantage: Information technologies, sourcing and management.* Oxford University Press, Oxford.

KPMG IMPACT Programme, Outsourcing Working Group (1995) *Best practice guidelines for outsourcing.* HMSO, London.

Lacity, M.C. and Hirschheim, R. (1995) *Beyond the information systems outsourcing bandwagon: The insourcing response.* John Wiley & Sons, Chichester.

Lacity, M.C. and Willcocks, L.P. (2001) *Global information technology outsourcing: In search of business advantage.* John Wiley & Sons, Chichester.

Mylott, T.R. (1995) *Computer outsourcing: Managing the transfer of information systems*. Prentice-Hall, New Jersey.

Neely, A., Mills, J., Gregory, M., Richards, H., Platts, K. and Bourne, M. (1998) *Getting the measure of your business*. Findlay Publications, Swanley.

Office of Government Commerce (2001) *Service delivery*. The Stationery Office, London.

Office of Government Commerce (2002) *IS management and business change guides: How to manage service acquisition*. Format Publishing, Norwich.

Reeves, J. (ed.) (1999) *Outsourcing IT: Business guide*. Caspian Publishing, London.

Reeves, J. (ed.) (2002) *The emergence of e-sourcing*. Caspian Publishing, London.

Remenyi, D., Money, A. and Sherwood-Smith, M. (2000) *The effective measurement and management of IT costs and benefits*. Butterworth-Heinemann, Oxford.

Ventralla, T. (1994) *A contractor's guide to contract law*. Dannick Publications, London.

White, R. and James, B. (1996) *The outsourcing manual*. Gower, Aldershot.

Willcocks, L. and Graeser, V. (2001) *Delivering IT and e-business value*. Butterworth-Heinemann, Oxford.

Willcocks, L.P. and Lacity, M. (1998) *Strategic sourcing of information systems: Perspectives and practices*. John Wiley & Sons, Chichester.

Index

270

.

Lightning Source UK Ltd.
Milton Keynes UK
24 January 2011

166254UK00005B/30/P